THE
ALPHABET

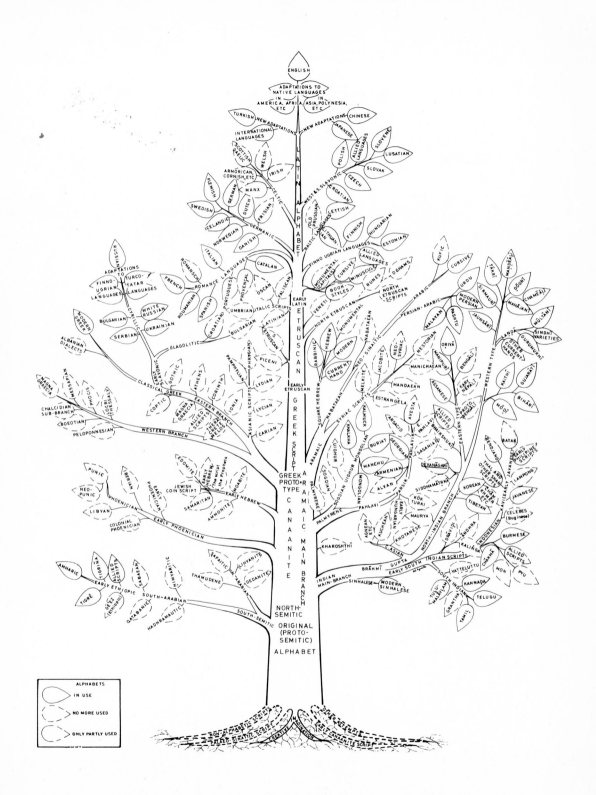

THE
ALPHABET

A Key to
the History of Mankind

DAVID DIRINGER

D.Litt. (*Flor.*), M.A. (*Cantab.*)

THIRD EDITION

completely revised with the collaboration of

REINHOLD REGENSBURGER

VOLUME 2

FUNK & WAGNALLS
NEW YORK

Published by Funk & Wagnalls, *A Division of*
Reader's Digest Books, Inc.

First published by Hutchinson & Co.
(Publishers) Ltd. in April 1948

Second edition, revised April 1949
Reprinted (with amendments) January 1953
Reprinted (with amendments) October 1953
Third edition (completely revised, in two volumes) 1968

Printed in Great Britain

CONTENTS

IN this illustration volume the sections are numbered to correspond exactly with the chapter headings in the text volume, and the illustrations are numbered serially within sections. Each illustration is marked with two numbers separated by a dot. The first is the section number and the second is the specific number. The index to the whole work is in the text volume, where illustrations are referred to by page numbers shown in italic type.

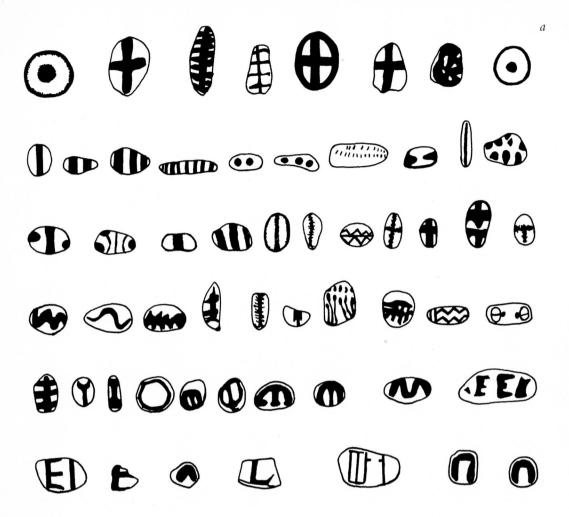

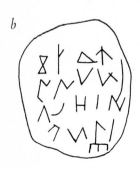

Introd. 1. *a* Azilian signary: coloured pebbles from Mas d'Azil, Ariège (Southern France). *b* Prehistoric geometric signs from Portugal.

a

b

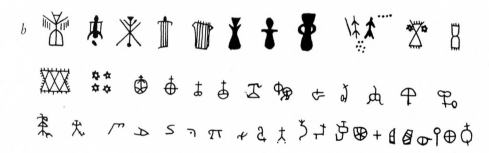

Introd. 2. Prehistoric conventionalized figures and geometric symbols from *a* Italy and *b* Spain.

2

a

b

c

Introd. 3. Prehistoric rock-carvings from Val Cammonica (Italian Alps). *a* Fish trapped. *b* Plan of village. *c* Work in the fields.

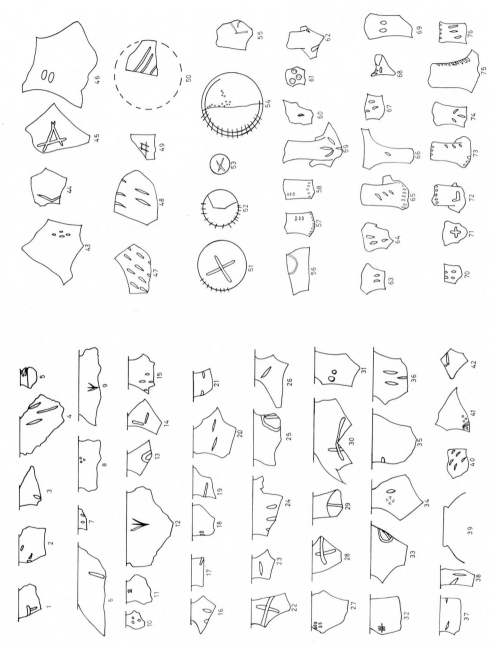

Introd. 4. Prehistoric geometric symbols from Palestine.

4

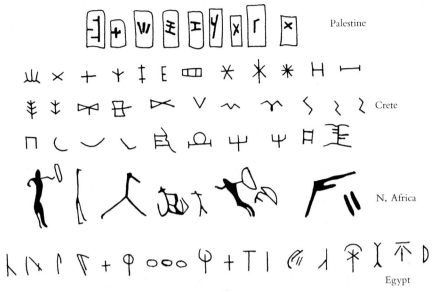

Introd. 5. *a* Prehistoric geometric symbols and conventionalized figures.

Introd. 5. *b* Prehistoric geometric symbols from Southern Rhodesia.

5

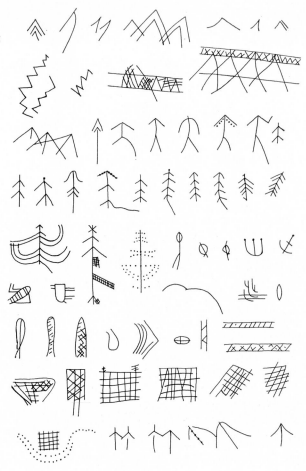

Introd. 6. Prehistoric symbols from Katanga (Congo) *a* engraved, *b* punched, and *c* painted.

6

Introd. 7. Petroglyphs from Afghanistan.

7

Introd. 8. Petroglyphs from Hoshangabad (India).

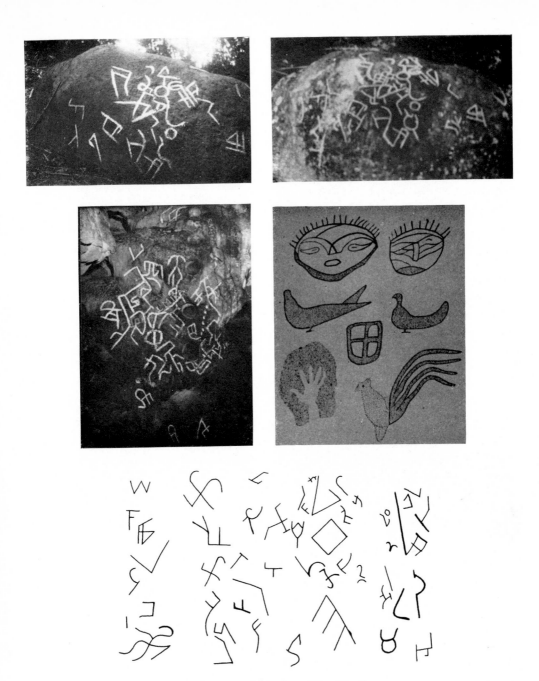

Introd. 9 Petroglyphs from Fijian Islands.

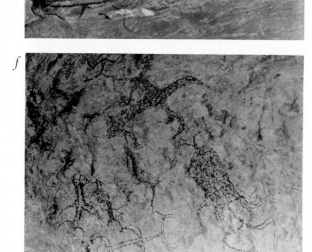

Introd. 10. Petroglyphs from New Zealand. *a* and *b* Weka Pass shelter, *c* Monkey Face Reserve, *d* Ford's shelter, *e* Awamoko Stream, *f* Dogsheads Rock Cave.

Introd. 11. Conventionalized figures of men and animals, animated objects and geometrical symbols from rock-paintings or carvings in the U.S.A. *a* to *d* California, *e* Arizona, *f* Bahamas, *g* Brazil, and *h* Australia.

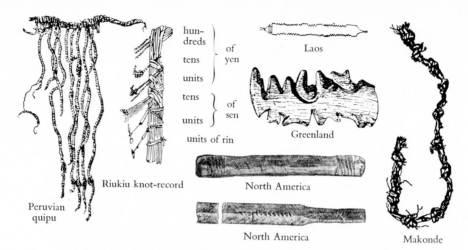

hun-
dreds
tens   of
            yen
units

tens   of
            sen
units

units of rin

Laos

Greenland

North America

North America

Riukiu knot-record

Peruvian
quipu

Makonde

Introd. 12. *a* Peruvian *quipu*; Riukiu knot-record; notched stick from Laos; 'geographical map' from Greenland; Makonde knot-record; notched sticks from North America.

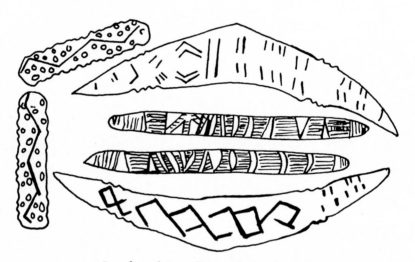

Introd. 12. *b* Australian notched sticks.

Introd. 12. *c* The Penn Wampum belt (Historical Society of Pennsylvania).

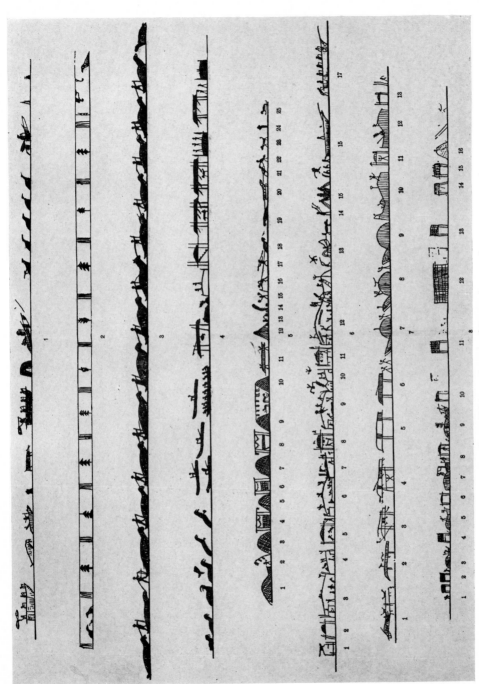

Introd. 13. Eskimo pictographic carvings on ivory.

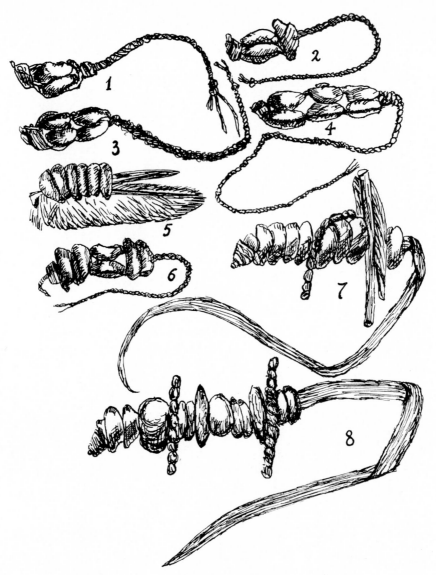

Introd. 14. *Aroko* or symbolic epistles of the Yoruba people.

1 Two cowries, strung back to back (message of reproof for non-payment of debt).
2 Two cowries, face to face, followed by one above, facing upwards (message from
a creditor to a bad debtor). 3 Four cowries, in pairs, face to face (message of good will
from a native to his brother abroad, asking for a personal interview). 4 Six cowries,
face to face (message from a general of the Jebu force to a native prince abroad).
5 Letter from a native prince of the Jebu Ode to one of his cousins abroad. 6 Another
Jebu message. 7 Message from the king Awnjale to his nephew abroad. 8 Message of
peace and good news from the king of Jebu to the king of Lagos, after his restoration to
the throne, on the 28th December, 1851.

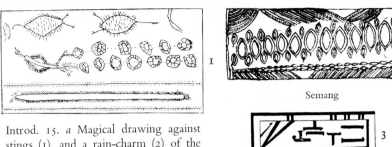

Introd. 15. *a* Magical drawing against stings (1), and a rain-charm (2) of the Semang people (East Malacca). 3 Samoyed 'document' representing a requisition of property.

Semang

Samoyed

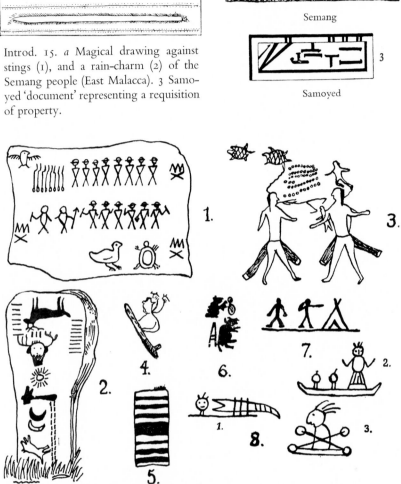

Introd. 15. *b* Ideographic documents of North American native tribes.

1 Indian expedition. 2 Tomb-board of Indian Chief. 3 Letter of a man called Turtle-Following-His-Wife to his son named Little-Man. 4 The French General Maynadier (a man with a hat, indicating a European; the two heads of a deer at the top right-hand side, indicate the name 'Many Deer'). 5 The winter 1858–59 as indicated in a Dakota (a North American Indian tribe) 'winter count': the Dakotas bought in that winter many *Mexican blankets* from John Richard. 6 Message of a North American Indian: 'Bad-Bear (a name) died at a buffalo hunt'. 7 Message of a native from Alaska: 'No eating is in tent'. 8 (1 to 3) Ideographs from the Delaware 'Chronicle' *Walam Olum*.

Introd. 16. The modern and astute advertiser turns to a pictographic appeal for his rubber goods.

a

b

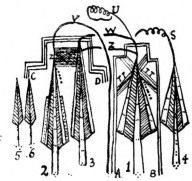

c

Introd. 17. Picture stories of native tribes: *a* ideographic document of North American Indians; *b* symbolic proverbs of the Ewe (West African people); *c* sad love-story of a Yukaghir girl; *d* Dakota 'winter-count' chronicle (drawing by Kedma Diringer).

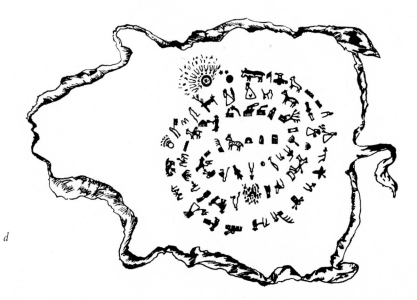

d

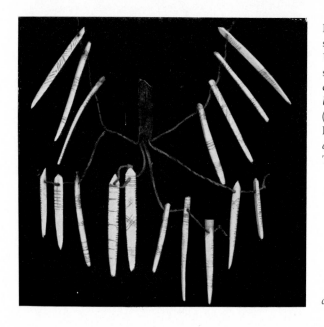

Introd. 18. *a* 1, Song Record-stick from Ogaga, Oklahoma, U.S.A. 2, Cheyenne Record-stick (Museum of the American Indian, New York).
b Arapahoe Record-sticks (Museum of the American Indian, New York).
c Marked bone spikes from Tahltan (Alaska).

18

Development of Cuneiform Signs

Meaning in Sumerian	English	Original Pictograph	Pictograph after turning 90°	Archaic form (c. 2500 - c. 2350) on clay	Archaic form (c. 2500 - c. 2350) on stone or metal	Ancient Babylonian	Classic Assyrian
gir	dagger, lancet, razor						
an, dingir	heaven, god						
lú	man						
sal, munus	pudendum woman						
kur	mountain						
gem	slave-girl						
sag	head						
ka, dug	mouth, to speak						
a	water						
du, gub	to go, to stand						
mushen	bird						
ha, ha	fish, may						
gud	ox						
she	barley						

1.1. Origin of cuneiform characters.

1.2. Archaic Sumerian pictorial tablets, from Kish (*a* obverse; *b* reverse), Uruk-Warka (*c* and *d*), possibly from Umma (*e*) and Jemdet Nasr (*f*).

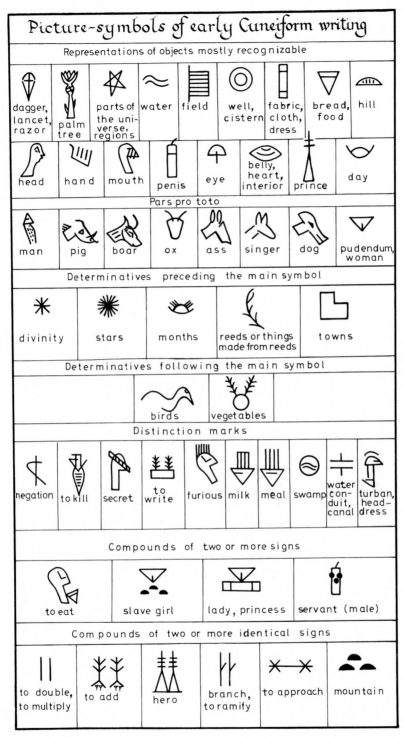

1.3. Sumerian pictorial symbols.

NO.	A	TU	GAR	NO.	A	TU	GAR
1				9			
2			(REC 417)	10			
3				11			
4				12			
5				13			
6				14			
7				15			
8				16			

1.4*a*. Examples of cuneiform homophones.

1	2	3	4	5	6
7	8	9	10	11	12
13	14	15	16	17	18

1.4*b*. Examples of cuneiform determinatives (for full explanation see text, p. 18).

1	2	3	4	5	6
7	8	9	10	11	12
13	14	15	16	17	18
= a 19	= e 20	= i 21	= o 22	= u 23	

1.4*c*. Assyrian cuneiform symbols (1–18) for syllables and (19–23) vowels (1, ba; 2, da; 3, ga; 4, kha 5, ka; 6, qa; 7, la; 8, ma; 9, na; 10, pa; 11, ra; 12 and 13, sa; 14 and 15, sha).

I.5. Early cuneiform writing on soft material: inscribed brick of Eannadu, King of Lagash (modern Tell Lo, southern Mesopotamia).

1.6. Assyrian sculptures from the royal palace at Ashur, representing scribes. (*above*) Scribes in the act of writing; (*below*) two scribes writing out lists of booty.

1.7. *a–e* Cuneiform tablets of various shapes; *f* Extract from Hammurabi's *Code of Laws* showing the stylus.

1.8. *a* Pillar on which is inscribed Hammurabi's Code of Laws (18th cent. B.C.). *b* Baked clay prism of Sennacherib, King of Assyria (705–681 B.C.), inscribed with the account of his invasion of Palestine and the siege of Jerusalem.

a

b

1.9. *a* Nippur archaic cylinder and grammatical text; *b* Sumerian flood tablet from Nippur (both from University Museum, Philadelphia).

a

b

a

b

1.10. *a* Fragments of the Lipit-Ishter Law Code, the oldest law-code in man's history; *b* Sumerian tablet from Nippur with the story of the Creation and the Flood (both from University Museum, Pennsylvania).

1.11b. Fragmentary tablet containing the Babylonian account of the Flood (British Museum K3375).

1.11a The Fourth Tablet of the Assyrian account of the Creation and the Flood (British Museum No. 93016).

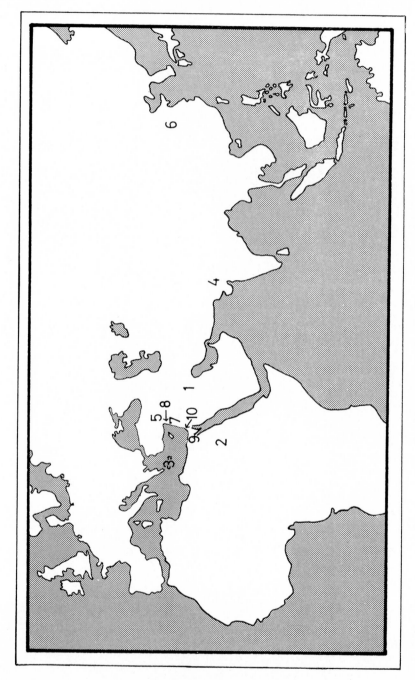

Map I. MAIN SYSTEMS OF WRITING 3000–1000 B.C.

1 Cuneiform scripts (Mesopotamia and surrounding countries). 2 Egyptian scripts (Hieroglyphic, Hieratic, Demotic). 3 Cretan and Mycenaean scripts. 4 Indus Valley scripts. 5 Hittite Hieroglyphic scripts (Asia Minor and N. Syria). 6 Chinese scripts. 7 Byblos pseudo-hieroglyphic script. 8 Ugarit cuneiform alphabet. 9 Palaeo-Sinaitic script. 10 North Semitic alphabet.

1.12b. Neo-Babylonian chronicle; Fall of Nineveh
British Museum 21901).

1.12a. Letter from Tushratta, King of Mitanni to
Amenophis III, King of Egypt (British Museum 29791).

1.13. The 'Sun-god Tablet', showing the worship of the 'sun-god', and inscribed with a record of the restoration of the temple of Sippar by the Babylonian king Nabu-apal-iddina (ca. 870 B.C.).

a

1.14a. Dudu, Sumerian scribe. Inscription on back of above statue identifying him as a professional scribe. Dudu, a Sumerian, of ca. 2350 B.C. who lived in Lagash (Bagdad, Iraq Museum).

b

c

d

e

f

1.14b–f. Cuneiform seals preserved in the British Museum.

33

1.15*a*. Proto Elamite tablet (British Museum 120486).

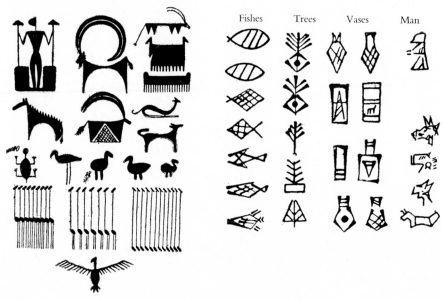

1.15*b*. *Left* Elamite decorative motifs, *right* early Elamite pictorial symbols.

1.15*c*. Inscribed Elamite brick (British Museum 90529).

1.16*a*. Darius inscription.

1.16*b*. Slab with inscription in Persian Cuneiform script, with text of Xerxes; *right*, part of a tree (from Persepolis, British Museum 118841), *see* also 11.1.

(1) $D(a)-a-r(a)-y(a)-v(a)-u-š(a)$ (2) $x(a)-š(a)-a-$
$y(a)-\vartheta(a)-i-y(a)$ (3) $v(a)-z(a)-r(a)-k(a)$ (4) $x(a)-$
$š(a)-a-y(a)-\vartheta(a)-i-y(a)$ (5) $x(a)-š(a)-a-y(a)-\vartheta(a)-i-y(a)-a-n(a)-$
$a-m(a)$ (6) $x(a)-š(a)-a-y(a)-\vartheta(a)-i-y(a)$ (7) $d(a)-h(a)-y(a)-u-$
$n(a)-a-m(a)$ (8) $Vi-i-š(a)-t(a)-a-s(a)-p(a)-h(a)-y(a)-a$ (9) $p(a)-$
$u-ç(a)$ (10) $H(a)-x(a)-a-m(a)-n(a)-i-š(a)-i-y(a)$ (11) $h(a)-y(a)$
(12) $i-m(a)-m(a)$ (13) $t(a)-č(a)-r(a)-m(a)$ (14) $a-ku-u-n(a)-a-u-š(a)$

*Dārayavauš xšāyaθiya vazrka xšāyaθiya xšāyaθiyā-
nām xšāyaθiya dahyunām Vištāspahya puça Haxāmanišiya hya imam
tačaram akunauš*

1.17a. Darius inscription, *above* transcribed from 1.16a, *below* deciphered. Translated into English, this reads:—

Darius, the great King, the King of Kings, the King of the countries, son of Hystaspes, the Achaemenid, who built this palace.

(1) $X(a)-š(a)-y(a)-a-r(a)-š(a)-(\dot{a})-a$ (2) $x(a)-š(a)-a-$
$y(a)-\vartheta(a)-i-y(a)$ (3) $v(a)-z(a)-r(a)-k(a)$ (4) $x(a)-š(a)-a-y(a)-$
$\vartheta(a)-i-y(a)$ (5) $x(a)-š(a)-a-y(a)-\vartheta(a)-i-y(a)-a-n(a)-a-m(a)$ (6)
$D(a)-a-r(a)-y(a)-v(a)-h(a)-u-š(a)$ (7) $x(a)-š(a)-a-y(a)-\vartheta(a)-i-$
$y(a)-h(a)-y(a)-a$ (8) $p(a)-u-ç(a)$ (9) $H(a)-x(a)-a-m(a)-n(a)-i-$
$š(a)-i-y(a)$

*Xšayāršā xšāyaθiya vazrka xšāyaθiya xšāyaθiyānām
Dārayavahauš xšāyaθiyahya puça Haxāmanišiya*

1.17b. Xerxes inscription, *above* transcribed, *below* deciphered. Translated into English, this reads:—

Xerxes, the great King, King of Kings, of Darius, the King's son, the Achaemenid.

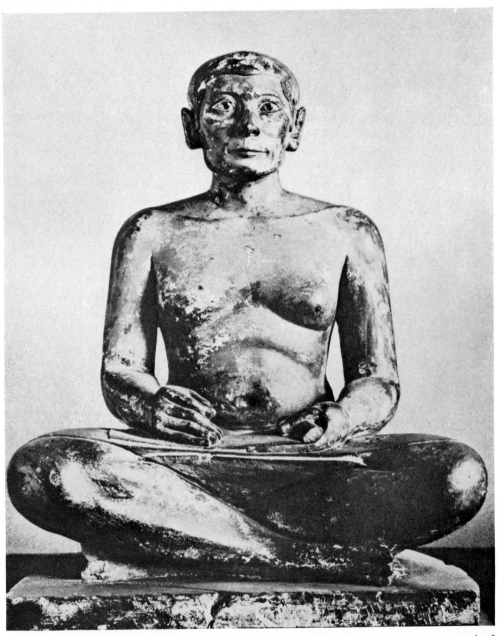

2.1. Egyptian scribe. This statuette only 5.3 cm. high, was found by Mariette at Saqqara in a tomb of the period of the Fifth Dynasty. (Louvre Museum, Salle du scribe).

2.2a. Limestone relief: Four scribes with papyrus rolls and reed pens (18th Dynasty).

2.2b. Limestone relief: Scribes and village elders (Saqqara, 6th Dynasty).

2.3a. Both sides of the ceremonial palette of King Narmer (c. 2900 B.C.).

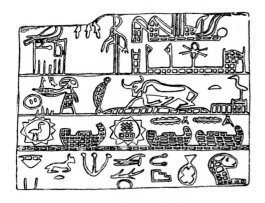

2.3b. The plaque of Akha or Akhai (c. 3000 B.C.).

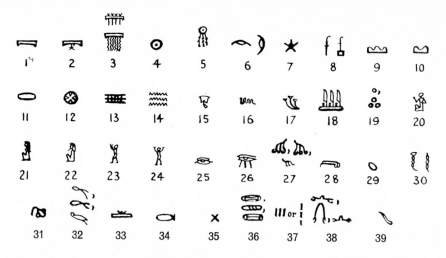

2.4. Hieroglyphic determinatives.

1. Heaven, Sky, Ceiling, what is above. 2. Night sky with a star hanging like a lamp from it, darkness, night. 3. (above) Sky slipping down over its four supports, storm, hurricane; (below) rain or dew falling from the sky. 4. Sun, the sun-god Ra, day period, time in general. 5. Shine, rise (of a luminary), being of light. 6. Moon, month. 7. Star, morning star, hour, time for prayer, pray. 8. Flourish, blooming, year, time in general, last year of a King's reign. 9. Foreign country, desert. 10. Mountain. 11. Island. 12. City, town. 13. Nome, District. 14. Water, watery mass of the sky. 15. Skin, hide. 16. Worm. 17. Plant, vegetable, herb, dried up. 18. Field, garden. 19. Grain, corn. 20. Man, first person sing. 21. Woman, first and second person sing. 22. God or divine person. 23. Pray, worship, adore, entreat, praise. 24. High, lofty, exalt, make merry. 25. To see. 26. To weep, tear, grief. 27. Hair (of men and animals), bald, lack, want, lacuna (in manuscripts), colour, complexion. 28. Phallus, front, male, masculine, procreate. 29. Women, godessess, cities. 30. Sweet, pleasant. 31. Incense. 32. Roll of papyrus, tie up, bind together, come to an end. 33. Roll of papyrus (tied round the middle), book, deed, document, register, group together, abstract ideas. 34. Oval round a royal name, known as *cartouche*. 35. Pair of tallies, count, tally, reckon, pass by, depart. 36. Bread, cake. 37. Sign of the plural 38. Negation, no, not, nothing, lack, want, need. 39. Horn.

soldier (army) eye giraffe horn swallow beetle flower sun

mountain corner foot sandal arch plough bread

to beat to fly to eat to go to fight to row to weep

to dominate to direct upper Egypt to find old age fresh
to govern south

m – n m – s sh – n – w kh – n w – kh – m – i – t – y

2.5a. Hieroglyphic word signs. 1, symbols representing things shown
2, ideographs representing actions associated with things shown; 3, symbols
representing abstract ideas; 4, hieroglyphic bi-consonantal signs.

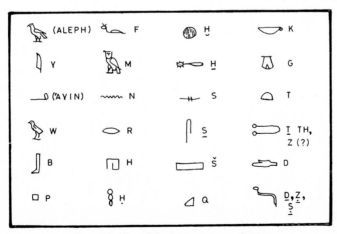

2.5b. Earliest hieroglyphic consonantal signs.

a

b

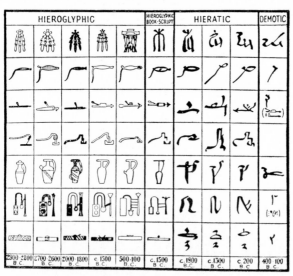

c

2.6. *a* The Palermo Stone. *b* The Stone of Israel. *c* Development of Egyptian signs (from G. Moeller).

2.7b. Offering cene from the Mastaba of Ptah-hotep at Saqqara. 5th Dynasty.

2.7a. False door from the tomb of Iry, an official connected with the Great Pyramid of Cheops at Giza, fifth–sixth Dynasties.

2.8a. Egyptian hieroglyphic papyri: Ani Papyrus, sheet 3 (British Museum, Pap. 10470).

2.8b. Egyptian hieroglyphic papyri: Khă Papyrus (Turin Egyptian Museum).

2.9. Papyri written in late hieroglyphic writing.

a Nu Papyrus (British Museum, 10447).

2.9*b*. *Book of the Dead* written in the so-called cursive hieroglyphs, belonging approximately to the Eighteenth Dynasty (Trinity College Library, Dublin).

45

2.10a. *Book of the Dead* of the Saitic period (Trinity College Library, Dublin).

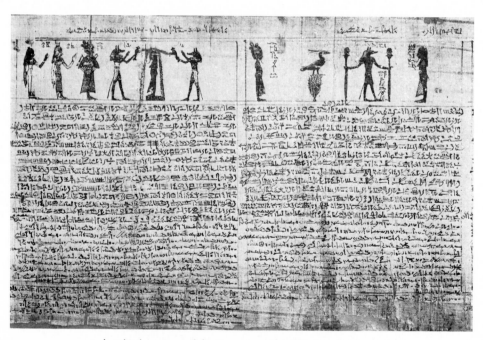

2.10b. *Rhind papyrus*, of the Roman period (Edinburgh Museum).

46

2.11*a*. Earliest known fragments of hieratic Papyri (Cairo Museum).

2.11*b*. Early hieratic Papyrus, Fifth Dynasty (Berlin Papyrus 9874).

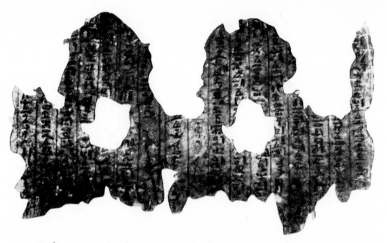

2.12*a*. Earliest extant book written on leather. Hieratic manuscript attributed to Sixth Dynasty (Cairo Museum).

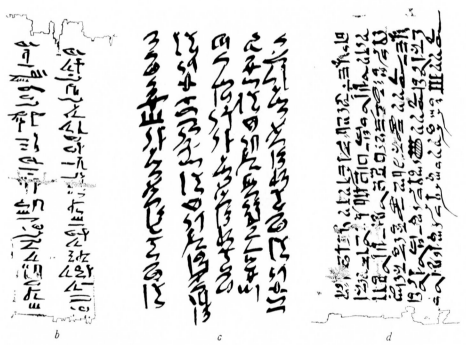

| *b* | *c* | *d* |

2.12*b*. *left* Portion of Berlin Papyrus 9010, attributed to the period of the Sixth Dynasty, *centre* Berlin Papyrus 3024, attributed to the period of the Middle Kingdom, *right* Berlin Papyrus 3033, Early New Kingdom.

2.13. a (*above*) *Papyrus Anastasi 7*, half of sheet 6, *recto* (British Museum 10222).
b (*below*) *Rhind Mathematical Papyrus* (British Museum 10057 and 10058).

49

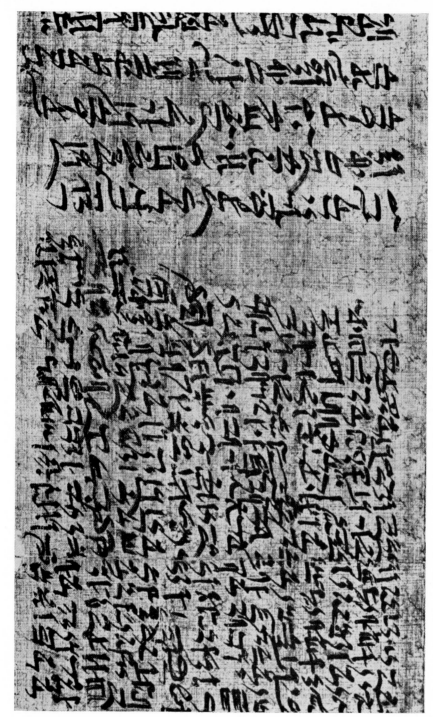

2.14. *Story of Si-nuhe*, portion of a copy dating from the Twelfth or Thirteenth Dynasty. (Berlin Papyrus 3022).

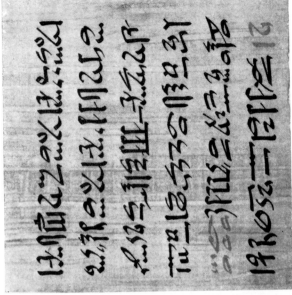

2.15. a (*left*) *Papyrus Ebers*, belonging to the period of the early Eighteenth Dynasty (University of Leipsig). b (*above*) Portion of *Papyrus Ebers*.

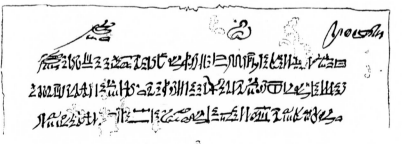

2.16a. Page of hieratic writing from the *Great Harris Papyrus* (British Museum).

2.16b. Detail from a school exercise book written in hieratic, with the teacher's corrections.

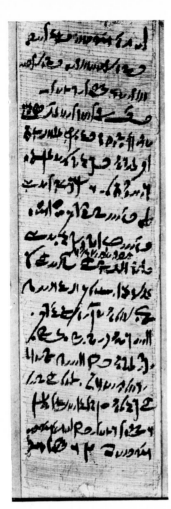

obverse

reverse   *b*

obverse

reverse   *c*

2.17. *a* Demotic document on wood. *b, c* Two wood labels of mummies written in demotic. Note the two lines of Greek on the reverse of *c*.

2.18. Rosetta stone (British Museum).

PTOLEMY

(P T O L M I S)
 1 2 3 4 5 6 7

HIEROGLYPHIC

DEMOTIC

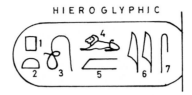

CLEOPATRA

(K LE O PAT R A)
 1 234 567 8 9

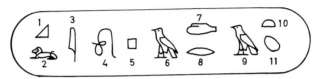

10 FEMININE ENDING
11 DETERMINATIVE FOLLOWING A FEMININE NAME

BERENICE

ALEXANDER

AUTOCRATOR

TIBERIUS

DOMITIAN

GERMANICUS

TRAJAN

2.19. Decipherment of Egyptian hieroglyphic writing: decipherment of certain imperial names and titles.

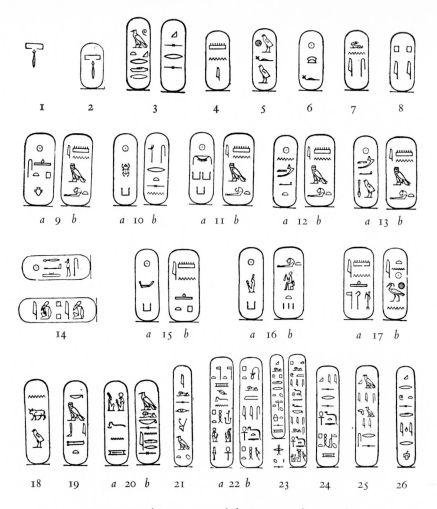

2.20. Egyptian royal names. *a* royal-divine name; *b* personal name.

1-2, Pharaoh. 3, *Autókratos* and Caesar (*Kaísaros*). 4, Mena or Menes (1st dyn.). 5, Khufu or Cheops (4th dyn.). 6, Khaf-ra or Chephren (4th dyn.). 7, Unas or Unis (5th dyn.). 8, Pepi I (6th dyn.). 9, Amen-em-hat I (12th dyn.). 10, Usertsen I or Sesonchosis (12th dyn.). 11, Amen-em-hat II (12th dyn.). 12, Amen-em-hat III (12th dyn). 13, Amen-em-hat IV (12th dyn.). 14, Apepa I or Apophis (a chief king of the Hyksos). 15, Amen-hetep or Amenophis I (18th dyn.). 16, Hat-shepset-khnem-Amen (Queen Hatshepsu). 17, Amen-hetep Neter Heq Uast or Amenophis IV (Akhnaton) (18th dyn.). 18, Necho (26th dyn.). 19, Cambyses (27th dyn.). 20, Alexander the Great. 21, Queen Arsinoë (Ptolemies). 22, Ptolemy V Epiphanes. 23, Cleopatra VII with her son Caesarion. 24, Augustus. 25, Caligula. 26, Claudius.

Class A

Class B

3.1. Cretan pictographic inscriptions.

57

3.2a. Main symbols of Linear A.

3.2b. Linear A sign list according to Caratelli.

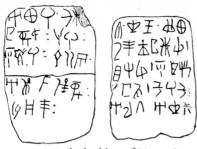

3.3a. Inscribed tablets of Linear A.

3.3b. Inscription in ink of Linear A.

Linear A

3.3c. Vase from Orchomenus (an ancient city in Boeotia) with inscription in Linear A.

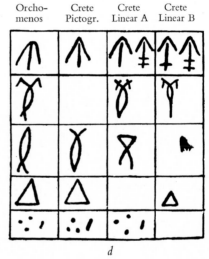

d

3.3d. The Orchomenus signs compared with Cretan symbols: Cretan pictographic signs, Linear A and Linear B.

side *a*　　　　3-4. Phaistos Disc (from a cast).　　　　side *b*

3.5. The symbols of both faces of the Phaistos disc, according to Professor Schwartz. *a* corresponds to 3.4*a* and *b* corresponds to 3.4*b*.

3.6b table:

NO.	PICTOGRAM	I	M	F	T
1	[pictogram]	19	0	0	19
2	[pictogram]	0	13	4	17
3	[pictogram]	2	3	1	6
4	[pictogram]	1	3	7	11
5	[pictogram]	0	7	5	12
6	[pictogram]	1	4	1	6
7	[pictogram]	0	5	1	6
8	[pictogram]	8	3	0	11
9	[pictogram]	1	5	0	6
10	[pictogram]	4	6	8	18
11	[pictogram]	0	2	1	3
12	[pictogram]	0	1	0	1
13	[pictogram]	2	1	3	6
14	[pictogram]	5	8	2	15
15	[pictogram]	0	1	0	1
16	[pictogram]	0	1	4	5
17	[pictogram]	2	2	0	4
18	[pictogram]	2	3	0	5
19	[pictogram]	0	3	3	6
20	[pictogram]	0	4	3	11
21	[pictogram]	0	2	7	2
22	[pictogram]	0	2	0	3
23	[pictogram]	1	3	1	11
24	[pictogram]	0	9	0	3
25	[pictogram]	1	1	1	11
26	[pictogram]	0	3	3	4
27	[pictogram]	0	0	0	1
28	[pictogram]	2	4	1	3
29	[pictogram]	2	2	3	7
30	[pictogram]	2	0	0	2
31	[pictogram]	0	4	0	4
32	[pictogram]	0	0	2	2
33	[pictogram]	0	2	0	2
34	[pictogram]	0	1	0	1
35	[pictogram]	0	2	0	2
36	[pictogram]	4	1	0	5
37	[pictogram]	0	0	1	1
38	[pictogram]	0	2	0	2
39	[pictogram]	2	0	0	2
40	[pictogram]	0	0	1	1
41	[pictogram]	1	0	0	1
42	[pictogram]	0	1	0	1
43	[pictogram]	1	0	0	4
44	[pictogram]	1	1	0	2
45	[pictogram]	0	1	0	1

3.6b. The frequency of the various symbols (I = initial, M = medial, F = final, T = total) according to Prof. Schwartz.

3.6a. Professor Schwartz' attempted decipherment of the Phaistos disc.

(Chart with columns A, E, I, O, U and rows Y, W, R, M, N, P, T, K, S containing pictograms; THORN = (S); UNIDENTIFIED – 15.)

4.1. Selection of inscribed seals from Indus Valley.

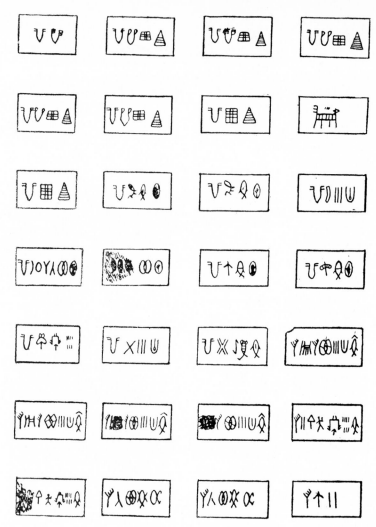

4.2. Seal inscriptions from Indus Valley.

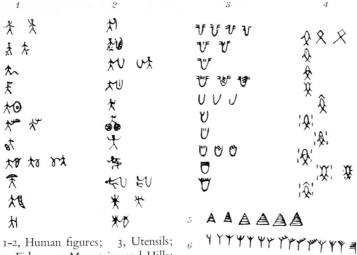

1-2, Human figures;   3, Utensils;
4, Fishes;   5, Mountains and Hills;
6, Trees.

4.3*a.* Stylized Indus Valley symbols.

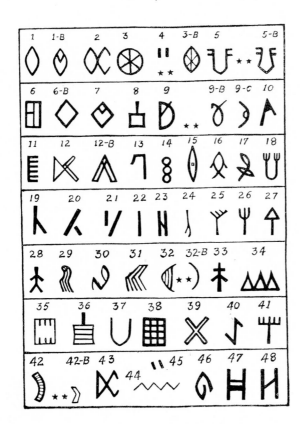

4.3*b.* Attempted decipherment by S. K. Ray, New Delhi: the uniliteral symbols of the Indus Valley.

Indus Valley	Easter Island	Indus Valley	Easter Island	Indus Valley	Easter Island	Indus Valley	Easter Island
I	II	III	IV	V	VI	VII	VIII

4.4. De Hevesy's comparison of Indus Valley symbols with Easter Island script.

5.1. Hittite hieroglyphic inscriptions carved in relief. *a*. The most beautiful inscription from Carchemish, ninth century B.C. *b*. Another Carchemish inscription, eighth century B.C.

a

b

5.2. Broken door jamb, in-
scribed in raised Hittite hiero-
glyphs: dedication of Temple of
Goddess Kubaba by Kaluwas,
King of Carchemish, c. 900 B.C.
(British Museum).

5.3*a*. Hittite hieroglyphic inscription engraved on stone.

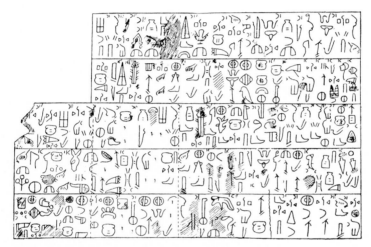

5.3*b*. Late Hittite hieroglyphic inscription, about 600 B.C., from Bulgar Dagh (Bulgarmaden).

Mon	Curs	Mon	Curs	Mon	Curs	Mon	Curs

5.4a. Comparison of Hittite hieroglyphic cursive signs with monumental symbols.

	Crete	Hitt.		Crete	Hitt.		Crete	Hitt.		Crete	Hitt.
1			11			21			31		
2			12			22			32		
3			13			23			33		
4			14			24			34		
5			15			25			35		
6			16			26			36		
7			17			27			37		
8			18			28			38		
9			19			29			39		
10			20			30			40		

5.4b. Comparison of Hittite hieroglyphic symbols wth Cretan pictographic signs.

70

5.5a. Hittite ideographic symbols.

5.5b. Hittite hieroglyphic syllabary according to I. J. Gelb.

5.6. Hittite inscription from Karatepe.

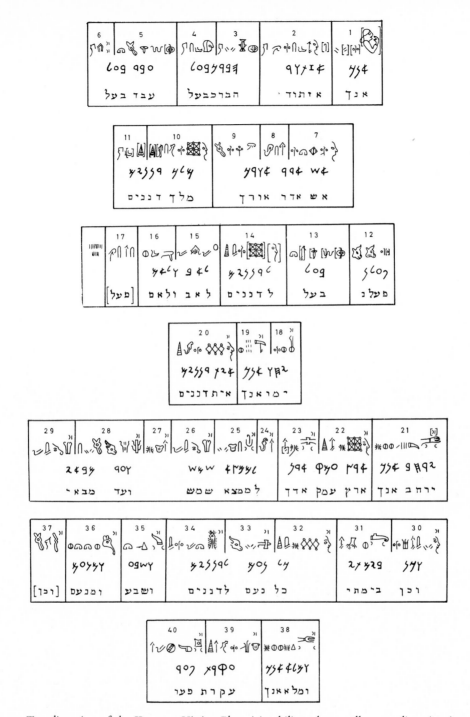

5.7. Transliteration of the Karatepe Hittite, Phoenician bilingual, as well as transliteration into modern hebrew.

73

(1) *kan*, sky, dry; *yang*, the first element, the creative element; Grand-father, life, favourable presage

(2) *tui*, water, sea, lakes, light

(3) *li*, fire, sun, heat, the creative element of heat and light

(4) *ch'en*, thunder, mother of lightning and heat, hard

(5) *hsü*, wind, movable, wood

(6) *k'an*, water, rivers, liquid element, cool, cold, moon

(7) *kên*, mountains, hills, element which hinders movement

(8) *kun*, earth, terrestrial element; *yin*, the second element, the element of destruction; Grand-mother, bad presage.

6.1*a*. Chinese mystic trigrams *pa kua*.

| command | vow, oath | refusal | refuse to marry | usur- pation |

6.1*b*. Chinese hand gestures.

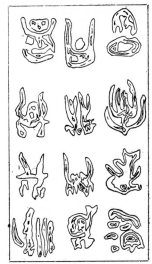

The 'Yü Tablet'

Stone drum inscription

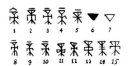

Archaic characters on
bronze and bone

character *ti*, 'sovereign ruler'

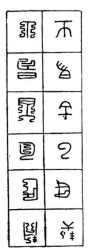

Hsiao   Ta
chuan   chuan

Bronze inscrip-
tion from Shang-
Yin period

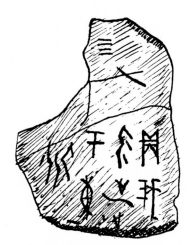

Ancient characters engraved on
fragments of bone

6.2. Early Chinese inscriptions on stone, bronze and bone.

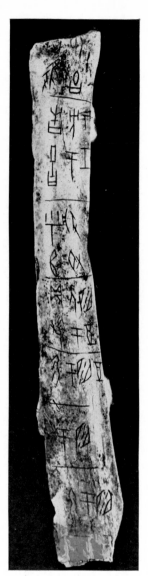

6.3. Oracle bone-inscriptions from the village of Hsiao-t'un, near An-yang (Honan). (University Library Cambridge).

6.4. Copy of the inscriptions of divination on the ventral part of a tortoise shell on the occasion of a hunt at Kwei, by King Wu-ting of the Yin (Shang) Dynasty, 1450–c. 1000 B.C. The hunt yielded one tiger, 40 deer, 164 foxes, 159 fawns, a brace of pheasants and 18 double-red birds.

Hsing shu.　K'ai shu.　Ts'ao shu.　Li shu.　Shan fang　Chuan
　　　　　　　　　　　　　　　　　　　　ta chuan

6.5. Main types of Chinese writing.

PICTOGRAMS							
MAN, ANIMALS, AND PARTS OF THE HUMAN BODY							
MAN	WOMAN	CHILD	MOUTH	NOSE	EYE	HAND	FOOT
HORSE	TIGER	DOG	ELEPHANT	DEER	SHEEP	SILKWORM	TORTOISE
NATURAL AND ARTIFICIAL OBJECTS							
SUN	MOON	RAIN	LIGHTNING	MOUNTAIN	RIVER	GRAIN	WOOD
VASE	TRIPOD	BOW	ARROW	SILK	BOOK	ORACLE	OMEN

IDEOGRAMS			
FIGHTING (MAN AGAINST MAN)	PLOUGHING (MAN+PLOUGH)	HUNTING (WEAPON + ANIMAL)	SUCKLING (WOMAN NURSING CHILD)
SUNSET (SUN+GRASSES)	BRIGHT (MOON+WINDOW)	WRITING BRUSH (HAND + BRUSH)	SCRIBE (HAND+OBJECT)
	ABOVE	BELOW	

PICTOGRAM + PHONETIC ELEMENT			
BLACK HORSE (HORSE + li)	SACRIFICE (SPIRIT + ssu)	PREGNANCY (WOMAN + Jen)	HUAN RIVER (RIVER +huan)

HOMOPHONES	
(lai," WHEAT," FOR) lai "TO COME"	(feng," PHOENIX," FOR) feng "WIND"

6.6. Examples of Chinese pictograms, ideograms, pictograms combined with phonetic elements, and homophones.

Ancient	Modern		Ancient	Modern	
⊙	日	*jih* sun	米	木	*mu* tree
☽	月	*yüeh* moon	雨	雨	*yü* rain
⏶	山	*shan* mountain	矢	矢	*shih* arrow
	子	*tzu* child	門	門	*mên* door, gate
	巴	*pa* great serpent	冊	冊	*ts'ê*, bundle of inscribed sticks, volume, book, scroll

Hsiang symbols

Ancient	Modern		Ancient	Modern	
	方	*fâng* zone square		言	*yên* word, to talk
	勿	*wu* no	中	中	*chung* middle
I	一	*yi* one	畺	畺	*chiang* border, limit, frontier
II	二	*erh* two			
III	三	*san* three			

Chih Shih symbols

Ancient	Modern	Ancient	Modern	Ancient	Modern
東	東	奻	奻	馬	馬

2 × East = everywhere (*tung*) 2 × women = quarrel (*wân*) 3 × horse = to gallop (*ch'êng*)

Ancient	Modern	Ancient	Modern		Ancient	Modern	Ancient	Modern	
口	口	鳥	鳴		人	言	信		

kô + *niaô* = *ming* mouth bird to sing

jên + *yên* = *sin* man word true

jih + *yüeh* = *ming* sun moon bright, clear

Hui i symbols

6.7. Classification of Chinese characters.

后　司　人　尸

hêú　*szü*　*jên*　*shih*
prince　officer,　man,　corpse
　　　　clerk　person

Chuan chou symbols

nine basic strokes of Chinese
writing

來　　足　　故　　古　　女　　汝

lâi　　*tsu*　　*ku*　used in-　*kú*　　*nü*　used in-　*jü*
grain,　foot,　cause　stead of　old　woman　stead of　you
also　also
to come　be sufficient

Chia chieh symbols

心忄 *hsin*　　　水氵 *shiú*　　言 *yên*

heart　　　　　water　　　　to talk

工 *kūng*　　忏 *k'ūng*　　江 *kiāng*　　訌 *hûng*

worker　　impatience　torrent, flood　quarrel

由 *yu*　　忦 *yeû*　　油 *yeû*　　詷 *chou*

from　　sad　　oil　　to pray

甫 *fou*　　惠 *fou*　　浦 *pu*　　誧 *fū*

table land,　to have fear　branch of　to talk together
huge　　　　　　　a river　　to decide

果 *kò*　　悇 *kò*　　猓 *k'o*　　課 *k'ó*

fruit　　to go　　river　　to examine
　　　　　　　　　　　to investigate

Hsing shêng symbols

6.8. Classification of Chinese characters.

6.9. 300 Chinese primary elements.

No.		No.		No.		No.		No.		No.		No.		No.		No.		No.	
1	一	31	匕	61	尢	91	子	121	斤	151	弗	181	缶	211	兆	241	亞	271	垂
2	丨	32	彐	62	尤	92	中	122	戶	152	冊	182	至	212	放	242	金	272	琴
3	丶	33	刀	63	廾	93	心	123	午	153	皿	183	辛	213	厽	243	來	273	旁
4	丿	34	力	64	刅	94	止	124	牛	154	且	184	衣	214	谷	244	兔	274	寅
5	乀	35	勹	65	才	95	丙	125	今	155	目	185	交	215	豆	245	希	275	魚
6	乁	36	乃	66	广	96	氏	126	不	156	曰	186	亥	216	呂	246	易	276	鳥
7	乙	37	又	67	弋	97	丑	127	木	157	臣	187	虫	217	克	247	炙	277	鹿
8	乚	38	乂	68	孔	98	互	128	开	158	四	188	朿	218	臣	248	函	278	亞
9	亅	39	㐅	69	凡	99	云	129	水	159	糸	189	束	219	畱	249	甾	279	率
10	く	40	卜	70	无	100	无	130	火	160	民	190	束	220	酉	250	果	280	离
11	ㄅ	41	丩	71	毛	101	井	131	犬	161	凸	191	虍	221	卵	251	俞	281	殼
12	二	42	丁	72	口	102	丹	132	爪	162	出	192	舟	222	臼	252	希	282	壺
13	亠	43	丂	73	口	103	丹	133	夭	163	丙	193	自	223	角	253	發	283	象
14	人	44	万	74	回	104	亢	134	壬	164	朮	194	自	224	囪	254	非	284	舄
15	入	45	三	75	厂	105	六	135	凶	165	禾	195	耳	225	豕	255	韭	285	焉
16	八	46	彡	76	尸	106	文	136	禾	166	乑	196	臣	226	豕	256	面	286	誉
17	儿	47	巛	77	己	107	方	137	矛	167	矛	197	而	227	采	257	革	287	爲
18	几	48	巜	78	弓	108	万	138	永	168	永	198	西	228	甬	258	肩	288	巢
19	九	49	彳	79	馬	109	勿	139	瓜	169	瓜	199	丙	229	弟	259	盾	289	樂
20	九	50	个	80	小	110	欠	140	玉	170	戊	200	西	230	車	260	鹵	290	鼠
21	九	51	勺	81	小	111	气	141	主	171	矢	201	西	231	貝	261	录	291	蜀
22	十	52	久	82	毛	112	毛	142	玄	172	冬	202	丹	232	肉	262	癸	292	齊
23	七	53	夂	83	手	113	手	143	白	173	正	203	肉	233	身	263	泉	293	壽
24	冂	54	夊	84	丯	114	半	144	囟	174	皮	204	臼	234	頁	264	者	294	齒
25	冖	55	夕	85	山	115	丰	145	瓦	175	穴	205	甘	235	辰	265	畏	295	嘼
26	凵	56	夊	86	屮	116	斗	146	田	176	它	206	囟	236	長	266	乖	296	龍
27	凵	57	女	87	斗	117	爿	147	由	177	宁	207	由	237	長	267	飛	297	龜
28	厶	58	互	88	土	118	丬	148	甲	178	米	208	曲	238	東	268	馬	298	燕
29	厶	59	大	89	干	119	牙	149	羊	179	羊	209	羽	239	隹	269	咼	299	翏
30	匚	60	夨	90	也	120	予	150	冉	180	冉	210	兆	240	倉	270	舉	300	爵

一 丨 丶 丿 乙 亅

二 亠 人 儿 入 八 冂 冖 冫 几 凵 刀 力 勹 匕 匚 匸 十

卜 卩 厂 厶 又 口 囗 土 士 夂 夊 夕 大 女 子 宀 寸 小 尢 尸 屮 山 巛 工

己 巾 干 幺 广 廴 廾 弋 弓 彐 彡 彳 心 戈 戶 手 支 攴 文 斗 斤 方 无 日

日 月 木 欠 止 歹 殳 毋 比 毛 氏 气 水 火 爪 父 爻 爿 片 牙 牛 犬 玄 玉

瓜 瓦 甘 生 用 田 疋 疒 癶 白 皮 皿 目 矛 矢 石 示 内 禾 穴 立 竹 米 糸

缶 网 羊 羽 老 而 耒 耳 聿 肉 臣 自 至 臼 舌 舛 舟 艮 色 艸 虍 虫 血 行 衣

西 見 角 言 谷 豆 豕 豸 貝 赤 走 足 身 車 辛 辰 辵 邑 酉 釆 里 金 長

門 阜 隶 隹 雨 青 非 面 革 韋 韭 音 頁 風 飛 食 首 香 馬 骨 高 髟 鬥

鬯 鬲 鬼 魚 鳥 鹵 鹿 麥 麻 黃 黍 黑 黹 黽 鼎 鼓 鼠 鼻 齊 齒 龍 龜 龠

6.10. The 214 keys of Chinese writing.

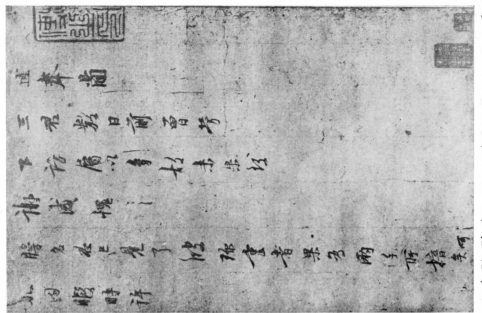

6.11b. Liu P'u (A.D. 967–1028) Sung Dynasty. Part of personal letter.
Born in Ch'ien Tung, led a hermit life at West lake. Emperor Sen Tsung conferred on him the posthumous title Ho-Chin Shing Sheng.

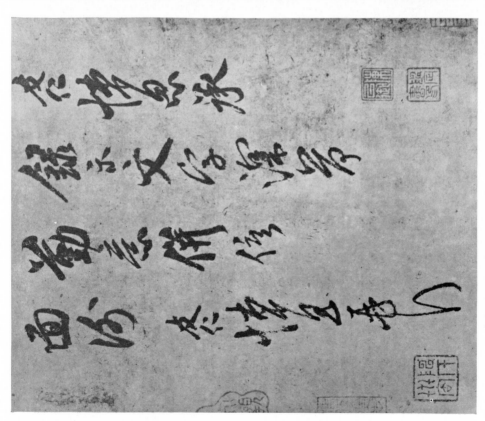

6.11a. Note of thanks to a friend, written by Mi Yu-Jen (son of Mi Fei) A.D. 1086–1165; vice minister of war under Emperor Kao Tsung—Southern Sung Dynasty.

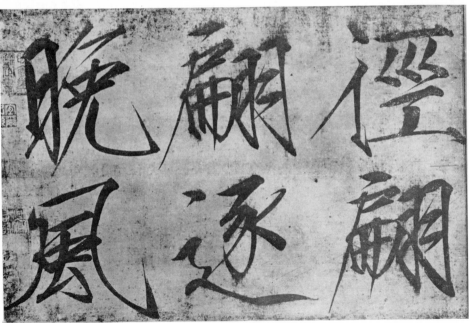

6.12. *a* (above) Part of a poem on *Autumn Flowers* by Emperor Huei Tsung (A.D. 1082–1135) the eighth ruler of the Sung Dynasty (1102–1125) named Chao Chih, the 11th son of Emperor Shen Tsung (A.D. 1068–1085). *b* (below) Part seven of the same poem.

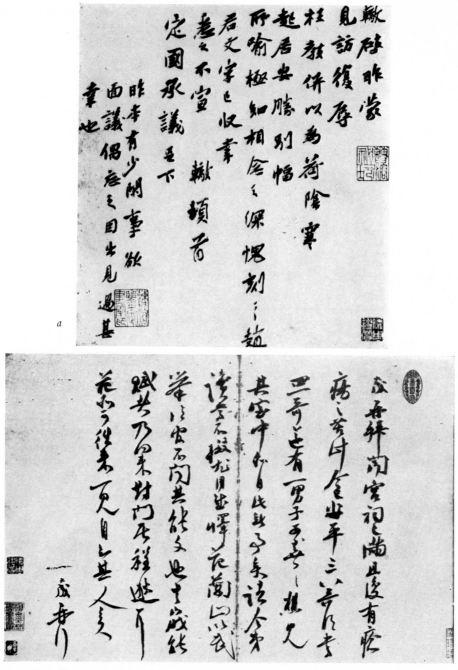

6.13. Sung Dynasty. *a* Su Ch'e's personal letter to Wang Kung (A.D. 1039–1112) younger brother of Su Shih, became a Chin-Shih in 1057, served as Deputy Premier under Emperor Cheh Tsung. Posthumously was given—by Emperor Hwei Tsung—the title Wen Ting. *b* Personal letter by Chang Chin-Chen (A.D. 1092–1159). Born on K'ai-Feng, topped the list of Chin-Shih 1132, vice minister of Rites, southern Sung Dynasty. Posthumous title: Wen-Chung.

86

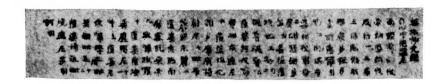

6.14a. The earliest preserved printing; Japanese Buddhist charms, in the Sanskrit language and in Chinese characters (c. A.D. 770).

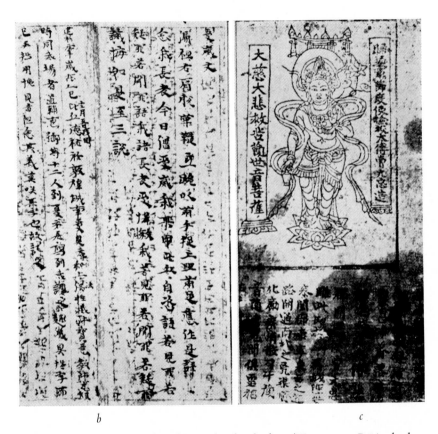

b   c

6.14. *b* Earliest example of a Chinese dated colophon (Vinaya text, *Prātimoksa* by Sarvāstivādin, dated 10.1.406); *c* printed and hand-coloured Chinese prayer-sheet dated 947; it gives the name (Lei Yen-mei) of the first known printer (or rather blockmaker). Both documents were found at the 'Caves of the Thousand Buddhas' and are preserved in the British Museum.

87

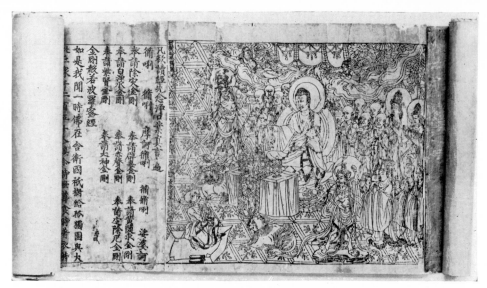

6.15a. The earliest preserved book: the *Diamond Sutra* in Chinese, A.D. 868 (British Museum).

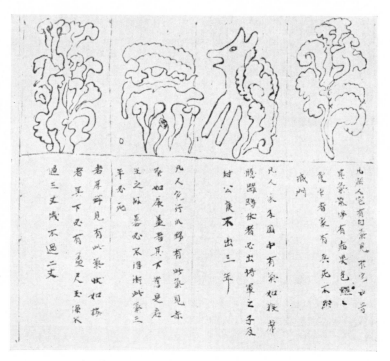

6.15b. Chinese Taoist text on divination from vapours.

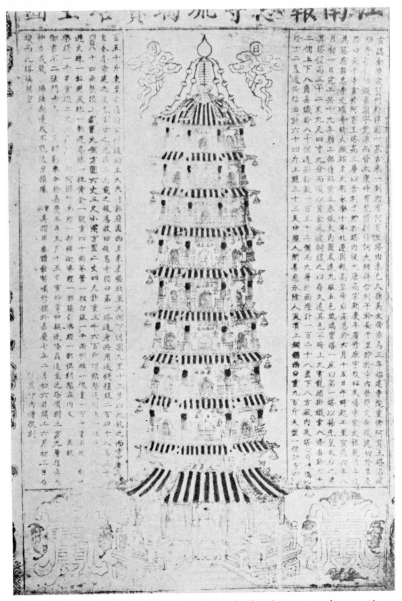

6.16. Page from a Chinese book (The John Rylands Library, Manchester, *Chin. No. 465*).

6.17. *a* Mahāprajñaparamitasûtra. Chap. 110, printed at Fêng-hua, A.D. 1162. (University Library, Cambridge). *b* Jade book: Diamond Sūtra, A.D. 1732 (Chester Beatty Library, Dublin).

6.17 *b* Jade Book: *Dirmond Sutra*, A.D. 1732 (Chester Beatty Library, Dublin).

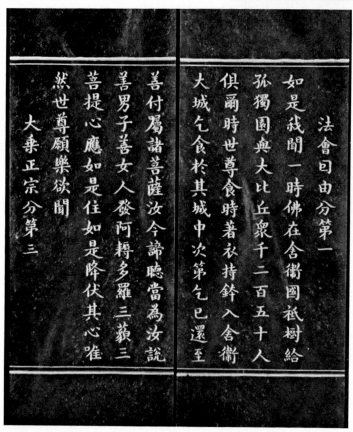

6.18*a*. 1, *Jên*, man, person, human. 2, *Nü*, girl, woman, female. 3, *Tzu*, child, son, posterity. 4 (composed of symbols 2 and 3), *Hao*, good, well, fond of, very. 5, *Kuo*, kingdom or country surrounded with boundaries. 6, *Chung*, centre, middle, inside. 7, *Ta* or *da*, great, noble, very. 8, *Ying*, superior used for Eng(land). 9, *I* (*ee*), one. 10, *Erh*, two. 11, *San*, three. 12, *Szu*, four. 13, *Wu*, 'five.' 14, *Lu*, six. 15, *Chi*, 'seven. 16, *Pa*, eight. 17, *Chiu*, nine. 18, *Shih*, ten.

6.18. Modern Chinese characters.

6.18*b*. 1. (2+1), *Nü-jên*, female+ person = woman. 2. (6+5), *Chung-kuo*, middle + kingdom = China. 3. (8+5), *Ying-kuo*, Ying (England)+ kingdom = England. 4. (8+5+1), *Ying-kuo-jên*, English + kingdom + man = Englishman.

口 = mouth

子 = child

日 = sun

mouth+vapour

words+tongue

pig+roof

言 = words

話 = speech

家 = house

a

'fang'
square

place

spinning

fragrant

enquire

hinder

方 square

坊 square+earth

紡 square+silk

芳 square+herbs

訪 square+words

妨 square+woman

pig+roof+woman = to marry

woman+broom+storm = wife

woman+roof = peace

2 women+roof = discord

3 women = intrigue

women+mouth+crooked = dangerous

word+mouth+mountain = slander

b

c

6.19. *a*, *b* and *c* Modern Chinese characters.

一 one (i)

十 ten (shih)

中 centre (chung)

女 woman, daughter (niü)

本 root, origin (pen)

仁 perfect virtue (jen)

河 river (ho)

栢 cypress (pai)

銀 silver (yin)

輪 wheel (lun)

字 characters (tzŭ)

思 to think (szŭ)

要 important must (yao)

買 to buy (mai)

集 to gather (chi)

反 to turn over, to turn back (fan)

店 inn, shop (tien)

眉 eyebrow (mei)

虐 harsh cruel (nüeh)

差 different (ch'a)

武 military, violent (wu)

式 fashion, rule (shih)

飛 to fly (fei)

或 or (huo)

成 success (ch'eng)

近 near (chin)

廸 to bring forward, to direct (ti)

建 to build to establish (chien)

逼 to annoy to press (pi)

避 to shun to avoid (pi)

回 to return (hui)

因 because (yin)

固 firm, strong (ku)

圓 round (yuan)

團 (a) mass, to coil (tuan)

閂 the bolt used to bar a door (shuan)

閃 to flash (shan)

問 to ask (wen)

開 to open (k'ai)

鬪 to flight (tou)

6.20. Modern Chinese characters: simple, and compounds of two elements.

93

衍 (yen) to overflow, to spread out
漪 (i) the ripples on water
樹 (shu) tree
謝 (hsieh) to thank
鐵 (tie) iron

稟 (ping) to inform
賣 (mai) to sell
器 (ch'i) vessel
算 (suan) to reckon, to calculate
靈 (ling) spirit, efficacious

咒 (chou) to curse, incantations
智 (chih) wisdom
豎 (shu) to set up
賢 (hsien) virtuous
瞽 (ku) blind

品 (p'in) conduct
森 (shen) overgrown, dark
晶 (ching) crystal, bright
焱 (yen) flames
鑫 (hsin) used as names

盟 (meng) oath, alliance
盤 (p'an) plate, dish
契 (ch'i) contract, to notch
染 (jan) to dye, to infect
點 (tien) dot, spot

符 (fu) to agree with, to tally
筋 (chin) sinews
萌 (meng) the budding of plants
莊 (chuang) sedate
箱 (hsiang) box, chest

6.21. Modern Chinese compound characters—three elements.

94

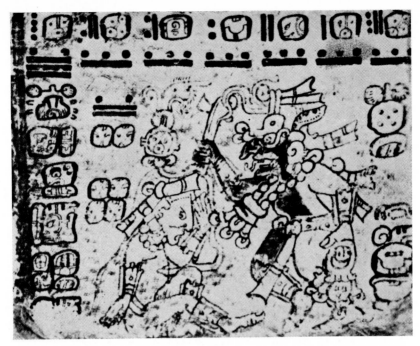

7.1*a. Codex Dresden.* Portion of divinatory almanac (4 *Ahau,* 12 *Lamat,* 7 *Cib,* 2 *Kan,* 10 *Eb,* 5 *Ahau,* 13 *Lamat,* South, God B, fire god, maize god, drought).

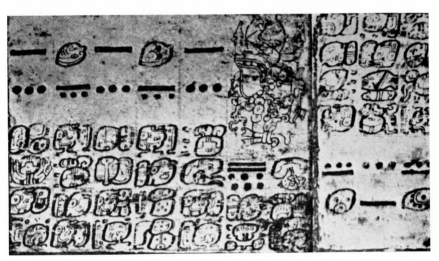

7.1*b. Codex Dresden.* Complete divinatory almanac with the four world directional colours: red, white, black, and yellow, and glyphs of various offerings to be made to the gods. (Explanation by J. Eric S. Thompson.)

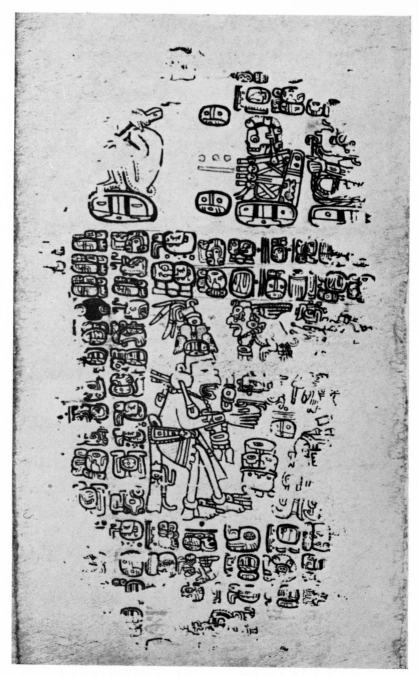

Fig. 7.2. *Codex Paris* (infra red photo of p. 4, the best preserved page of the manuscript). Represents events connected with the Maya *katun* (twenty-year period) 11 *Ahau*. (Explanation by J. Eric S. Thompson.)

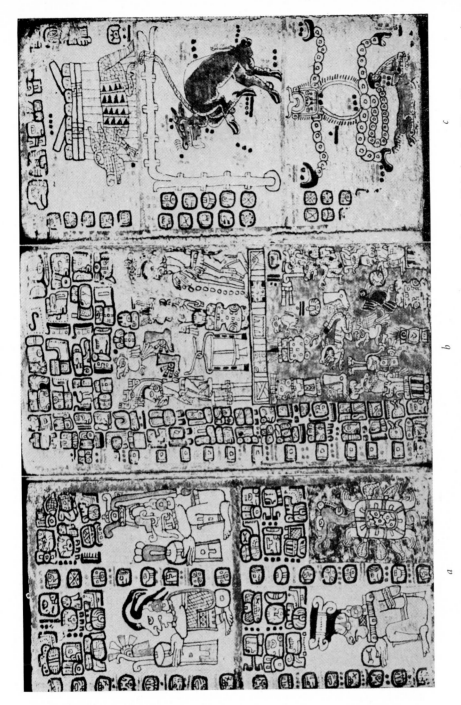

7.3. *Codex Tro-Cortesiano*. *a*, page 72 (page 38 of *Codex Cortesiano*). *b*, page 36 (page 21 of *Codex Tro*), showing New Year ceremonies for the *Kan* years, and including the unusual feature of a man walking on stilts and also a man sowing; *c*, page 48 (page 9 of *Codex Tro*), showing an *armadillo* in a dead-fall trap and a deer caught in a noose trap, and also the scorpion god. Each picture illustrates a divinatory almanac, presumably for hunters (Explanation by J. Eric S. Thompson).

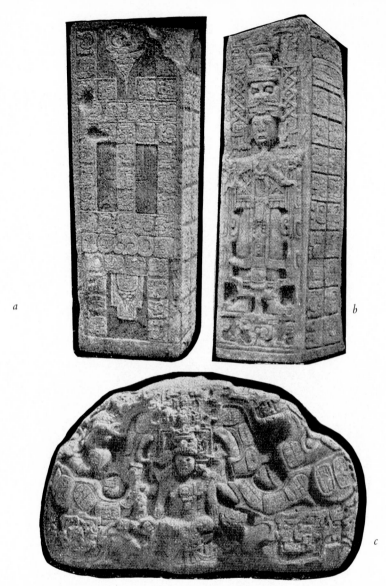

7.4. *a*, *b* Maya Stelae. *c* Maya altar.

7.5a. Maya 'hieroglyphs'. One of the few surviving texts in wood, from Tikal.

7.5b. Maya 'hieroglyphs'. Text from the left side of the cross at Palanque.

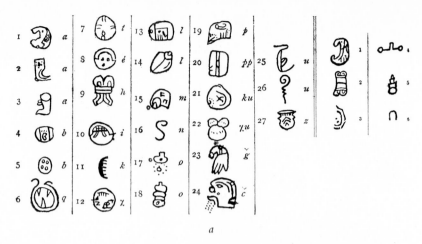

7.6a. The Maya 'alphabet' according to Bishop Diego de Landa.

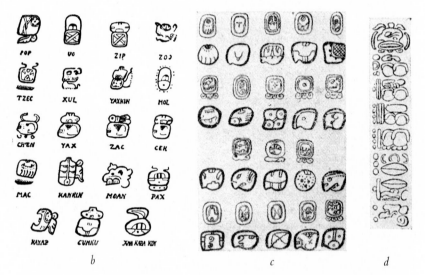

7.6. b Maya symbols of the months, according to the Dresden codex. c Maya symbols of the days, according to monuments (upper part) and manuscripts (lower part). d The highest number found in a Maya inscription: 1,841,639,800 days, corresponding to over 5,100,000 years.

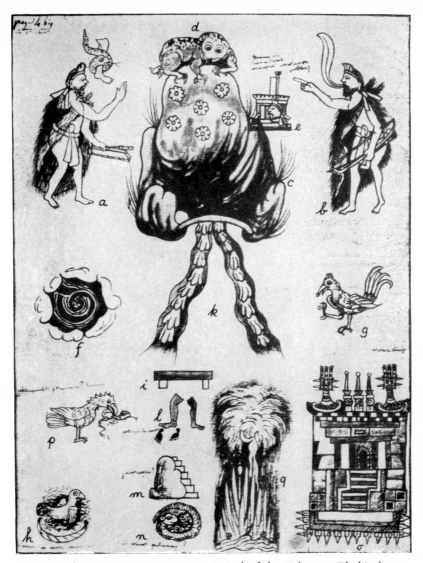

7.7. Page from an Aztec manuscript. Arrival of the Toltecs at Tlachiualtepec. *a*, Icxicouatl; *b*, Quetzalteueyeac at *c*, Tlachiualtepec, *e*, the seat of Aquiach-Amapane (K. Th. Preuss and E. Mengin, *Die Mexikanische Bilderhandschrift Historia Tolteca-Chichimeca*, Berlin, 1937, pl. IV).

7.8*a*. Portion of *Codex Zouche* (*Nuttall*) (British Museum).

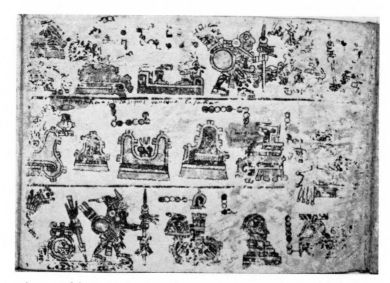

7.8*b*. Page of the pre-Columbian *Codex Colombino* (National Anthropological Museum, Mexico).

7.9. Post-Conquest *Codex Fernandez Leal* (National Anthropological Museum, Mexico), shows a *volador*; the frame on which the fliers sit—owing to ignorance of perspective—is shown vertical instead of horizontal. (Explanation by Dr. Bodil Christensen).

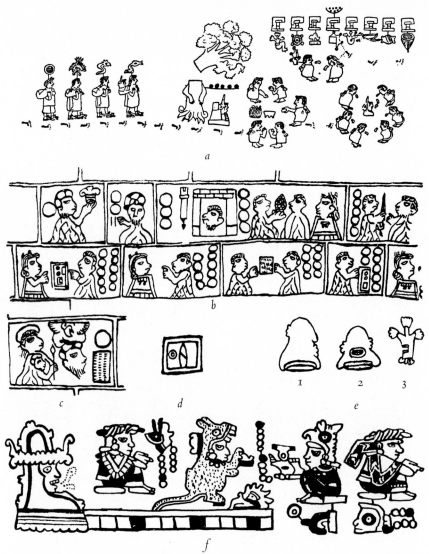

a

b

c   *d*   1   2   3

e

f

7.10*a*. The migrations of the Aztecs, as represented in native manuscripts.

7.10*b*. The Ten Commandments in Aztec post-Conquest manuscripts.

7.10*c*. The First Article of the Catholic dogma, in Aztec post-Conquest manuscripts.

7.10*d*. Year 1 of the Flint-knife, corresponding to A.D. 1168.

7.10*e*. The place-names Tepeyacac, Tepetitlan, and Qauhnauc; (1) *tepe(.tl)*, mountain+ *yaca(.tli)*, nose = Tepeyacac, On-the-Mountain-nose. (2) *tepe(.tl)*, mountain+ *tlan(.tli)*, tooth, denture = Tipetitlan, Between-the-Mountains. (3) *qua(i.tl)*, tree, forest+ *nau(a.tl)*, mouth = Qauhnauc, On-the-Trees.

7.10*f*. A suitor, named One House, brings presents to Nine Wind and Ten Eagle, the parents of princess Six Monkey, living at a place called Cloud-Belching-Mountain; Six Monkey turns her back on the wooer (H. G. Spinden, *Indian Manuscripts of Southern Mexico*, Washington, 1935, p. 436).

7.11*a*. Mexican symbols representing the twenty days.

7.11*b*. 'Paper' manufacture in modern Mexico: from San Pablito, Sierra Norte de Pueblo.

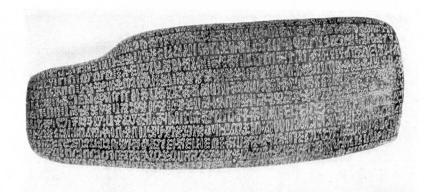

a

b

c

8.1. Easter Island writing. *a* Signatures of the native chiefs on the treaties with the Spaniards in 1770. *b–c* Specimens of *kohau-rongo-rongo* tablets.

8.2. Obverse and reverse of an Easter Island Tablet (Courtesy Smithsonian Institution, catal. no. 129773).

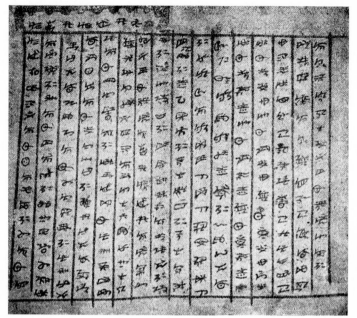

9.1*a*. Lo-lo horizontal script.

9.1*b*. Lo-lo vertical script.

9.1*c*. Lo-lo printed book, edited by Prince Len.

4   3   3   1

Kàng-siang-ying

Kiao-kyo

Yei-Ming-cheu

Local variant characters

The characters for 1, 'sun', 2, 'rain',
3, 'wind', and 4, 'mountain'.

a

b   *c*   *d*

sky   earth   moon   father   mother   person   heart   foot   tiger   dragon   door   to make   the same   name   family   hand   tree

e

I   1 2 3 4 5 6 7 8 9 10 11 12 13 14 15 16 17 18

II   1 2 3 4 5 6 7 8 9 10 11 12 13 14 15

f

9.2. *a* Lo-lo script: local variant characters. *b* The five known ideograms of
the Khitan script. *c* Niu-chih 'little' script. *d* Niu-chih 'national' character.
e Ideograms of the Yao script. *f* Miao-tzu ideograms.

109

a

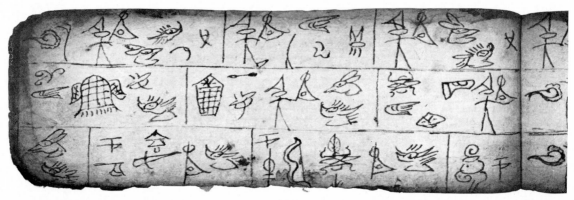

b

c

9.3. *a* First page of a Mo-so manuscript. *b*, *c*, Na-Khi book (Alphabet Museum, Tel-Aviv).

110

9.4. Si-Hia or Hsi-hsia syllabary.

III

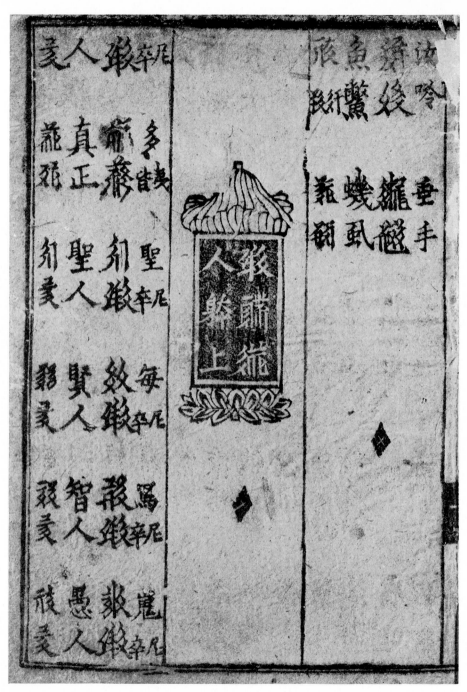

9.5 and 9.6. Chinese Si-Hia (Hsi-hsia) glossary.

9.6. Si-Hia glossary.

113

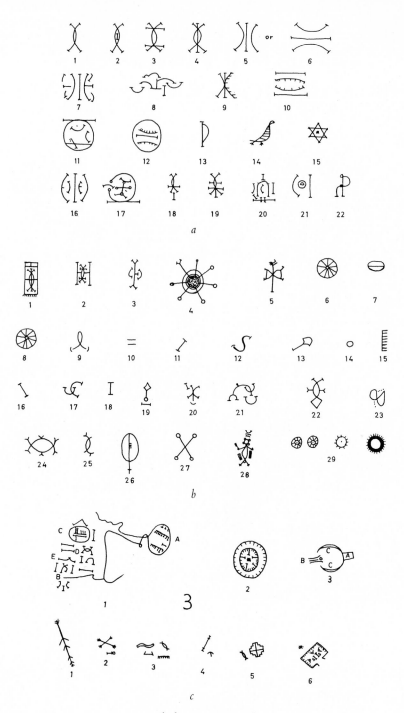

9.7. Nsibidi signs or records.

a. 1, Married love. 2, Married love, with pillow. 3, Married love with pillows for head and feet (a sign of wealth). 4, Married love with pillow. 5 and 6, Quarrel between husband and wife (a pillow is between them). 7, Violent quarrel between husband and wife. 8, One who causes a disturbance between husband and wife. 9, A woman with six children and a husband, and a pillow. 10, A man with two wives and their children, with the roof-tree of their house. 11. A house in which are three women and a man. 12, Two women with many children in the house with their husband. 13, A woman with child. 14, The same. 15, (shield of David), Ardent love. 16, Two women on each side of a house; one on each side has a child. 17, Two women who live in the same house have palaver every time they meet; a third woman is entering by the door. 18, A man comes to a woman who has a husband and asks her to live with him. 19, Three men who sought the same married woman. 20, A man committed adultery with a woman who lives apart from her husband; he has to pay compensation to the woman's family and to her husband. 21, A woman goes to bathe in the river at a ford, while her husband watches to see that no one shoots her. 22, fire.

b. 1, A man and a woman sleeping together on a native bed; it was very hot, so they put their arms outside, the short strokes at the bottom are the legs of the bed. 2, A boy kept a girl as his friend until they grew up. He then married her, and they lived together and made their bed with a pillow for the head and feet. 3, A man and his friend went into the town to get two girls; one of them got a girl and took her home with him; the other could not find one, and therefore they parted and went different ways. 4 and 5, A man's heart; he stands with his arms spread out to show that he knows more about Egbo than any other man; the dots represent the blood in the heart. 6, Young boys sitting in a Nsibidi house. 7, A palaver house.

An episode. 8, The young boys were sitting in the Nsibidi house. 9, there were two young women who sold their favours for money, 10, and they had two boys whom they used to send out to get the men to come to them, or to get money from them; 11, one of the boys took 12, a chewing stick, 13, a bottle of *tombo* and 14, a native glass; to 15, the young men sitting on the *ekfrat* stick; these young men sent 16, their boy to bring 17, a bag containing rods; 18, the boy took the bag of rods to the two men, who in turn took them to the women; 19, the young men sent their boy (with the sign of the comet) to meet them that night; 20, one of the young men met one of the women in an open place, where they rested to their mutual satisfaction and content; 21, the next day, the young man found the woman with a different man, and knew she was unfaithful.

22, Two young girls carrying water pots on their heads. 23, Large stone for grinding up medicine. 24, The sign of love: a man and woman sleeping together. 25, A sick boy and girl sleeping together. 26, Rat trap set to catch the rat which ate the corn in the house. 27, Two sticks crossed before the door of an Egbo house. 28, Husband and wife love each other ardently: they like to put their arms round one another (shown by extended hands); they are rich (having three pillows and a table on each side); the wife holds a comb. 29, Some representations of the Nsibidi house.

c. 1. A record of an *ikpe* or judgment case. The lines round and twisting mean that the case was a difficult one which the people of the town could not judge by themselves, so they sent to the surrounding towns to call the wise men from them, and the case was tried by them (*a*) and decided; it was a case of adultery (*b*); the court was held under a tree (*c*); (*d*), the party who won the case; (*e*) a man who thumbs as a sign of contempt.

2. The record of a trial by the Nsibidi club, drawn on a small calabash: the circles show the court-house, with verandah, round which, are the inner walls, the towns-folk are standing; also the executioners are represented (T-signs).

3. A stranger (B enters a town; he walks up the main street between two rows of houses (C–C) till he comes to Egbo House (A). As a consequence of the comet (4) lately seen, property (5, 6, 7) is strewn about in disorder, the Head Chief is dead and his body has been set in an armchair (8); before his house there is a seat. In the Egbo House (9), the townspeople have collected to decide between the two claimants to the office of Head Chief now vacant.

9.8a. Symbols of the Bamun ideographic script.

PHON. VALUE	MEANING	SYMBOL	PHON. VALUE	MEANING	SYMBOL	PHON. VALUE	MEANING	SYMBOL
si	BIRD		pe	CULLENDER		ngüê	LEOPARD	
baka	PLATE		nyam	HORSE		memfi	GOAT	
kuo	LADDER		wuo	STONE		mengob	COCK	
nôd	BODY		tu	HEAD		nyu	HAIR	
mon	CHILD		ndàb	THREAD		kuob	PALM-GROVE	
nuê	SNAKE					kom	RAZOR	
sie	DITCH		li	EYE		ndab	HOUSE	
tüt	EAR		mi	FACE		tâm	MUD	

9.8b. Development of Bamun characters.

Actual value	Word	Meaning	1907	1911	1916	1918
F, fa, 8	Fama	Eight				
F, fè	Fè	Burn & work				
F, fo	Fom	King				
F, fou	Fou	Measure				
G, ga	Ngè	(Chose-faite)				
G, go, 10	Ngom	Ten				

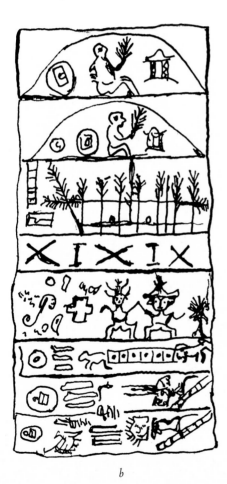

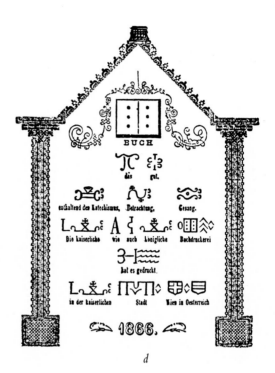

9.9. *a* Native pictographic writing of Paucar-tambo (Peru). *b* Minhassa ideographic script. *c* Aymarà ideographic script. *d* Micmac ideographic script.

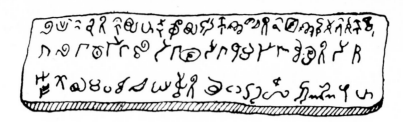

9.10*a*. Chukcha inscribed tablet.

Father	Mother	Son	Reindeer herd	On the river	Small, little
Rich	Poor	Good	Bad	I	My, mine,
Our	Food, to eat,	To live	To be	There	No
Only	Also	Various	kinds of	Fishes	Plate
Light	Tea-pot	Milk		Tobacco-pipe	Cigarette

9.10*b*. Chukcha ideograms.

118

10.1. *a* Bronze tablet inscribed in the pseudo-hieroglyphic syllabary of Byblos (*left*, obverse; *right*, reverse). *b* Pseudo-hieroglyphic inscription on stone (fragment g). *c* Bronze tablet in the script of Byblos (*above*, obverse; *below*, reverse). *d* Spatulae from Byblos with N. Semitic inscriptions and traces of pseudo-hieroglyphic character.

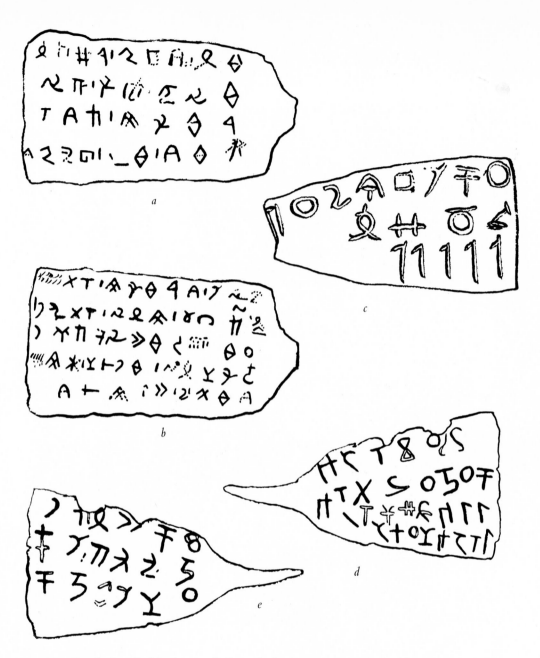

10.2. *Spatulae* inscribed in the pseudo-hieroglyphic syllabary of Byblos (a and e *obverse*, b and d *reverse*).

10.3. Stone inscriptions in the pseudo-hieroglyphic script of Byblos. *a* Fragment h, *b* Stele a, *c* fragment j, *d* 'Linear' pseudo-heiroglyphic on stone.

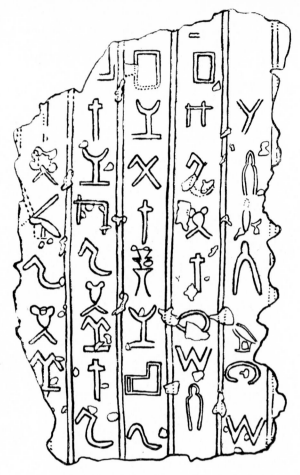

10.4*a*. Stone inscription from Byblos (stele g).

10.4*b*. The pseudo-hieroglyphic syllabary of Byblos according to Dhorme.

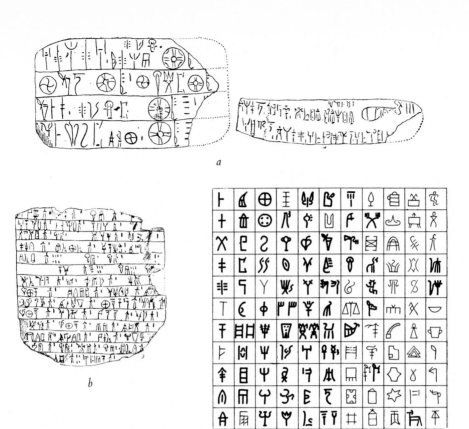

10.5. *a* and *b* Inscriptions in Linear B. *c* Symbols of Linear B drawn by the late Michael Ventris, before his decipherment.

10.6a. Tablets inscribed in Linear B. (Museum of Classical Archaeology, Cambridge).

a	e	i	o	u
a, a₂	e	i	o	u
ai				
ja	je		jo	
wa	we	wi	wo	
da	de	di	do	da₂
ka	ke	ki	ko	ku
ma	me	mi	mo	
na	ne	ni	no	nu / nu₂?
pa / pa₂?	pe	pi	po	pu
	qe	qi	qo / qo₂?	
ra / ra₂	re	ri	ro / ro₂	ru
sa	se	si	so	
ta / ta₂?	te / pte	ti	to	tu
	z?e		z?o / z?o₂	

10.6b. Experimental syllabic grid for Linear B., by Ventris and Chadwick (J.H.S. 1953, p. 86).

a (8)	e (38)	i (28)	o (61)	u (10)	a₂ (25)		ai (43)		
da (1)	de (45)	di (7)	do (14)	du (51)	dwe (71)		dwo (90)		
ja (57)	je (46)		jo (36)						
ka (77)	ke (44)	ki (67)	ko (70)	ku (81)					
ma (80)	me (13)	mi (73)	mo (15)	mu (23)					
na (6)	ne (24)	ni (30)	no (52)	nu (55)	nwa (48)				
pa (3)	pe (72)	pi (39)	po (11)	pu (50)	pte (62)		pu₂ (29)		
qa (16)	qe (78)	qi (21)	qo (32)						
ra (60)	re (27)	ri (53)	ro (2)	ru (26)	ra₂ (76)		ra₃ (33)	ro₂ (68)	
sa (31)	se (9)	si (41)	so (12)	su (58)					
ta (59)	te (4)	ti (37)	to (5)	tu (69)	ta (66)				
wa (54)	we (75)	wi (40)	wo (42)						
za (17)	ze (74)		zo (20)						

UNCERTAIN PHONETIC VALUE

18	19	22	34	35	47	49	56
63	64	65	79	82	83	88	89
	84	85	86	87			

10.7. The Mycenaean syllabary as deciphered by Ventris and Chadwick.

NUMBER	KNOSSOS	PYLOS	MYCENAE	THEBES	PHONETIC VALUE	NUMBER	KNOSSOS	PYLOS
1					da	31		
2					ro	32		
3					pa	33		
4					te	34		
5					to	35		
6					na	36		
7					di	37		
8					a	38		
9					se	39		
10					u	40		
11					po	41		
12					so	42		
13					me	43		
14					do	44		
15					mo	45		
16					qa	46		
17					za	47		
18					?	48		
19					?	49		
20					zo	50		
21					qi	51		
22					?	52		
23					mu	53		
24					ne	54		
25					a_2	55		
26					ru	56		
27					re	57		
28					i	58		
29					pu_2	59		
30					ni	60		

10.8. Linear B symbols from Knossos, Pylos, Mycenae and Thebes.

MYCENAE	THEBES	PHONETIC VALUE	NUMBER	KNOSSOS	PYLOS	MYCENAE	THEBES	PHONETIC VALUE
		sa	61					o
		qo	62					pte
		ra_3	63					?
		?	64					?
		?	65					(ju)?
		jo	66					ta_2
		ti	67					ki
		e	68					ro_2
		pi	69					tu
		wi	70					ko
		si	71					dwe
		wo	72					pe
		ai	73					mi
		ke	74					ze
		de	75					we
		je	76					ra_2
		?	77					ka
		nwa	78					qe
		?	79					(zu)?
		pu	80					ma
		du	81					ku
		no	82					?
		ri	83					?
		wa	84					?
		nu	85					?
		$?(pa_3)$	86					?
		ja	87					?
		su	88					?
		ta	89					?
		ra	90					dwo

10.9. Linear B symbols from Knossos, Pylos, Mycenae and Thebes.

CYPRIOTE SYLLABARY

Vowels	a	e	i	o	u
Vowels					
y + Vowel					
f + "					
r + "					
l + "					
m + "					
n + "					
p + "					
t + "					
k + "					
s + "					
z + "					
kh + "					

a

	A	E	I	O	U
Θ H					
J					
K					
L					
M					
N					
P					
Q					
R					
S					
T					
W					
X					
Z					

1. = FINAL S.
2. = (PROBABLY) ME.
3. = (POSSIBLY) WE AS WELL AS LE.
4. = (POSSIBLY) MA AS WELL AS ME.
5. = CLAY-BALL CHARACTER.

c

b

10.10. *a* Cypriote syllabary. *b* Cypro-Minoan or Cypro-Mycenaean symbols. *c* Suggestion for decipherment of Cypro-Minoan.

JAPANESE SYLLABARIES

PHONETIC VALUE	KATA KANA	HIRA GANA	PHONETIC VALUE	KATA KANA	HIRA GANA	PHONETIC VALUE	KATA KANA	HIRA GANA	PHONETIC VALUE	KATA KANA	HIRA GANA
i	イ	い	wa	ワ	わ	w(i)	ヰ	ゐ	sa	サ	さ
ro	ロ	ろ	ka	カ	か	no	ノ	の	ki	キ	き
fa (ha)	ハ	は	yo	ヨ	よ	o	オ	お	yu	ユ	ゆ
ni	ニ	に	ta	タ	た	ku	ク	く	me	メ	め
fo (ho)	ホ	ほ	re	レ	れ	ya	ヤ	や	mi	ミ	み
fe (he)	ヘ	へ	so	ソ	そ	ma	マ	ま	si (shi)	シ	し
to	ト	と	tu (tsu)	ツ	つ	ke	ケ	け	w(e)	ヱ	ゑ
ti (chi)	チ	ち	ne	ネ	ね	fu	フ	ふ	fi (hi)	ヒ	ひ
ri	リ	り	na	ナ	な	ko	コ	こ	mo	モ	も
nu	ヌ	ぬ	ra	ラ	ら	e	エ	え	se	セ	せ
ru	ル	る	mu	ム	む	te	テ	て	su	ス	す
(w)o	ヲ	を	u	ウ	う	a	ア	あ	n	ン	ん

10.11. Japanese syllabaries.

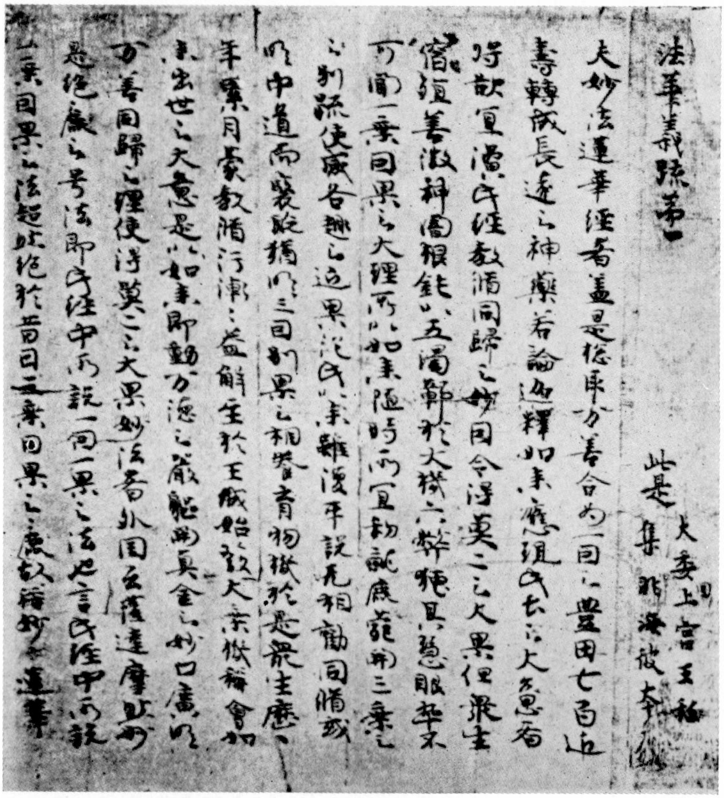

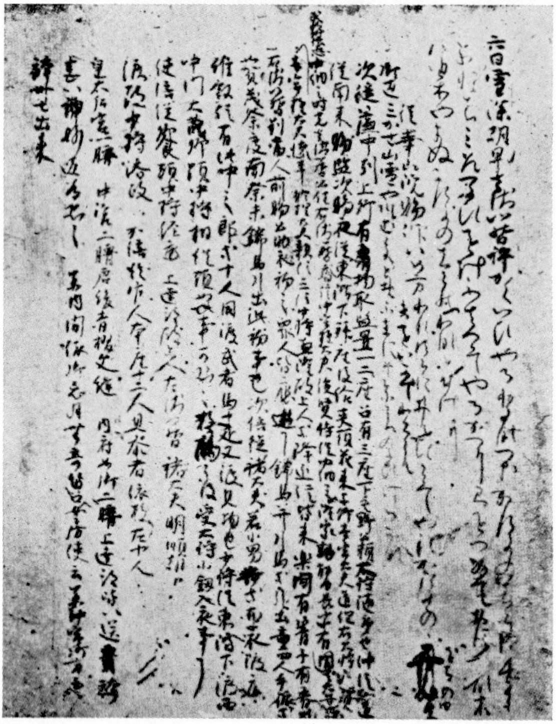

10.12a. (above) Earliest extant work written by a Japanese: *Commentary* on a Buddhist *sūtra* written in Chinese, Shotoku Taishi (or Prince Shotoku) A.D. 573–622. 12b. (left) Earliest extant Japanese manuscript of which both the date and the name of the writer are known: *Diary* by Fujiwara Michinaga (961–1095). The portion shown here is written in pure Japanese, in *Kana* script, and dated 6.2.1004 A.D., according to the lunar calendar.

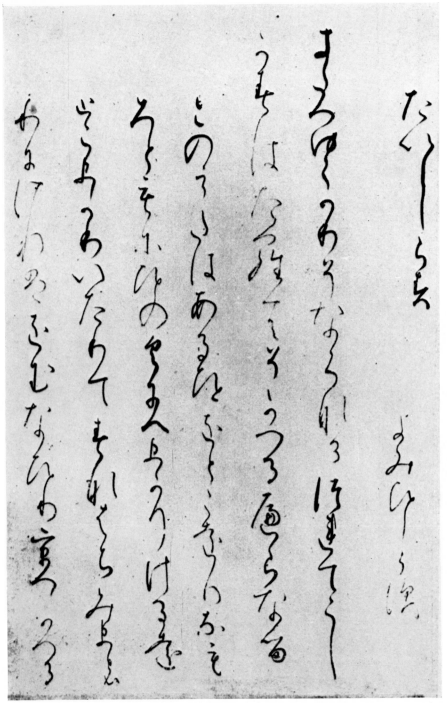

10.13. Hiragana calligraphy: Ki No Tsurayuki (Died A.D. 946), Poems from *Koninshu*, Book 9.

131

10.14. Cherokee syllabary.

a	e	i	o	u
ga	ge	gi	go	gu
ha	he	hi	ho	hu
la	le	li	lo	lu
ma	me	mi	mo	mu
na	ne	ni	no	nu
gwa	gwe	gwi	gwo	gwu
sa	se	si	so	su
da	de	di	do	du
dla	dle	dli	dlo	dlu
dza	dze	dzi	dzo	dzu
wa	we	wi	wo	wu
ya	ye	yi	yo	yu
ö	gö	hö	lö	nö
gwö	sö	dö	dlö	dzö
wö	yö	ka	hna	nah
s	ta	te	ti	tla

1848 1898

a
ā
è
e
ē, ɨ̃
i
ɨ
ō, ū

ba
»
bɑ
bè
be, bě
be, mbe
bi
bɨ
bò
»
bo
bó
bɔ̃

a

1848 1898

bu
bū
gba
gbe, gbè
gbi
»
gbī, gbě
gbo, gbò
gbu
ñgba
ñgbe
ñgbi
ñgbo

mba
mbe, mbè
mbě, mbi
mbi
mbò
mbo
mbō, mbū
mbu

b

	fe̱	pe̱	gbo	do̱
1849 (Forbes)				
1898 (Delafosse)				
1933 (Klingenheben)				

c

10.15. *a* and *b* The Vai syllabary. *c* Development of Vai characters.

tu, ta, ti   su,   sa,   si   du, da, di   u, a, i   bu, ba, bi   mu, ma, mi   wu, wa, wi   ku, ka, ki

kpe, nga   ho,   ha,   he   nu, na, ni   fu, fa, fi   yu, ya, yi   ju, ja, ji   lu, la, li

ndô, njô, mba, vi,   nyô, mê, nya, ngô, gba, tê, lo, hi, heⁿ, pê, pu, wo, kô, mbe, huⁿa, wô

yê, sô, fe, vô,   ko, fê, kpu, lê, mbê, gbo, gbô, tô, pi, ndô, pô, ke

he, kê, mo, gbê, kpa, tê, ndi, ndê, fo, huⁿ, ge, bo, ve,   le, hei, ngu, pe

le, vê, nga, mbô, yê, kpe, gbe, ngô, mbô, tô, bô, pô, fâ, e, pa, nye, do, be

ngua, wê, ndu, gbi, ndi, mbu, vo, ngo, nde, we, ne, se, ngê, wô, je, po

kua, wei, mbo, yô, ho, we, bo, ei, sô, ì, njô, fô, kpi, î, haⁿ, nda, hou

jê, gô, hi, gi, mua, lô, nja, vu, be, njê, gbu, o, nge, mbi, vô, jô

va, gu, gua, guei, vi, eⁿ, ngua, ô, nyi, dô, ê,   sê, be, jo, ga, kpo

nju   mue   bê   bu   hu   go   nge   ra   nyu   no

10.16. Mende syllabary.

134

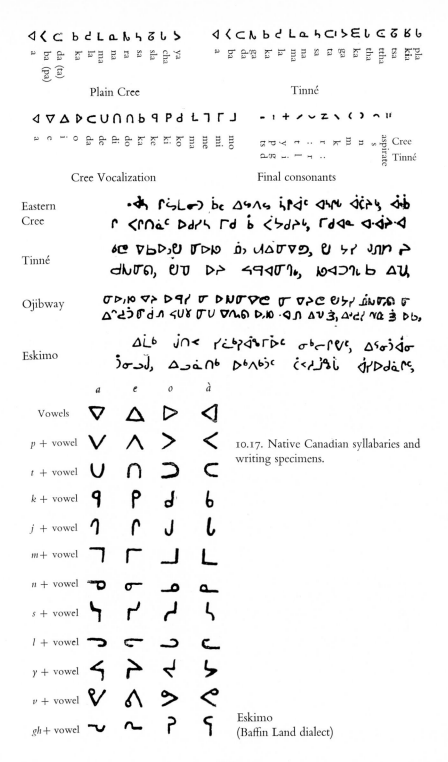

Plain Cree

Tinné

Cree Vocalization

Final consonants

Cree

Tinné

Eastern Cree

Tinné

Ojibway

Eskimo

	a	e	o	à
Vowels	▽	△	▷	◁
p + vowel	V	∧	>	<
t + vowel	U	∩	⊃	C
k + vowel	٩	P	ᑯ	ᑲ
j + vowel	ᒃ	ᒉ	J	ᒕ
m + vowel	⅂	ᒥ	⌐	L
n + vowel	ᓇ	ᓯ	ᓄ	ᓀ
s + vowel	ᔭ	ᔅ	ᔪ	ᔨ
l + vowel	ᓚ	ᓓ	ᓗ	ᓕ
y + vowel	ᔾ	ᐯ	ᐱ	ᐳ
v + vowel	ᐚ	ᐩ	ᐪ	ᐫ
gh + vowel	ᖕ	ᖖ	ᖏ	ᖐ

10.17. Native Canadian syllabaries and writing specimens.

Eskimo
(Baffin Land dialect)

135

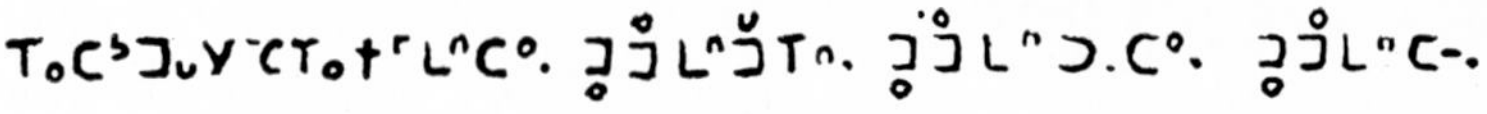

[Hwa Miao script sample]

Hwa Miao

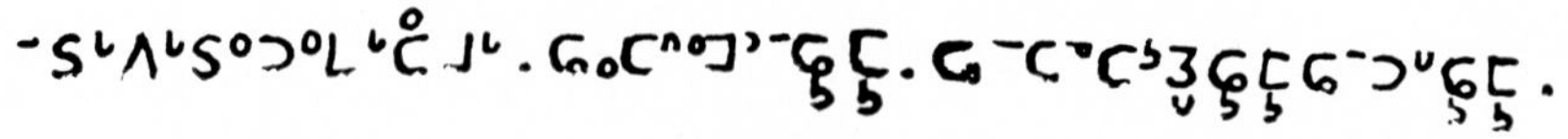

[Kopu script sample]

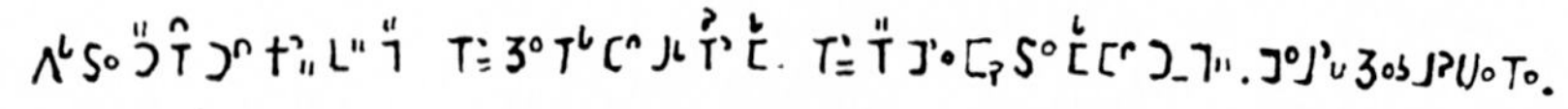

Kopu

[Laka script sample]

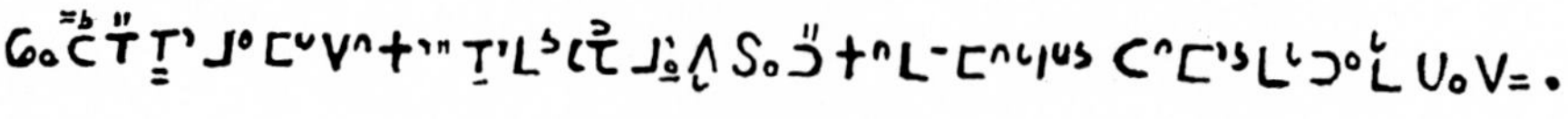

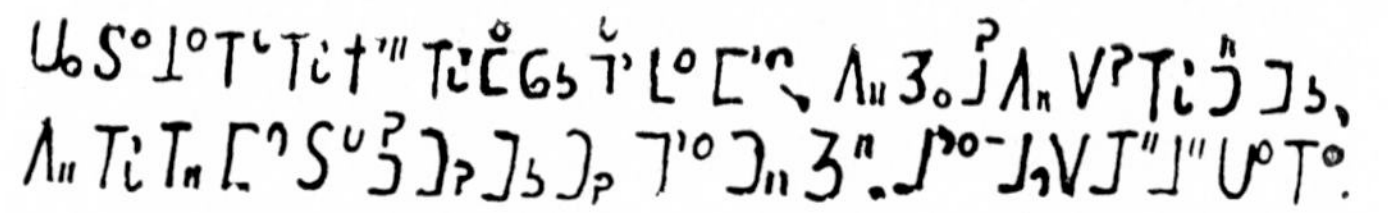

Laka

[Nosu script sample]

Nosu

[Lisu script sample]

Lisu

"A: M Λ– Mi=YI. TV. J�∩_ M L: ⅎO TV. M: dI:
YE FI SI.=II: ⅎI; II: P M SV; MY M7 FI_ BE=

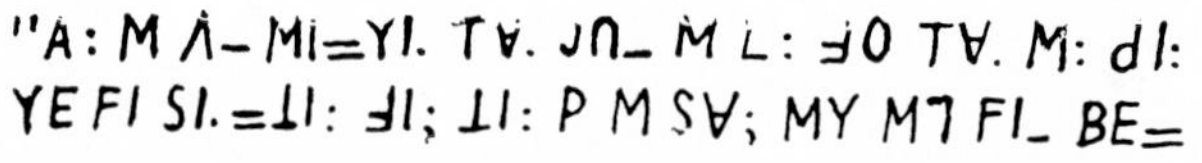

Hwa Lisu

VE GƎ SU–NDU NƓU ᴐᴖ BE, BE Nᴖ GƎ XI

Lᗺ. SE, ΛƎ GƎ A–BU, Gᴖ–Rᴖ ME–ME,

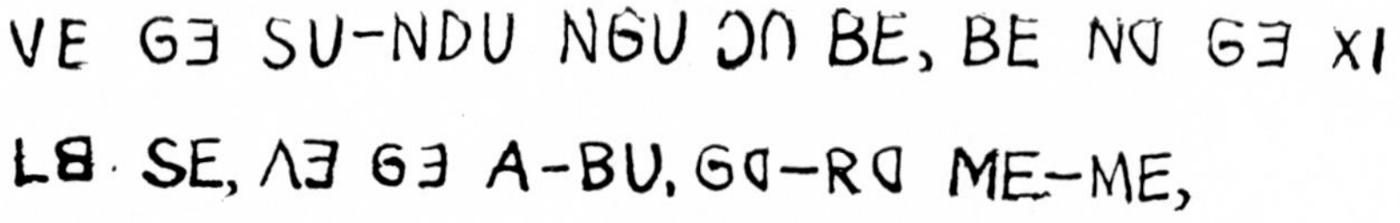

Lo-lo

10.18. Pollard and allied systems, of South Western China.

a

					CONSONANTS +						Closed Sylla-bles
a	aa	ä	o	oa	oo	oi	ö	u	ü	ui	
		bä		boa			bö				bag
				(2 symbols)							
	daı				doo			du			
		gä			goo						
								ku	kii		
		lä					lö				liih
ma (2symbols)		mä		moa	moo	moi					
		mmä									
na					noo						
		pä						pu		pui	
	raa	rä	ro					ru	rii		
		shä		soa							
		tä			too						tiit
va				voa							
		wä									warr
nga		ngä									
chra				chroa							
							shrö		shrii		
gkaa		chä									sthah
											uh

b

10.19. Woleai syllabary.
  a. symbols.
  b. phonetic values.

10.20. Specimens of Caroline writing *a* on the arms and legs of a man; *b* on a food bowl.

10.21. Page from a Caroline manuscript.

NO.	SYMBOL	PHON. VALUE	NO.	SYMBOL	PHON. VALUE
1		a	22		n(u)
2		b(a)	23		p(a)
3		č(a)	24		r(a)
4		d(a)	25		r(u)
5		d(i)	26		s(a)
6		d(u)	27		š(a)
7		f(a)	28		t(a)
8		g(a)	29		t(u)
9		g(u)	30		ṯ(a)
10		h(a)	31		u
11		ḫ(a)	32		v(a)
12		i	33		v(i)
13		j(a)	34		y(a)
14		j(i)	35		z(a
15		k(a)	36		tr(a)
16		k(u)	37		ḫšāyaϑia "king"
17		l(a)	38		dahyu "country" (two forms)
18		m(a)			
19		m(i)	39		Awra - Mazda (divine name)
20		m(u)	40		bumi "earth"
21		n(a)	41		word-divider

11.1. Early Persian character (*See* also 1.16*b* and 17).

11.2. Meroitic writing. *a* The Meroitic scripts. *b* Comparison of Meroitic hieroglyphic letters with Egyptian hieroglyphs. *c–d* Meroitic inscriptions.

Hierogl.	Derived	Differen-tiated
	North-Semitic Letters	

a

12.1. Origin of the alphabet. *a* Halévy's Egyptian Hieroglyphic theory, *b* Taylor's Egyptian Hieratic theory.

Phon. Value	Egyptian Hierogl.	Hieratic	Semitic Letters	Phon. Value
'(a)				'
b				b
k(g)				g
t(d)				d
h				h
f				w
z				z
x(kh)				ḥ
o(th)				ṭ
i				y
k				k
l				l
m				m
n				n
s				s
'a				'
p				p
t(ts)				ṣ
q				q
r				r
sh				sh
t				t

b

Meaning	Name	Semitic	Cretan Linear	Cretan Hierogl.
ox	aleph			
house	beth			
door	daleth			
hook	waw			
fence	he			
fence	heth			
hand	yod			
palm of hand	kaph			
fish	nun			
mouth	pe			
head	resh			
tooth	shin			
eye	'ayin			
mark	taw			

Egypt	Crete	N.-S. Alph.	Modern Hebrew

Phon. Value	Semitic	Cretan Linear	Cretan Hierogl.
g			
z			
ṭ			
l			
s			
q			
ṣ			

12.2. *a* (*above left*) Sir Arthur Evans Cretan theory: Derivation of North Semitic letters of known meaning and *b* (*left*) letters of uncertain meaning. *c* (above) Grumach's Egyptian–Cretan theory.

143

KEY	PREHISTORIC LINEAR	PALAEO-SINAITIC	PHOENIC.

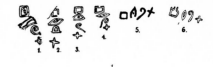

b

Phonetic Value	g	ḥ	z	s	ʻ	sh
N. Sem. Letters						
Cuneiform Letters						

c

12.3. *a* Gaster's prehistoric-geometric theory. *b* Gardiner's identification of Baʻalat. *c* Ugarit signs resembling N. Semitic letters.

a

EGYPT HIER.	SINAI	SOUTH-SEMITIC	NORTH-SEMITIC	MEANING IN SEMITIC	SINAITIC SYMBOLS	MEANING IN SEMITIC	HEBREW
𓃀	𓃀		𐤀	ox	𓃀	ox אלף	א ב ג ד ה ו ז ח ט י כ ל מ נ ס ע פ צ ק ר ש ת
☐ □	□	⊓⊽	𐤁	house	□ □ ☐	house בית	
					∞8○	nose-ring	
					⇨	fish דג	(Cowley)
Y	Y		Y	hook nail	─○		? (Sayce)
	⟂	I I ⟂	I I ⟂		I =		? (Gardiner)
					8		? (Cowley)
⟿	(0)		ㄹ	hand	+○		? (Sayce)
⟿	⅄		⅄	bent hand			
	)	⟩⟩Ⱡ	(		ℂ ─ᵒ	goad	
〰	⌁		ꜧ	water	᙭	water מים	
🐟	🐟	𐤃	⅄ⅎ	fish			
﹨	⌐			snake	⌐	snake נחש	
⬮	◉ 0	◇ ○	○	eye	◉○◎○	eye עין	
○	◇	0	⼇	mouth			
					ω	bow קשת	
𓁶	𐤉		⊲	head	𐤉	head ראש	
	ω	⧽⧼	⩗	tooth	⌁⌁	tooth שן	
	+	+ +	✕+	mark	+	cross תו	
					⚥	determinative of goddess	

12.4. Sinaitic theory of Gardiner, with Cowley's and Sayce's additions.

Modern Hebrew	South Arabic	Se'irite-Sinaitic	Canaanite–Phoenician	Ras Shamra Cuneiform
1				
2				
3				
4				
5				
6				
7		= (?)		
8				
9				
10				
11				
12				
13				
14				
15				
16				
17				
18				
19				
20				
21				

12.5. The relation of the Early Sinaitic (Se'irite-Sinaitic) script to the South Semitic (South Arabic), North Semitic (Canaanite–Phœnician) and Ugarit (Ras Shamra) alphabets, according to Martin Sprengling.

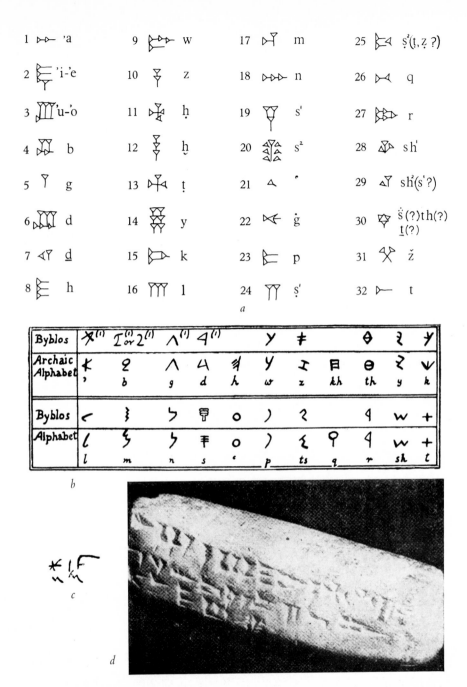

Byblos	X⁽¹⁾	I or 2⁽¹⁾	Λ⁽¹⁾	◁⁽¹⁾			Y	ǂ		θ	?	Ψ
Archaic Alphabet	𝕂 '	𝒬 b	Λ g	⊔ d	⌐ h	Y w	I z	目 kh	θ th	? y	∨ k
Byblos	⌐	?	ﾅ	?	o	)	?		ᐅ	w	+
Alphabet	ℓ l	? m	ﾅ n	∓ s	o '	) p	? ts	? q	ᐅ r	w sh	+ t

b

12.6. *a* The Ugarit cuneiform alphabet (15th–13th century B.C.). *b* Dunand's theory of the derivation of the Alphabet from the pseudo-hieroglyphic script of Byblos (1) 'Linear' variety of the same script. *c* Alphabet 'incunabula' according to Dunand. *d* Ugaritic ABC tablet.

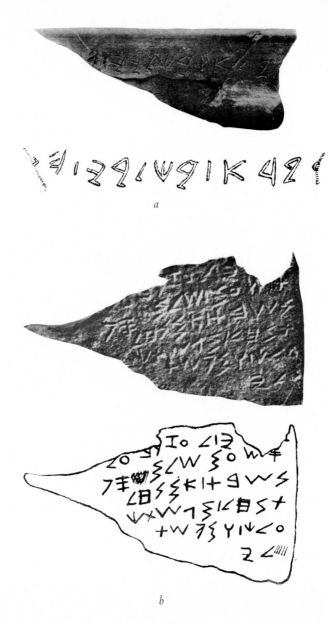

12.7. Early North Semitic inscriptions. *a* Abdo fragment, photograph and transcription. *b* Asdrubal spatula, photograph and transcription.

12.8*a*. Shafatba'al Inscription, photograph.

12.8*b*. Shafatba'al Inscription, transcribed.

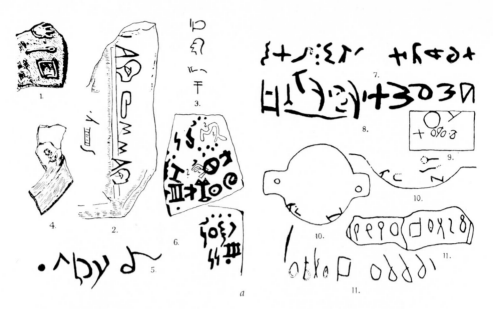

12.9. *a* Early Canaanite inscriptions, 1, Gezer Potsherd; 2, Shechem Plaque; 3, Lachish Dagger; 4, Tell el-Hesy; 5, Tell el-'Ajjul; 6, Beth Shemesh Ostracon (obverse above, reverse below); 7, 8, inscriptions from Lachish; 9, signs painted or engraved in the foundations of the Temple of Jerusalem; 10, 11, different drawings of some Lachish inscriptions. *b* Lachish Bowl No. 1 (transcription in 9*a*[8] above).

b

12.10*a*. Lachish ewer (transcription shown in 12.9*a*[7]).

12.10*b*. Inscription from Lachish (transcription shown in 12.9*a*[11]).

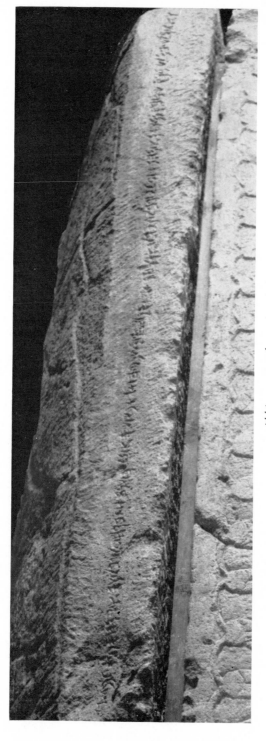

12.11a. Akhiram sarcophagus inscription.

12.11b. Transcription from Akhiram sarcophagus.

12.11c. Akhiram graffito.

12.11d. Abiba'al inscription.

PHON. VALUE	ʿABDÔ	ŠHAFATBAʿAL	ASDRUBAL	AḤIRAM	YEḤIMILK	RUEISSEH	ABIBAʿAL	ELIBAʿAL	MEŠAʿ
ʾ									
b									
g									
d									
h									
w									
z									
ḥ									
ṭ									
y									
k									
l									
m									
n									
s									
ʿ									
p									
ṣ									
q									
r									
š									
t									

12.12. Early development of the North Semitic alphabet according to Maurice Dunand.

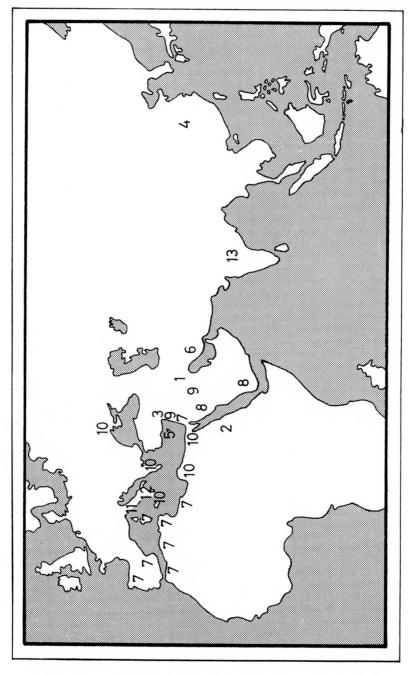

Map. 2. Early Development of alphabet *c.* 1000–1 B.C.

1 Cuneiform Scripts	6 Persian Semi-alphabetic Cuneiform Script
2 Egyptian Scripts	7 Canaanite Alphabetic Branch
3 Hittite Hieroglyphics	8 S.-Semitic Alphabetic Branch
4 Chinese Scripts	9 Aramaic Alphabetic Branch
5 Cyprus Syllabary	10 Greek Alphabet

11 Etruscan Alphabet
12 Latin Alphabet
13 Indian Branch

Phon. Value	Sabaean	Lihyanian	Thamudene	Safaitic	Early Ethiopic
'	𐩱 𐩱	𐩱 𐩱 ˅	𐩱 𐩱 Ж Ж I	ХХ Ж Ҝ Ϝ	𐩱 𐩱
b	⊓ ⊓	⊓ ⊓	⊓ ⊐ ⊐⊏	)⊂⊐ ∪ ∪	⊓ ⊓
g	⅂	⅂	□ ◻ ◻ ◢	∧∩0◻◻	⅂ ⅂
ḏ	Ħ Ħ	Ⱳ Ⱳ Ħ Ⱳ	⅄ Ⱳ⅄ Ⱳ⅄	⅄Y⅄	Ħ
d	⬧⬧	ϑ ϑ ϑ	⬧⬧ͼ ⌐	⅃⅃⅃	⧈ ⅌ ⅌
h	⅄ⅎⅎⅎ	⅄⅄⅄⅄	⅄ⅎ⅄ⅎⅎ⅄	⅄ⅎⅎⅇⅇ	∪ ∪ ∪ ⅄
w	Ⴑ ∞	Ⴑ ⬧ ⬇	Ⴑ θ ⊕ ⊞	Ⴑ θ θ θ	Ⴑ ⬇ ∞ ⬩
z	Ħ Ⴟ Ħ 𐩢	⊦⊦	Ŧ⅃⅃Ŧ	Ŧ⅃Ŧ⅃	Ħ Ħ Ħ
ḥ	Ⴘ ⅄	⋀⋀⋀⋀	⊓Ⴣⅿ⊏⅄	⋀⅄⋜ ⊓Ⴣ	⊞
ḫ	⅏ Ⴘ⅄ Ⴘ	Ⴑ Ⴑ Ⴑ Ⴑ Ⴑ	Ж	Ж Ж	Ⴑ Ⴘ
ẓ	𐩣𐩣𐩣	⊦⊦⊦	𐩢⅃⅃(?)	⅃⅃∪⅃	⊓ ⊓
ṭ	⊞	⊞	⧻ ⧻ ⧻⋀	Ħ℣Ⅳ	⊓ ⊓
y	φ	φ φ φ	φ⅃ Ᵽ	φ φ⅃⅃	⅌φⅬφφ
k	⊓⊓⊓	⊌⊌ ⊌	⊓ ⊓⊓	⅃⅃⅃⅃⋐	⊓⊓⊓⊐
l	⅃⅃	⅃⅃⅃⅃	⅃⅃⊓⅃⅃⅃	⅃⟮⟯⅃ ⅃⅃	⋀
m	⧈⅌⅍	𐩣⅍⅌⅌⅌	⅃⌐𐩣⅌⅍	⅃(⟨⅃⅃⅍⅍	𐩣𐩣⌐ ⅍
n	⅄⅄⅄⅄	⟨⟨⟨⟨⟨	⅄⅃⟨⅄⋅⅂⅃⅄	⅃	⅄ ⅄ ⅄
s	⊓ ⅏	⊓⅏⅍⅏⅏	⊓⟩⊤	⋀℣⋜⊐⊓	⊓ ⅃
g	⅃⅃	⊓ ⋈	ϡ⅃ϝ	⟨⟩⟨	
'	○ ◇	○ ◇	○·❖	○◁·○◁	○ ○ ▽
p	◇⬦○	◇∩○	⟿⅃⅃⋀⊓	⟨⟩ ⟨⟩	⟨⅃⅃⅃⟨
ḍ	⊟		⧻ Ж Ħ	Ħ Ħ	
ṣ	⅄⅄⅄⅄Ⱳ⅄	⅄⅄	⅄ ⅄ ⅄⅄⅄⅄	⅄⅄⅄⅄⅄	Ⴑ⅄Ⴑ
q	φ φ	φ φ	φ φ φ	φ φ Ⱡ	φ φ ⅌
r	⟩⟩⟨⟮	⟩⟩	⟩⟨⟩⟨⟨⟩	⟩⅃⟩⟩⟨⟮	⟮⟨⟮⟩⟮
š	⟨⟩⟨	⟩⟩⟩⟩	⟨⟩⟩⟩⟩	⟨⟩	⅏ ⅏ ⟩ ∪
ṯ	⅃	⊹ ⊹	⅃ ⅃	⅃⅃⅌⅃⅃	
ṱ	× ×	×	× ⊹ ⊹	⊹ ×	⊹ Ж ⊹ Ж ⊹

13.1. The South Semitic Alphabets.

a

d

13.2. *a*, *b* Sabaean inscriptions. *c* Minaean inscription. *d* Himyaritic inscription.

b

c

Original Letter	Ethiopic	ሰ	ጥ	፝	ከ	ዘ	ፈ	ጠ
	Phon. Value	sa	ta	na	ka	za	da	ṭa
Derived Letter	Amharic	ሸ	ጭ	ኘ	ኸ	ዠ	ጀ	ጨ
	Phon. Value	sha	cha	ña	kh'a	ja or zha	dja	ṭcha

a

b

c

d

e

f

g

h

i

j

13.3. *a* Derivation of modern Abyssinian additional letters. *b, c* South Semitic inscription from Ethiopia. *d* to *h* Thamudene inscriptions. *i* The earliest, still unvocalized Ethiopic inscription from Matara, Eritrea. *j* Page from an Ethiopic gospel, 1675–6 (British Museum Or. 510, f. 51a).

	a	*û*	*î*	*â*	*ê*	*e**	*ô*
h	ሀ	ሁ	ሂ	ሃ	ሄ	ህ	ሆ
l	ለ	ሉ	ሊ	ላ	ሌ	ል	ሎ
ḥ	ሐ	ሑ	ሒ	ሓ	ሔ	ሕ	ሖ
m	መ	ሙ	ሚ	ማ	ሜ	ም	ሞ
sh	ሠ	ሡ	ሢ	ሣ	ሤ	ሥ	ሦ
r	ረ	ሩ	ሪ	ራ	ሬ	ር	ሮ
s	ሰ	ሱ	ሲ	ሳ	ሴ	ስ	ሶ
q	ቀ	ቁ	ቂ	ቃ	ቄ	ቅ	ቆ
b	በ	ቡ	ቢ	ባ	ቤ	ብ	ቦ
t	ተ	ቱ	ቲ	ታ	ቴ	ት	ቶ
kh	ኀ	ኁ	ኂ	ኃ	ኄ	ኅ	ኆ
n	ነ	ኑ	ኒ	ና	ኔ	ን	ኖ
'a	አ	ኡ	ኢ	ኣ	ኤ	እ	ኦ
k	ከ	ኩ	ኪ	ካ	ኬ	ክ	ኮ
w	ወ	ዉ	ዊ	ዋ	ዌ	ው	ዎ
'	ዐ	ዑ	ዒ	ዓ	ዔ	ዕ	ዖ
z	ዘ	ዙ	ዚ	ዛ	ዜ	ዝ	ዞ
y	የ	ዩ	ዪ	ያ	ዬ	ይ	ዮ
d	ደ	ዱ	ዲ	ዳ	ዴ	ድ	ዶ
g	ገ	ጉ	ጊ	ጋ	ጌ	ግ	ጎ
t	ጠ	ጡ	ጢ	ጣ	ጤ	ጥ	ጦ
p	ጰ	ጱ	ጲ	ጳ	ጴ	ጵ	ጶ
ṣ	ጸ	ጹ	ጺ	ጻ	ጼ	ጽ	ጾ
ḍ	ፀ	ፁ	ፂ	ፃ	ፄ	ፅ	ፆ
f	ፈ	ፉ	ፊ	ፋ	ፌ	ፍ	ፎ
p	ፐ	ፑ	ፒ	ፓ	ፔ	ፕ	ፖ

13.4. The Ethiopic character (the form marked * also expresses the pure consonant).

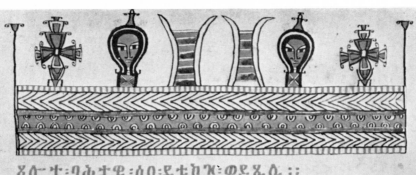

ጸሎ–ተ፡ባሕታዊ፡ሰበ፡ደቲክኘ፡ወደጊሲ ፡፡
ወደክዑ፡ቅድመ፡እግዚእብሔር፡ስእሉ ፡፡

ያስ ስምባኔ፡እግዚኡ፡ጸሎትየ ❖
ወደብጻሕ፡ትድሚክ፡ገ ረ ❖

ወኢትመ ዎ፡ገጸ ክ፡እ ኒ ፡፡
በዕለ ተ፡መን ደ ቢ፡እ ም ዕ፡እ ክ፡ ቢ ፡፡
እመ፡ዕለተ፡እ ው ባ ከ፡ፍ ዑ ኔ፡ስ ም ኔ ❖
እስመ፡ ል ተ፡ከመ፡ ስ፡መ ዕ ል ❖
ወ ት ጸ፡ከመ፡ ዕ ር፡እዕጸም ትየ ❖
ተ ሰ ፍ ኩ፡ወ ስ፡ከመ፡ ዕ ር፡ ብ ❖
እ ም፡ተ ረ ስ ኔ፡ በ ሲ ❖
እ ም ቀ ሰ፡ገ ረ የ፡ወ ጋ ፡ ጋ የ ዲ በ፡እ ጸ ም ትየ ❖
ወ ኮ ኩ፡ከመ፡እ ግ፡ ረ ብ፡ ገ ደ ም ❖
ወ ኮ ኩ፡ከመ፡ ጋ፡ወ ስ ተ፡ ት፡ ሊ ት ❖
ተ ገ ከ፡ወ ኮ ኩ፡ከመ፡ ዕ ፡ ሕ ታ ዊ፡ወ ስ ተ፡ ሕ ❖
ወ ስ፡እ ሪ፡ደ ዕ ኔ፡ጸ ለ ትየ ❖
ወ ስ ኔ፡ ደ ኔ፡ ስ ከ ተ፡ ዕ የ ❖
እ ስ መ፡ ወ ደ፡ከ መ፡እ ስ፡ ማ ኩ ❖

13.5. Ethiopic manuscript: psalms, 17th cent. (Chester Beatty MS. 908).

159

LETTER-NAME	PHON. VALUE	NORTH-SEMITIC	EARLY PHOEN-ICIAN	LATE PHOEN-ICIAN	NEO-PUNIC
aleph	ʾ	✷	✶	✶	X
beth	b	⅁	⅃	⅃	⅁ʾ
gimel	g	⅂	∧	∧	∧
daleth	d	△	◁	◁	⅁ʾ
he	h	Ⅲ	ⅢY	⅃Y	ℛ
waw	w	Y	Y	Y	Ƴ
zain	z	I	I	⅄	⅂
ḥeth	ḥ	⊟	⊟	ⅢⅢ	ʾ⅀\ ʾ⅝ |||
ṭeth	ṭ	⊕	⊗	☉	⊖
yod	y(i)	⅄	⅄	⅄ ⅄	⅄
kaph	k	Ѵ	Ѵ	⅃Ѵ	⅄
lamed	l	⅃	⅃	⅃	⁄
mem	m	⅚	⅏	Ѵ ⅚	✕
nun	n	⅄	Ⴑ	⅄	⅃
samek	s	ⅲ	ⅲ	ⅲ	Ⴑ
ʿain	ʿ	○	○	○	○
pe	p (ph)	⅂	⅂	⅂	⅃
ṣade	ṣ	⅂	⅄	⅄	⅂
qoph	q	Φ	Φ	Ϙ	Ϙ
reš	r	⅄	⅄	ⅾ	⅁ʾ
šin	sh-s	Ѡ	Ѡ	Ѵⅶ	∧
taw	t	+	✕	⅃ⅼ	⅃⅃

14.1. Origin and development of the Phoenician alphabet.

	GEZER	MONUMENTAL	CURSIVE	BOOK–HAND	COIN–SCRIPT	SAMARITAN	MOD.–HEBREW
1	𐤀	𐤀𐤀𐤀	𐤀𐤀𐤀	𐤀𐤀𐤀	𐤀𐤀𐤀	𐤀𐤀𐤀	א
2	𐤁	𐤁𐤁𐤁	𐤁𐤁𐤁	𐤁𐤁𐤁	𐤁𐤁𐤁	𐤁𐤁𐤁	ב
3		𐤂𐤂𐤂	𐤂𐤂𐤂		𐤂𐤂𐤂	𐤂𐤂𐤂	ג
4	𐤃	𐤃𐤃𐤃	𐤃𐤃𐤃	𐤃𐤃𐤃	𐤃𐤃𐤃	𐤃𐤃𐤃	ד
5		𐤄𐤄𐤄	𐤄𐤄𐤄	𐤄𐤄	𐤄𐤄𐤄	𐤄𐤄𐤄	ה
6	𐤅𐤅	𐤅𐤅𐤅	𐤅𐤅𐤅	𐤅𐤅𐤅	𐤅𐤅𐤅	𐤅𐤅𐤅	ו
7	𐤆	𐤆𐤆𐤆	𐤆𐤆𐤆	𐤆𐤆	𐤆𐤆𐤆	𐤆𐤆𐤆	ז
8	𐤇𐤇	𐤇𐤇𐤇	𐤇𐤇𐤇	𐤇	𐤇𐤇𐤇	𐤇𐤇𐤇	ח
9		𐤈𐤈𐤈	𐤈𐤈𐤈		𐤈	𐤈𐤈𐤈	ט
10	𐤉𐤉	𐤉𐤉𐤉	𐤉𐤉𐤉	𐤉𐤉𐤉	𐤉𐤉𐤉	𐤉𐤉𐤉	י
11	𐤊	𐤊𐤊𐤊	𐤊𐤊𐤊	𐤊𐤊	𐤊𐤊𐤊	𐤊𐤊𐤊	כ
12	𐤋	𐤋𐤋𐤋	𐤋𐤋𐤋	𐤋𐤋𐤋	𐤋𐤋𐤋	𐤋𐤋𐤋	ל
13	𐤌	𐤌𐤌𐤌	𐤌𐤌𐤌	𐤌𐤌	𐤌𐤌𐤌	𐤌𐤌𐤌	מ
14		𐤍𐤍𐤍	𐤍𐤍𐤍	𐤍𐤍𐤍	𐤍𐤍𐤍	𐤍𐤍𐤍	נ
15	𐤎	𐤎𐤎𐤎	𐤎𐤎𐤎		𐤎𐤎	𐤎𐤎𐤎	ס
16	𐤏	𐤏𐤏𐤏	𐤏𐤏𐤏	𐤏	𐤏𐤏𐤏	𐤏𐤏𐤏	ע
17	𐤐	𐤐𐤐𐤐	𐤐𐤐𐤐	𐤐	𐤐	𐤐𐤐𐤐	פ
18	𐤑𐤑	𐤑𐤑𐤑	𐤑𐤑𐤑	𐤑	𐤑𐤑𐤑	𐤑𐤑𐤑	צ
19	𐤒𐤒	𐤒𐤒𐤒	𐤒𐤒𐤒	𐤒	𐤒𐤒𐤒	𐤒𐤒𐤒	ק
20	𐤓𐤓	𐤓𐤓𐤓	𐤓𐤓𐤓	𐤓𐤓	𐤓𐤓𐤓	𐤓𐤓𐤓	ר
21	𐤔𐤔	𐤔𐤔𐤔	𐤔𐤔𐤔	𐤔𐤔	𐤔𐤔𐤔	𐤔𐤔𐤔	ש
22	𐤕𐤕	𐤕𐤕𐤕	𐤕𐤕𐤕	𐤕𐤕	𐤕𐤕𐤕	𐤕𐤕𐤕	ת

14.2. Development of early Hebrew alphabet.

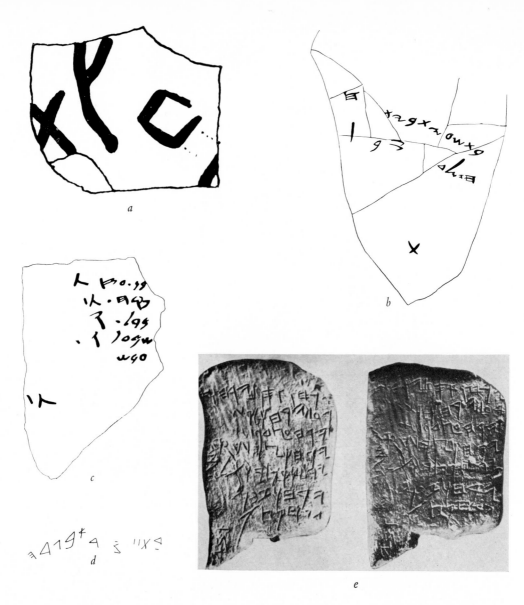

14.3. Early Hebrew alphabet. *a* 'Incunabula' (?) from Lachish. *b, c* Samarian ostraca. *d* Earliest Hebrew ABC. *e* Gezer calendar.

14.4*a*. Seal of Jereboam.

14.4*b*. Seal of Hananyahu son of 'Akhbor.

14.4*c*. Siloam inscription.

14.4*d*. Tomb inscription from Siloam (British Museum).

163

14.5. Early Hebrew royal and private jar handle, stamps and weights.

14.6. Early Hebrew ostracon from Metsad Khasha-vyahu; photograph and transcription.

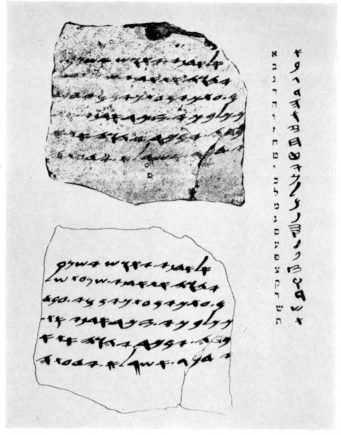

אל אדני . יאוש ישמ֫ע .
יהוה ، את אדני . ש[ו]מ֫ת של
ם . עת ֗ . כים עת כים מי . עב֫ד
ך . כלב . כי . זכר ֗ . אדני . את .
[ע֗]בדה . יבכר . יהוה . את . א
[.֗?] י דבר . אשר לא . ידעתה

c

14.7. Lachish letter. *a* photograph;
b transcription; *c* transliteration into
modern Hebrew; *d* style of writing.

14.7. *e, f* Hazor inscription; photograph and transcription.

	I	II	III	IV	V	VI
א						
ב						
ג						
ד						
ה						
ו						
ז						
ח						
ט						
י						
כ						
ל						
מ						
נ						
ס						
ע						
פ						
צ						
ק						
ר						
ש						
ת						

14.8. *a* (left) Early Hebrew cursive alphabet, as it appears in Lachish letters 1–6. *b* (below) Pottery vessel inscription from Lachish: liquid measure, reading from right to left, *bt lmlk* = 'bath of the king' = Royal bath.

167

Leviticus 19: 31-33

Leviticus 20: 20-23

14.9*a.* Early Hebrew fragments from *Leviticus*.

Leviticus 21: 24-25   *Lev. 22: 4-5*

a

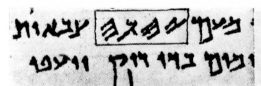

b

14.9. *b* Portion of a Dead Sea scroll, written in Square Hebrew character: within squares, *left*, Tetragrammaton (Hebrew divine name) and *right*, 'el (= God), both in early Hebrew script. *c* Coin of the small autonomous state of Judah, inscribed in early Hebrew script.

c

168

14.10. *a* Earliest Samaritan inscription. *b* Samaritan pentateuch written in 622 (A.H.) = A.D. 1225 (Chester Beatty MS. 751).

14.11. *a* Samaritan Pentateuch, Deuteronomy (Alphabet Museum, Tel-Aviv).
b Modern Samaritan character: beginning of Genesis.

14.12. Copper plate (inscribed in modern Samaritan character) presented to the second President of Israel by the Samaritan community of Holon.

14.13. *a* Jewish coins and Ammonite seal (centre). *b* Script from Maccabean and Bar-Kochba coins.

Coins of Year Four	Silver Shekels Year-Two-Three	Maccab. Coins	Phon. Value	
✗	F	✗ ✗	א	ʾ
𝄐	𝄐	ʔ ʔ	ב	b
٦	٦	﹁ ˄	ג	g
ʓ	ʓ	ʓ ʓ	ו	w
∿	∿	ʒ ɀ	י	y
⊟	⊟	B ʙ	ח	ḥ
‹ ⌐	‹ ⌐	ι↙	ל	l
ʏ	ʅ	ʅʅ	נ	n
ʒ ⱽ	ʒ ⱽ		צ	ṣ
ο	ο		ע	ʿ
٩	٩	٩ ι	ר	r
W	W	W ⱳ	ש	š
✗	✗	✗ ✗	ת	t
ʏ F∿ʒ	ʒ F⅄ⱽ		ציון	ṣyon
✗⅄W	✗⅄W		שנות	šnt
∿ʒ⊟	∿ⱳ⊟		חצי	ḥṣi

172

14.14. The Mesha' Stone.

Phon. Value	Punic or Carthagin	Libyan		Iberian		
		Ancient	Tifinagh	North-	South-	Turdetan
'						(ʌ)
b						
g						(?)
d						
ḥ						
w						
z						
ḥ						
ṭ						
y						
k						
l						
m						(?)
n						
s						
'						
p						
ṣ						
q						
r						
š						
t						
ca(z)						
ce						
du						

14.15. Descendants of Phoenician alphabet.

a

14.16. *a* (left) Yehaw-milk inscription, c. 5th–4th century B.C. (Beirut Museum). *b* (below) Kharaib inscription (Beirut Museum).

b

175

14.17. Karatepe, with the Phoenician, Hittite and other inscriptions engraved on the row of stones shown on the right: see also 5.7.

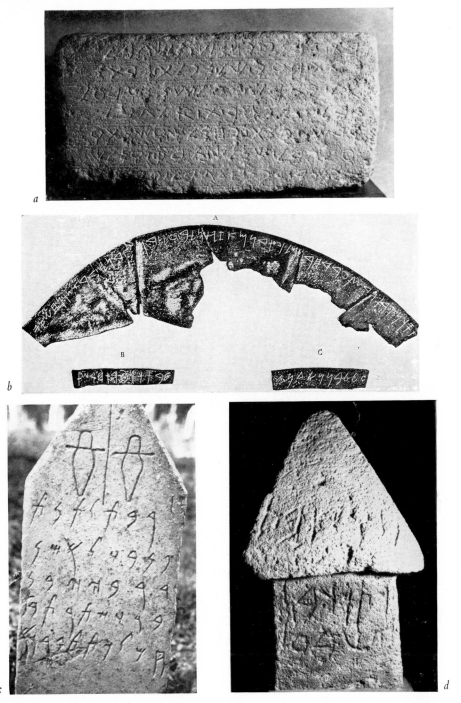

14.18. *a* Kharaib inscription. *b* Cypro-Phoenician inscription of c. 735 B.C. *c* Tunisian tombstone, Bardo Museum. *d* Sardinian tombstone.

14.19. Early Phoenician inscription found in 1838 at La Marmora (Nora), Sardinia.

a

b

14.20. *a* Another early inscription from Nora. *b* Early Phoenician
inscription on gold from Sulcis, now at Cagliari, Sardinia.

a

b

c

d

e

14.21. *a* Part of a Phoenician *stele* from Sidon. *b* Part of a Sidonian inscription from Piraeus (96 B.C.). *c–e*, Punic inscriptions fromdinia Sarand Tunisia.

b

a

14.22. Neo-Punic inscriptions, *a* Salambo inscription, *b* Latin–neo-Punic bilingual inscription.

14.23. *a* Punic inscription from North Africa. *b* Punic inscription from Gozo, Malta (200–100 B.C.) *c, d* Neo-Punic inscriptions.

14.23. *e, f, g* Libyan inscriptions.

Letter	Phon. Value	Letter	Phon. Value	Letter	Phon. Value	Letter	Phon. Value	Letter	Phon. Value
ᛈ	a	ᛉ	m	ᛋ	ds tz	ᚼ	bo po	⊙	gu ku
ᛒ	e	ᚾ	n	ᛇ	ds tz	ᚦ	bu pu	✕	da ta
ᛏ	i	ᛏ	nn	ᛏ	z	ᛘ	ga ka	◇	de te
ᚻ	o	◁	r	ᛁ	ba pa	ᚸ	gue ke	ᛡ	di ti
↑	u	ᛩ	rr	ᛩ	be pe	ᛃ	gui ki	ᛤ	do to
ᛰ	l	ᛗ	sx	ᚱ	bi pi	ᛡ	go ko	ᚷ	du tu

a

b

c

14.24. *a* The Iberian alphabet. *b* Iberian stone inscription. *c* Iberian pottery inscription.

‡Х‡ꓶ⊓ᗷΙꓕꓕꓕꓔꓕꓚꓯΛꓥꓯꓕꓯΙΛꓕꓯꓥꓕꓥꓕꓯꓕꓕꓕꓔ⊓ꓕꓔ⊠‡
⊓‡ΙꓕΧꓕꓕꓕꓕꓕꓪꓯꓦ⊓Λꓓꓕꓦ⊠‡Ι‡⊓
ꓕꓕꓤꓷꓕꓰꓯꓚꓔꓔꓕꓕ⊟ꓚꓕ‡Οꓕꓦꓕ

lecoebueniirabuedueabeairicaaltiolecoe
nanonabekeonacuisiincoelebu
eiitioremaroteotiaṡiieenii

14.25. Turdetan inscription on stone from Bensafrim near Lagos, S.W. Portugal preserved in the Municipal Museum of Figueira da Foz (Courtesy of Manuel-Gomez Moreno). Top to bottom; photograph, transcriptions, transliteration.

PHONETIC VALUE	EARLY ARAMAIC			PALMYRENE	NABATAEAN
	8th. CENT. B. C.	6th. CENT. B. C.	4th. CENT. B. C.		
ʾ					
b					
g					
d					
h					
w					
z					
ḥ					
ṭ					
y					
k					
l					
m					
n					
s					
ʿ					
p					
ṣ					
q					
r					
š(sh)					
t					

15.1. Aramaic, Palmyrene and Nabataean alphabets.

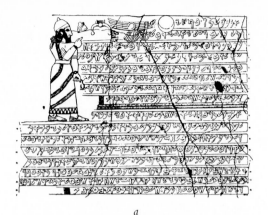

15.2. Royal Early Aramaic inscriptions (9th and 8th centuries B.C.). *a* Canaanite–Aramaic inscription of Kilamuwa, son of Khaya (?), king of Ya'di. *b* Zakir, king of Hamath and La'sh. *c* Bar-Rekub, king of Samal. [Samal was a small state of considerable importance at that time—it is now the Kurdish hamlet of Zenjirli.] *d* Earliest royal inscription: the stele of the Aramaean king Ben Hadad.

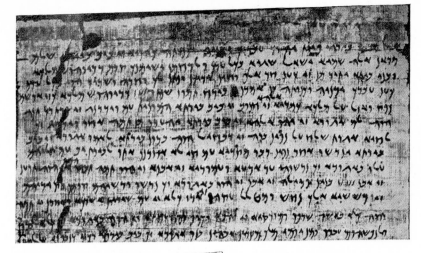

a

b

15.3. *a* Aramaic papyrus from Elephantine, a Jewish military colony in Egypt (5th century B.C.). *b* Rock inscription from Cilicia (5th century B.C.).

15.3*c*. Aramaic letter written on leather, 5th century B.C. (Bodleian Library, Oxford).

15.4. Aramaic papyrus of the 5th century B.C., from Egypt (Brooklyn Museum).

	V. CENT.	III. CENT.	PAP. NASH	HERODIAN	DURA
א				א (א)	
ה				ה (ה)	
ח				ח	ח
ל				ל (ל)	
מ				מ ם (ם)	
נ				נ ן	
צ				(צ)	
ק				(ק)	
ת				ת (ת)	

b Comparative table of selected characters, from the 5th century B.C. to 3rd century A.D.

MODERN HEBREW	660-50 B C	600-550 B C	515-4 B C	494-3 B C	PHON. VALUE
א					$'$
ל					h
ם					$ṭ$
.					y
ח					k
ם					m
ם					s
ם					$'$
ר					q
א					$š$

a The most characteristic letters used from the middle of the 7th century B.C. to the early 5th century B.C., according to Prof. W. F. Albright.

15.5. Development of Cursive Aramaic script.

15.6b Greek–Aramaic bilingual, from Armazi. (Courtesy, Acad. George Tseret'eli).

15.6a. Armazi Aramaic inscription No. 1.

	SQUARE HEBREW (MONUMENTAL)	MEDIEVAL FORMAL STYLES	RABBINIC STYLES	CURSIVE STYLES	CONTEMPORARY	
					CURSIVE	PRINT
1						
2						
3						
4						
5						
6						
7						
8						
9						
10						
11						
12						
13						
14						
15						
16						
17						
18						
19						
20						
21						
22						

* FINAL LETTERS

15.7. Main styles of the [square] Hebrew alphabet.

Phon. Value	Eleph. Pap.	Louvre Pap.	Edfu Ostr.	4 Q Sam.[b]	4 Q Jer.[a]	4 Q XII[a]	Nash Pap.	1 Q Is.[a]	Man. Disc.
'									
b									
g									
d									
h									
w									
z									
ḥ									
ṭ									
y									
k									
l									
m									
n									
s									
'									
p									
ṣ									
q									
r									
š									
t									

* Final Letters

15.8

1 Q Is.ᵇ	Hab. Comm.	Hod.	1V Q Dent.ʲ	Běnê Ḥēzîr	Kedron	Uzziah Slab	Queen Sara (Helena)	Ossuary Inscriptions	Mod. Hebr.
									א
									ב
									ג
									ד
									ה
									ו
									ז
									ח
									ט
									י
									כ
									ל
									מ
									נ
									ס
									ע
									פ
									צ
									ק
									ר
									ש
									ת

15.8 and 9. Early development of the Square Hebrew alphabet, based partly on various Dead Sea scrolls, and partly on ancient papyri and funerary inscriptions.

a   *b*

 זה ר‍וחש‍א דלאלערמטװ וטעריחזורה לעצ רוחנ
טזרחה לז דרעַ ‍וג ‍ואלעור טמחה
ו מטצ אזור

c

d   *e*

15.10. *a* Sepulchral inscription from 'Araq el-Emir. Late 6th or early 5th century B.C. *b* The 'Gezer boundary'. First half of the 1st century B.C. *c* Early Square Hebrew tomb inscription. *d* Uzziah plaque. *e* Chufutkale (Crimea) sepulchral inscription. *f* Jericho synagogue inscription. *g* Toledo synagogue inscription.

f

g

a   b

15.11. *a* Nash papyrus. *b* Dead Sea Scrolls: Manual
of discipline. *c* Dead Sea Scrolls: Isaiah A.

c

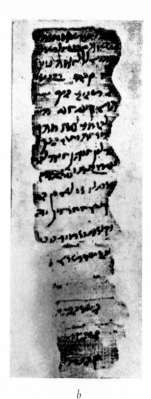

a   *b*

c

15.12. *a* Dead Sea Scrolls: Isaiah B. *b* Marriage contract, written in a hitherto unknown Hebrew cursive script, from Muraba'at. *c* Dead Sea Scrolls: Children of Light and Children of Darkness.

a

משמעון בן כוסבה לישע 1

בן גו[ל]גלה ולאנשי הכרך 2

שלו[ם] מעיד אני עלֿיתֿשמים 3

יפקד] מן הגללאים שהצלכם 4

כל אדם שאני נתנתכבלים 5

ברגלכם כמה שעקיבא] 6

לבן עפלול 7

[ש]מעון 8

b

1 From Simeon ben Kosba to Jeshua
2 ben Ga[l]gola and the men of the
   fortress,
3 Gree[tings]. I call Heaven to witness
   against me < that if >
4 of the Galileans, who are at your
   place, there should be missing
5 (even) a single one, I will put fetters
6 on your feet, as Akiba < did >
7 to Ben Aflul.
8 [Si]m̄eon b̄[en Kosba]

c

15.13. *a* Photograph of letter from Simon Bar-Kochba (2nd century A.D.).
b transliteration into modern Hebrew. *c* Tentative translation into English.
d Papyrus letter from the administrators of Bēth Māshkhô, found at Muraba'at.

15.14. *a* Incantation text on a bowl from Babylonia, attributed to 8th century A.D. *b* Divorce letter (*get*) of the year 1128 (Cairo Genizah). *c* Legal Document of the year 1137, from Léon (Spain). *d* Italian cursive hands of the 16th century: signatures of 3 Italian rabbis (Codex Livorno No. 27).

a

c

 וְשִׁפְטֵי טְמוּנֵי
חוֹל וּלְגָד
אָמַר בָּרוּךְ דו
מַרְחִיב גָּד י
כְּלָבִיא שָׁכֵן
וְטָרַף זְרוֹעַ אַף
קָדְקֹד וַיַּרְא
רֵאשִׁית לוֹ כִּי
שָׁם חֶלְקַת מְחֹקֵק
סָפוּן וַיֵּתֵא רָאשֵׁי
עָם צִדְקַת יהוה
עָשָׂה וּמִשְׁפָּטָיו
עִם יִשְׂרָאֵל

b

15.15. *a* Hebrew papyrus book (University Library, Cambridge). *b* Formal Hebrew alphabet: Leningrad pentateuch (Codex 85), dated to 1132 (from Jerusalem). *c* Apparently the oldest Hebrew Bible in Vellum codex form, late 9th or early 10th century. (British Museum, Or. 4445).

15.16. Hebrew Bible of Tiflis (Genesis 5, 28 to 6, 12) with Massoretic annotation assuming the form of decoration of the pages.

15.17. Titled Bible, Model Codex of the Pentateuch (formerly Gaster Collection No. 85, now in the Brit. Mus.).

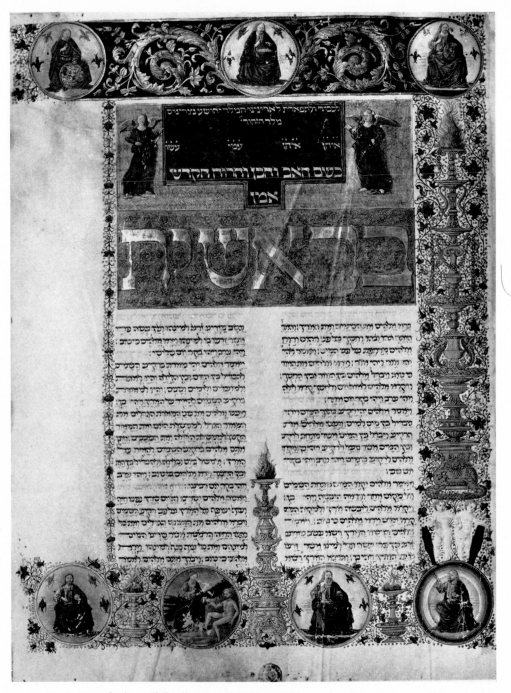

15.18. Beginning of a beautifully illuminated Hebrew Bible produced by Francesco d'Antonio del Cherico (worked from about 1455 to 1485), Laurentian Library, Florence, MS. Plut. 1,31.

15.19. Earliest extant incunabula of Hebrew Bible, by Joshua Saloman, Soncino, 1488. (Biblioteca Palatina, Parma).

a

26 וְגַם־מִקְנֵנוּ יֵלֵךְ עִמָּנוּ לֹא וְגַם־מִקְנֵנוּ יֵלֵךְ עִמָּנוּ לֹא
תִשָּׁאֵר פַּרְסָה כִּי מִמֶּנּוּ נִקַּח לַעֲבֹד אֶת־יְהוָה אֱלֹהֵינוּ
27 וַאֲנַחְנוּ לֹא־נֵדַע מַה־נַּעֲבֹד אֶת־יְהוָה עַד־בֹּאֵנוּ שָׁמָּה: וַיְחַזֵּק
28 יְהוָה אֶת־לֵב פַּרְעֹה וְלֹא אָבָה לְשַׁלְּחָם: וַיֹּאמֶר־לוֹ פַרְעֹה
לֵךְ מֵעָלָי הִשָּׁמֶר לְךָ אַל־תֹּסֶף רְאוֹת פָּנַי כִּי בְּיוֹם
29 רְאֹתְךָ פָנַי תָּמוּת: וַיֹּאמֶר מֹשֶׁה כֵּן דִּבַּרְתָּ לֹא־אֹסִף עוֹד
רְאוֹת פָּנֶיךָ: ס

11 וַיֹּאמֶר יְהוָה אֶל־מֹשֶׁה עוֹד נֶגַע אֶחָד אָבִיא עַל־פַּרְעֹה
וְעַל־מִצְרַיִם אַחֲרֵי־כֵן יְשַׁלַּח אֶתְכֶם מִזֶּה כְּשַׁלְּחוֹ כָּלָה
2 גָּרֵשׁ יְגָרֵשׁ אֶתְכֶם מִזֶּה: דַּבֶּר־נָא בְּאָזְנֵי הָעָם וְיִשְׁאֲלוּ
אִישׁ מֵאֵת רֵעֵהוּ וְאִשָּׁה מֵאֵת רְעוּתָהּ כְּלֵי־כֶסֶף וּכְלֵי
3 זָהָב: וַיִּתֵּן יְהוָה אֶת־חֵן הָעָם בְּעֵינֵי מִצְרָיִם גַּם הָאִישׁ
מֹשֶׁה גָּדוֹל מְאֹד בְּאֶרֶץ מִצְרַיִם בְּעֵינֵי עַבְדֵי־פַרְעֹה וּבְעֵינֵי
4 הָעָם: ס וַיֹּאמֶר מֹשֶׁה כֹּה אָמַר יְהוָה כַּחֲצֹת הַלַּיְלָה אֲנִי
5 יוֹצֵא בְּתוֹךְ מִצְרָיִם: וּמֵת כָּל־בְּכוֹר בְּאֶרֶץ מִצְרַיִם
מִבְּכוֹר פַּרְעֹה הַיֹּשֵׁב עַל־כִּסְאוֹ עַד בְּכוֹר הַשִּׁפְחָה אֲשֶׁר
6 אַחַר הָרֵחָיִם וְכֹל בְּכוֹר בְּהֵמָה: וְהָיְתָה צְעָקָה גְדֹלָה
בְּכָל־אֶרֶץ מִצְרָיִם אֲשֶׁר כָּמֹהוּ לֹא נִהְיָתָה וְכָמֹהוּ לֹא
7 תֹסִף: וּלְכֹל בְּנֵי יִשְׂרָאֵל לֹא יֶחֱרַץ־כֶּלֶב לְשֹׁנוֹ לְמֵאִישׁ
וְעַד־בְּהֵמָה לְמַעַן תֵּדְעוּן אֲשֶׁר יַפְלֶה יְהוָה בֵּין מִצְרַיִם
8 וּבֵין יִשְׂרָאֵל: וְיָרְדוּ כָל־עֲבָדֶיךָ אֵלֶּה אֵלַי וְהִשְׁתַּחֲווּ־לִי
לֵאמֹר צֵא אַתָּה וְכָל־הָעָם אֲשֶׁר־בְּרַגְלֶיךָ וְאַחֲרֵי־כֵן אֵצֵא
9 וַיֵּצֵא מֵעִם־פַּרְעֹה בָּחֳרִי־אָף: ס וַיֹּאמֶר יְהוָה אֶל־מֹשֶׁה
לֹא־יִשְׁמַע אֲלֵיכֶם פַּרְעֹה לְמַעַן רְבוֹת מוֹפְתַי בְּאֶרֶץ
10 מִצְרָיִם: וּמֹשֶׁה וְאַהֲרֹן עָשׂוּ אֶת־כָּל־הַמֹּפְתִים הָאֵלֶּה
לִפְנֵי פַרְעֹה וַיְחַזֵּק יְהוָה אֶת־לֵב פַּרְעֹה וְלֹא־שִׁלַּח אֶת־
בְּנֵי־יִשְׂרָאֵל מֵאַרְצוֹ: ס

b

הוּפַר הַשֶּׁקֶט בִּגְבוּלֵנוּ הַדְּרוֹמִי. הֻסְתְּמוּ
מוֹקְשִׁים, וְאַף מִסְתַּנְּנִים חָדְרוּ, מֵעֵבֶר
לַגְּבוּל. נִרְאֶה, כִּי מִתְחַדְּשׁוֹת פְּעֻלּוֹת
הָרֶצַח הַמִּצְרָיוֹת.

הָאַחְרָיוּת הַמְּלֵאָה לַהַפִיכָתָהּ-מֵחָדָשׁ
שֶׁל רְצוּעַת־עַזָּה לְקֵן מְרַצְּחִים מֻטֶּלֶת
בְּכָל חֻמְרָתָהּ עַל מוֹסְדוֹת אוּ"ם וְעַל
כֹּחַ־הַחֵרוּם שֶׁלּוֹ, שֶׁחוֹבָתָם הִיא לִמְנֹעַ
אֶת חִדּוּשָׁם שֶׁל מַעֲשֵׂי־הָאֵיבָה הַמִּצְ־
רַיִים, לִשְׁמֹר עַל הַשֶּׁקֶט וְהַבִּטָּחוֹן בַּגְּ־
בוּל. רוֹבֵץ מִצְרַיִם נָחֵל כַּמָּה כִּשְׁלוֹנוֹת
מְדִינִיִּים בַּתְּקוּפָה הָאַחֲרוֹנָה, וְנִרְאֶה, כִּי
הוּא שׁוֹאֵף "לְתַקֵּן אֶת מַזָּלוֹ" עַל־יְדֵי
חִדּוּשׁ הַהִתְנַקְּשֻׁיּוֹת הָרַצְחָנִיּוֹת בְּחַיֵּיהֶם
שֶׁל חַקְלָאִים וְאֶזְרָחִים יִשְׂרְאֵלִיִּים. מִמֶּ־
שֶׁלֶת יִשְׂרָאֵל הֵבִיאָה אֶת הַתַּקְרִית
הַחֲמוּרָה לִידִיעַת מוֹעֶצֶת הַבִּטָּחוֹן.
מִמּוֹסְדוֹת אוּ"ם וְהַגּוֹרְמִים הַקּוֹבְעִים
בָּהֶם תִּתְבַּע הָאַחְרָיוּת לַמַּצָּב שֶׁנּוֹצַר
וְלַסַּכָּנוֹת הַנִּשְׁקָפוֹת מִמֶּנּוּ לִשְׁלוֹם הָאֵ־
זוֹר.

בְּרִיטַנְיָה וְיַרְדֵּן

פְּנֵי יַרְדֵּן לִבְרִיטַנְיָה בְּבַקְּשַׁת סִיּוּעַ
כַּסְפִּי הִיא עוֹד עֵדוּת אַחַת לְהִתְפָּרְקו־
תָהּ שֶׁל הַלִּיגָה הָעַרְבִית כְּגוֹרֵם "אַנְטִי־
אִימְפֶּרְיָאלִיסְטִי", כּוֹתֵב "דָּ בָ ר". בְּמַ־
אֲמָרוֹ הָרָאשִׁי מִיּוֹם ו'. סֵמֲלֵי הַדָּבָר
לַמַּצָּב שֶׁנּוֹצַר בָּאֵזוֹר, כִּי פְּנִיַּת רַבַּת־
עַמּוֹן לְלוֹנְדּוֹן בָּאָה יוֹם אוֹ יוֹמַיִם לִפְנֵי
פְּנוֹת הַכֹּחוֹת הַבְּרִיטִיִּים מִן הַבָּסִיס הַגָּ־
דוֹל בְּמַפְרֶק. קָרוֹב לְוַדַּאי, כִּי בְּבַקְּשַׁת
הָעֶזְרָה לֹא תִּמְנַע אֶת הַמֶּלֶךְ חוּסֵין
מִלָּשֵׂאת בַּחֲגִיגוֹת הַפִּנּוּי נְאוּם "אַנְטִי־
אִימְפֶּרְיָאלִיסְטִי", שֶׁיְּפָאֵר אֶת הַמַּאֲבָק
לְעַצְמָאוּת אֲשֶׁר נִפְתַּח עִם הַדָּחָתוֹ שֶׁל
גֶּנֵרָל גְּלָב...

לֹא נַכְחִישׁ, מִצִּיּוּן הֶעָתוּק, כִּי אָנוּ חוֹ־

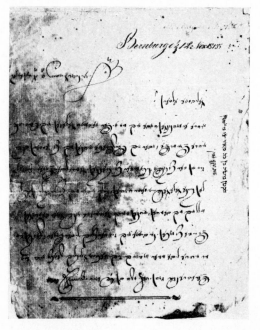

c

15.20. Hebrew character: *a* Vocalised modern Hebrew Bible. *b* Vocalized modern Hebrew for children. *c* Yiddish letter, 1818.

PHONETIC VALUE	NABATAEAN	NEO-SINAITIC	EARLY ARABIC	A.D. 8th CENTURY	KUFIC	EARLY NASKHI	MAGHRIBI	QARMATHIAN	MODERN NASKHI
'									
b									
g (ǧ)									
d (ḏ)									
h									
w									
z									
ḥ (ḫ)									
ṭ (ẓ)									
y									
k									
l									
m									
n									
s									
' (ġ)									
(p) f									
ṣ (ḍ)									
q									
r									
sh-š									
t (ṯ)									

ARABIC ADDITIONAL LETTERS	PERSIAN	پ p چ tš ژ ž گ g	PUSHTU	څ ts ږ z' ښ ch
	URDU	ٹ ṭ ڈ d ڑ r APART FROM PERSIAN ADDITIONAL LETTERS	MALAY	ڠ ñ ڤ p ث ñ ڬ g چ tš

15.21. Development of the Arabic alphabet.

15.22. *a* Important Nabataean inscriptions from Petra. *b, c* Minor Nabataean inscriptions. *d–f* Neo-Sinaitic inscriptions.

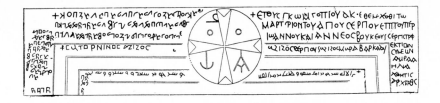

15.23. *a* Earliest extant Arabic inscription: Greek-Syraic-Arabic trilingual, A.D. 512. *b* Comparison of *left*, Kufic and *right*, Qarmathian scripts. *Koran*, Sura 3, 1–2. *c* Modern Kufic character. *d* Sepulchral epigraphic in Kufic character dated 445 A.H. [A.H. = in the year of the Hegira (*English* flight). The Moslem era, A.H., is reckoned from Mohammed's flight from Mecca to Medina in A.D. 622].

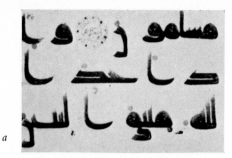

a

b

c

d قوتُ الغَنِي في أعزّ مثل حَياتِهِ وَعِيشُهُ في الذّلِ عَين مَمَاتِهِ

e قوتِ الغني في العزّ مثل حياته وعيشه في الذلّ عين مماته

f قوت الغني في العزّ مثل حياته وعيشه في الذلّ عين مماته

g قوتُ الغني في العزّ مثل حياته وعيشه في الذلّ عين مماته

h قوتُ الغني في العزّ مثل حياته وعيشه في الذلّ عين مماته

i قوت الغني في العزّ مثل حياته وعيشه في الذلّ عين مماته

j قوت الغني في العزّ مثل حياته وعيشه في الذلّ عين مماته

k قوت الغني في العزّ مثل حياته وعيشه في الذلّ عين مماته

l قوت الغني في العزّ مثل حياته وعيشه في الذلّ عين مماته

15.24. *a* Earliest dated Kufic manuscript in England, bearing the dedication of Amadjur, Governor of Damascus, A.D. 870–7. (University Library, Cambridge, *Add.* M.S. 1116). *b* Koran Sura 24, verses 32–6. 8th century Kufic on vellum. (British Museum, Dr. 2165, f. 676). *c* Oldest dated Christian Arabic manuscript: *Treatise on Christian Theology* A.D. 876, attributed to Theodorus Abū Kurrah, bishop of Harran (British Museum, Or. MS. 4950). *d* to *l* Varieties of Naskhi script.

d Naskhi current hand
e Diwani
f Naskhi-Djerisi
g Thuluth
h Ryq'a
i Ta'liq current hand
j Kalemi-Rasd
k Djeri
l Syakat

15.25. Page of a very elegant copy of the Koran, by a copyist who names himself, Husain Fakhkhâr. The pages measure 13¼ by 8½ inches, and some are entirely gilt, or written on a dyed ground, or ornamented with gold, blue, etc. The text is written in *Naskhi*, but the first, middle and last lines are written in large *Thuluth* (Courtesy S. C. Sutton, Librarian, India Office Library. No. 32A).

209

15.26. Copy of the Koran, probably early 10th century. (In a private collection at Izmir: Courtesy Glyn Meredith-Owens.)

15.27b. Koran with glosses, in Kanembu, N. Nigeria. (Courtesy Glyn Meredith-Owens.)

15.27.a. A medical encyclopaedia, A.D. 1085. The second earliest dated Persian MS. (Courtesy Glyn Meredith-Owens.)

15.28. Old Ottoman Naskhi: opening of the Koran with the ex-libris of the poet (Courtesy Glyn Meredith-Owens).

15.29. Old Ottoman translation of the Koran (Courtesy Glyn Meredith-Owens).

213

15.30. Luxurious 16th century Persian MS., ornamented in gold (Rylands Persian MS. 35; courtesy, Librarian John Rylands Library).

15.31. Çağatay or Old Uzbek MS. Divān of Mīr ʾAli Shīr Nevāʾi (Courtesy Glyn Meredith-Owens).

15.32a. Urdu: *Amwaj-i-khūdi*, A.D. 1667
(India Office Library, *Hindust.* B.2.)

15.32b. Malay: *Shair jaran Tamas*, c.
1800 (India Office Library, *Malay*,
D.6).

15.32c. Sindhi: Shab-i-Mi'rāj, A.D. 1807
(India Office Library, *Sindhi* 14).

15.32d. Pashtu: *Qissah-i-Bahramgor*, A.D.
1750 (India Office Library, *Pash.* B.28).

15.33a. Arabic adapted to a non-Semitic language: letter written in Urdu.

15.33b. Arabic adapted to a non-Semitic language: letter written in Swahili.

Phon. Value	Palmyrene	Syriac — Early Syriac	Estrang.	West-Syrian or Serta	East-Syrian or Nest.	Jacob.	Christ. Palestin or Palestin Syriac	Mand.	Manichaean
'									(ʾâ)
b									
g									
d									
h									
w									(v, û ô)
z									(ǯ ẓ ǧ) (ž)
ḥ									
ṭ									
y									(j, î, ê)
k									(kh)
l									(l)
m									
n									
s									
ʿ									
p									(ph)
ṣ									(č) (ǧ)
q									
r									
sh									
t									

15.34. Various offshoots of the Aramaic alphabet.

b

c

15.35. *a* Latin–Palmyrene inscription discovered in a Roman camp at South Shields near Newcastle, and the transcription of the Palmyrene text. *b, c* Palmyrene inscriptions.

a

15.35*d*. Palmyrene inscription in the background of a stone carving (Fitzwilliam Museum, Cambridge).

a

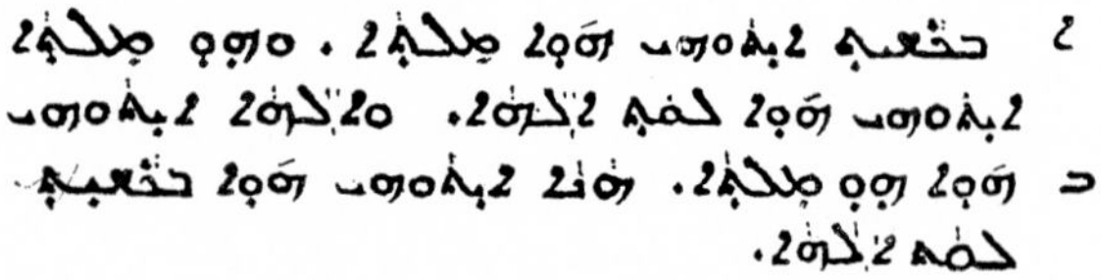

b

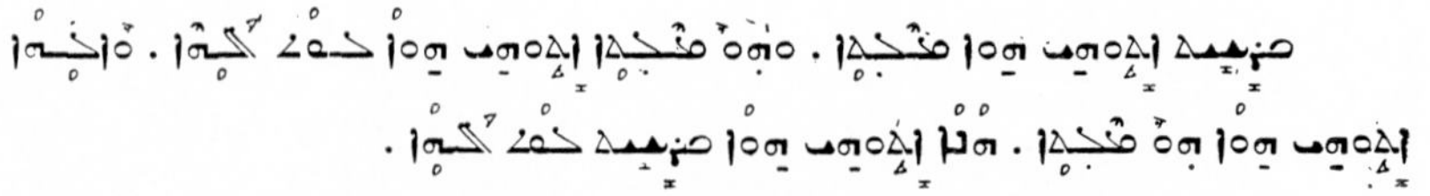

c

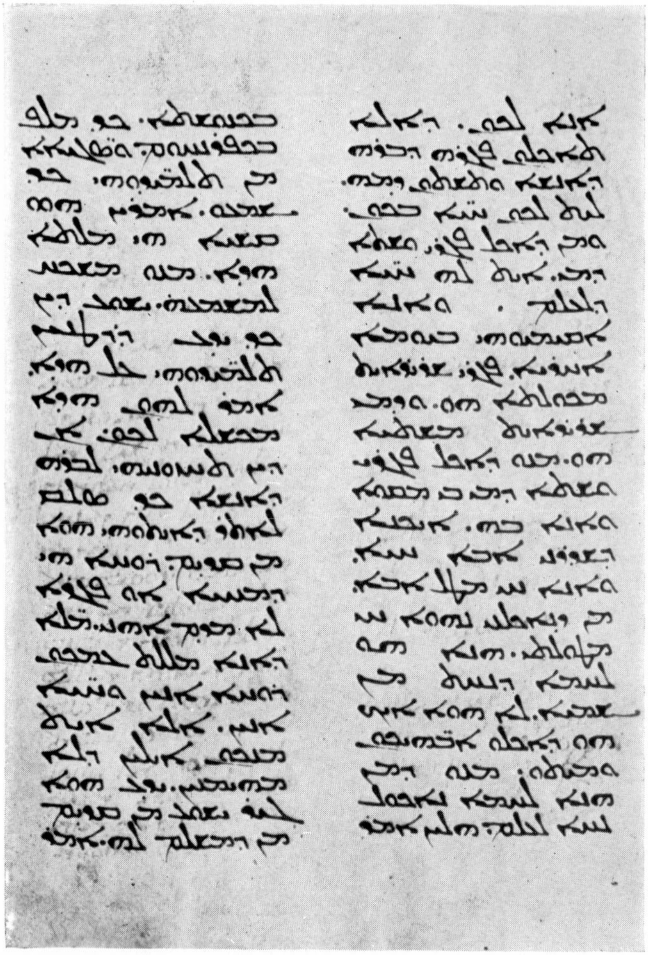

15.36. Syriac inscriptions and manuscripts: *a* Early Syriac, from Edessa, attributed to 4th century A.D. *b* Printed Nestorian script (St. John's Gospel I, 1–2). *c* Jacobite script. *d* Curetonian Gospels, 5th century A.D. (British Museum).

d

15.37. Rabbūlā Gospels, folio 6r. Written and illuminated by the monk Rabbūlā in A.D. 586 at the monastery of St. John at Zagba in Mesopotamia. Laurentian Library, Florence (Cod Plut. 1.56).

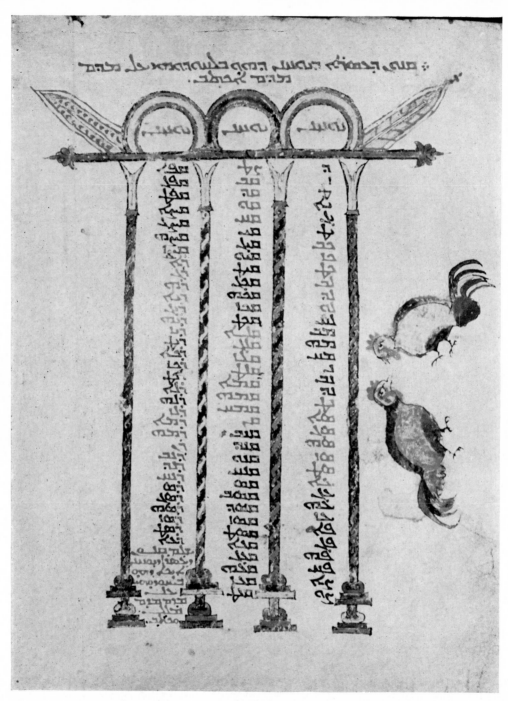

15.38. Illuminated Syriac MS.: courtesy Sir Chester Beatty. (MS. 16.)

222

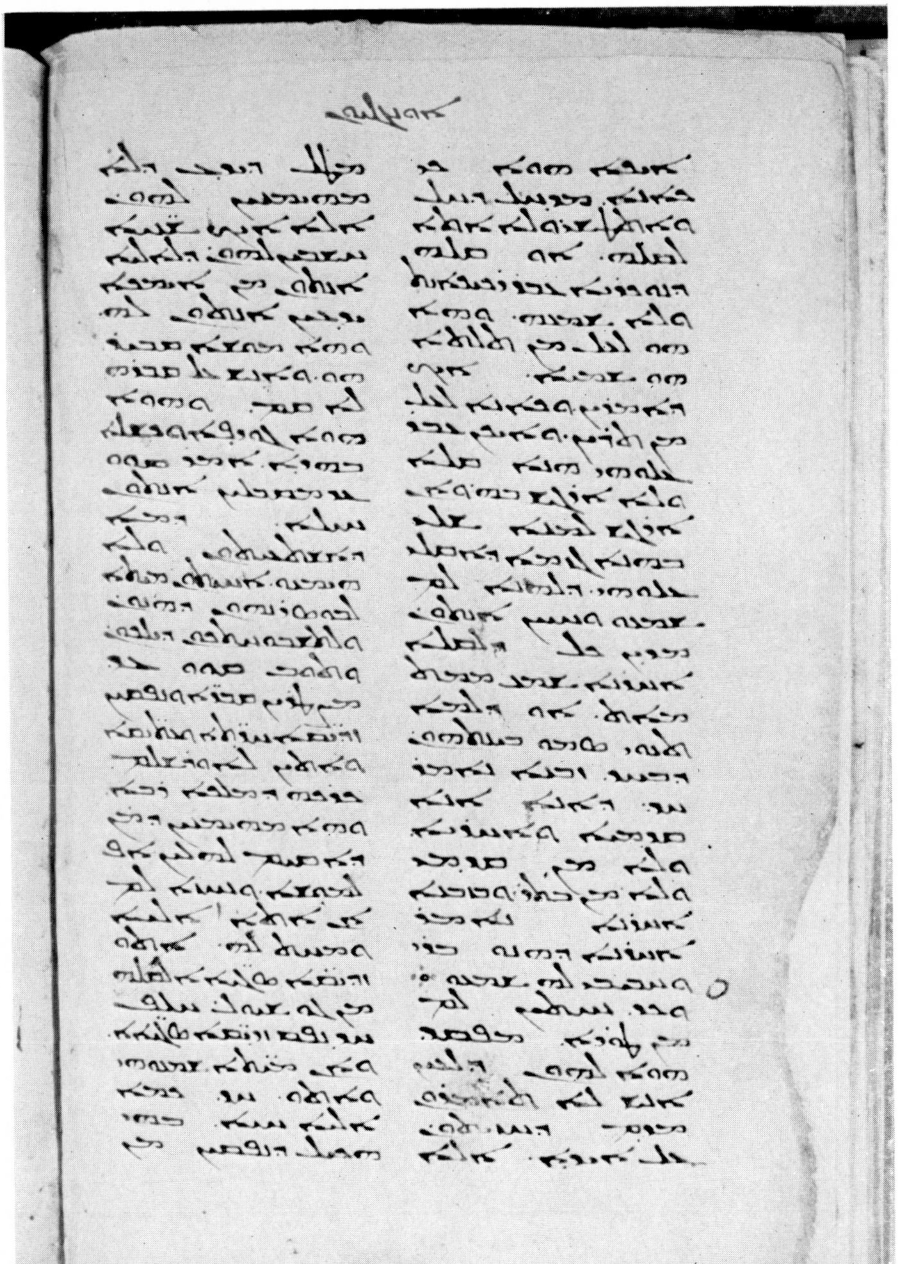

15.39. Syriac Codex: courtesy, Sir Chester Beatty. (MS 17.)

223

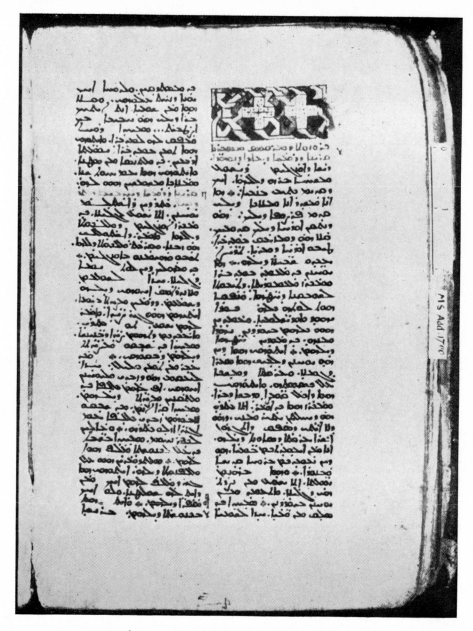

15.40. Harqleian version of the New Testament. Written in a neat
regular Jacobite cursive hand, it contains 216 leaves of vellum, each
measuring 9½ by 6½ inches. It is dated A.Gr 1481, corresponding to
A.D. 1170. (University Library, Cambridge, *Add. MS.* 1700.)

15.41. Nestorian book, written by a secluded monk, completed in the year 892. It contains meditations, prayers, sermons, Christian chronology, and so on. (Courtesy, Rev. A. E. Goodman.)

15.42a. Yezidi cryptic alphabet.

15.42. *b* Yezidi specimen from *Kitab-al-Jalweh*. *c* Yezidi specimen from *Miskhaf Resh*. *d* Somali alphabet.

Chā zernah, khudā-si khuri bui-kha
« What say-if, God-by his son-on
chhes-luh lya-khan kun mi shi, do-
faith-sort making all not die, that-
patse khong-lah hrtane . duk-pi
from him-to faithful being-ones-of

khson-luk thop-tuk, zere, khuri bu chik-bu mins; ditse khosi mi-
living-short receive, saiying, his son only-one gave; thus him-by men-
yul-po-lah rgas.
land-to liked ».

15.42e. Balti script. Specimen from St. John's Gospel, 3, 16, with transliteration and translation into English, according to G. A. Grierson.

226

No.		No.		No.		No.		No.		No.		No.	
1	a	2	am	3	ā	4	i	5	u	6	um	7	r̥
8	e	9	o	10	ka	11	ka	12	kā	13	kr̥	14	ko
15	kā	16	kum	17	ḱe	18	kha	19	khi	20	khu	21	ga
22	gu	23	gam	24	ǵa	25	ǵu	26	ḡam	27	gha	28	ghe
29	ca	30	ca	31	cam	32	ci	33	ce	34	co	35	cha
36	chi	37	cham	38	cha	39	cha	40	cham	41	chu	42	chum
43	ja	44	ja	45	jam	46	jā	47	ji	48	ja	49	ji
50	jha	51	jha	52	jhu	53	ña	54	ñi	55	ñi	56	ñe
57	ta	58	tam	59	tum	60	tha	61	tham	62	thu	63	tha
64	thi	65	tho	66	ḍa	67	ḍa	68	ḍa	69	ḍi	70	ḍem
71	dha	72	ḍha	73	ḍhi	74	ṇa	75	ta	76	tam	77	ti
78	te	79	tai	80	tä	81	taḥ	82	tha	83	thā	84	tha
85	da	86	da	87	du	88	de	89	do	90	dha	91	dham
92	dhik	93	dhiḥ	94	na	95	ni	96	ni	97	na	98	ne
99	pa	100	pi	101	pum	102	pū	103	pha	104	pha	105	phu
106	ba	107	bim	108	bu	109	bha	110	bhi	111	bhu	112	bhom
113	ma	114	ma	115	mam	116	mu	117	mr̥	118	me	119	me
120	mo	121	ya	122	yam	123	yi	124	yu	125	ya	126	yo
127	ra	128	ram	129	ru	130	ret	131	ro	132	rom	133	la
134	le	135	va	136	vim	137	vi	138	vu	139	vo	140	vr̥
141	va	142	vu	143	ve	144	ba	145	bam	146	bamñ(?)	147	bi
148	bu	149	be	150	bai	151	ba	152	ba	153	bam	154	bo
155	ba	156	bam	157	bim	158	bu	159	bū	160	bom	161	ba
162	bi	163	ha	164	hā	165	hi	166	hu	167	ha	168	ho
169	kha	170	khrā	171	kma	172	kra	173	krā	174	kva	175	khva
176	k'tṣi	177	gtsi	178	gra	179	ǵnu	180	ghra	181	nka	182	nga
183	cma	184	cva	185	jhbo	186	jhmo	187	ñǵe	188	tma	189	tya
190	tra	191	tva	192	tsa	193	tsma	194	dra	195	dryu	196	dvi
197	dhya	198	ng	199	nǵe	200	pte	201	pgu	202	pǵu	203	pǵe
204	pre	205	prá	206	pru	207	pro	208	mge	209	mya	210	mṣo
211	rta	212	rtha	213	rdha	214	rmi	215	rya	216	rura	217	rṣa
218	rsu	219	lpa	220	lpi	221	lpi	222	lme	223	lme	224	lve
225	vyā	226	brā	227	bru	228	brr	229	bvam	230	ṣṭha	231	ṣǵa
232	ṣǵe	233	ṣṭa	234	ṣḍhi	235	ṣṭa	236	ṣrá	237	ṣva	238	ṣpa
239	sta	240	stra	241	sthi	242	sthai	243	spa	244	opa	245	opu
246	oma	247	oya	248	ora	249	ova	250	ñsa	251	ñsam	252	ñse
253	1	254	1	255	1	256	2	257	2	258	3	259	3
260	3	261	4	262	4	263	10	264	20	265	100	266	1,000

16.1. The Kharoshthi character according to E. J. Rapson.

227

a Kharoshthi inscription. *b* Kharoshthi book on wood, found at Niya (Ruin 24, 7), Eastern Turkestan, by Sir Aurel Stein's expedition of 1906–8.

16.3a. Pahlavi alphabets compared with the Sogdian and Aramaic scripts. S, Sogdian, 1, phonetic value, 2, Elephantine Aramaic, 3, Pahlavik, 4, Avrománian, 5, Parsik, 6, Avesta, 7, phonetic value.

16.3b. Avesta alphabet.

16.3c. Parchment Document from Avromán, Kurdistán, found with Greek deeds dated B.C. 88 and 22/21. The earliest specimen of Pahlavi (Middle Persian): some words are actually Aramaic but were read as Persian, just as we write e.g. = *exempli gratia* and say 'for example'.

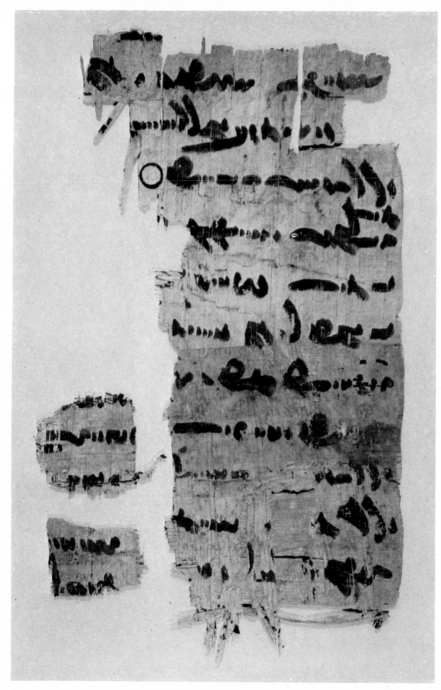

16.4. Pahlavi papyrus (Brooklyn Museum, 351452-A).

16.5. Iranian manuscripts
  a Cursive eastern Pahlavi.
  b Khordan Avesta, A.D. 1723 (India Office Library, Z & P. 21)
  c Pazand: Strikand Gumani Vigar, A.D. 1737 (India Office Library, Z & P. 23)

16.6. Specimens of *a* Manichaean writing. *b* Kök Turki runes and *c* Sogdian writing.

16.7. The Sogdian and Uighur alphabets compared with the Aramaic script.
(1) *Palmyrene* alphabet (2) phonetic values (3) *Sogdian* initial signs (4) medial signs
(5) final signs (6) phonetic values (7) *Uighur* initial signs (8) medial signs (9) final
signs of the script employed in Eastern Turkestan (10) *Qutadghu* initial signs (11) final
signs (12) phonetic value.

Figure a — table of Orkhon/Yenisei runes with phonetic values:

ORKHON	YENISEI	PHON. VALUE	ORKHON	YENISEI	PHON. VALUE	ORKHON	YENISEI	PHON. VALUE
		$a\ ä$			d^6			r^7
		$y\ \iota$			d^7			l^6
		$o\ u$			p			l^7
		$ö\ ü$			b^6			$č$
		k^1			b^7			$\underline{ič}$
		k^2			j^6			s^6
		k^3			j^7			s^7
		k^4			i			$š$
		k^5			$\frac{ng}{\underline{n}}$			z
		g^6			n^6			$\underline{nd}$
		g^7			n^7			$\underline{nč}$
		t^6			m			$\underline{ld}$
		t^7			r^6			

a

Figure b — comparison of Germanic (RUNES) with Kök Turki:

Value	RUNES	KökTurki	Value	Value	RUNES	KökTurki	Value	Value	RUNES	KökTurki	Value
f			g'	h			k	t			k
u			š	n			d	b			k'
th			y	ī			s	e			lt
a			k	y			y̆	m			
r				e			a	l			j
		ng	P			ng	o			b'
g			d'	R			č	o			b'
w			y''	s			r	dh			

b

16.8. *a* Kök Turki runes. The figures $^{1-7}$ indicate the shapes of the letters when they precede or follow these vowels ^{1}a, ^{2}y, ^{3}o or u, ^{4}ä, e or i, ^{5}ö or ü, ^{6}a, o, u or y, ^{7}e, i, ä, ö, or ü. *b* Comparison of Germanic with Kök Turki runes. *c* Early Hungarian script.

c

Syriac	Uighur			Mongolian turned horizontally			Mongolian			Kalmuck		Manchu	
	1	2	3	1	2	3	1	2	3	1	2	1	2

16.9. *a* The Mongolian, Kalmuck and Manchu alphabets compared with the Syriac and Uighur scripts. *b* Portion of The Gospel of St. John, in Manchu.

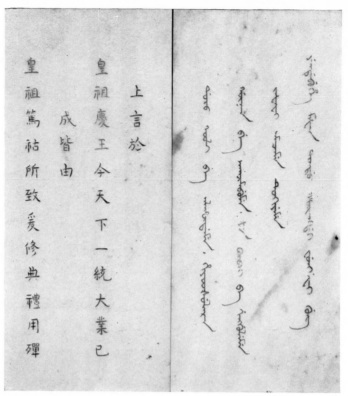

16.10*a*. Jade book, 1648, *right*, Manchu, and *left*, Chinese: Emperor Fu-Lin (Shuh-Chih) confers posthumous title on ancestor of the 6th generation (Chester Beatty 30).

16.10*b*. Mongolian, early 18th cent.: translation of Buddhist Sūtra *T'ar-Pa C'en-Po*. (Chester Beatty 29). Courtesy, Sir Chester Beatty.

a

b

a	γa	ba	la	da	tsa	sa	ra
ä	kä	bä	lä	dä	tsä	sä	rä
i	ki	bi	li	di	tsi	si	ri
o	γo	bo	lo	do	tso	so	ro
u	γu	bu	lu	du	tsu	su	ru
ö	kö	bö	lö	dö	tsö	sö	rö
ü	kü	bü	lü	dü	tsü	sü	rü
na	ga	ma	ta	ya	dza	ša	
nä	gä	mä	tä	yä	dzä	šä	
ni	gi	mi	ti	yi	dzi	ši	
no	go	mo	to	yo	dzo	šo	
nu	gu	mu	tu	yu	dzu	šu	
nö	gö	mö	tö	yö	dzö	šö	
nü	gü	mü	tü	yü	dzü	šü	

16.11. *a* Uighur book. *b* Mongolian manuscript, *Altasamba*, *c.* 1860 (India Office Library, R.305). *c* Kalmuck syllabic alphabet.

c

237

NO	MAJUSC.	MINUSC.	PHONETIC VALUE	NAMES OF LETTERS
1	Ա	ա	a	aïp
2	Բ	բ	b–p	bien
3	Գ	գ	g–k	gim
4	Դ	դ	d–t	da
5	Ե	ե	e	eč (yeč')
6	Զ	զ	z	za
7	Է	է	e (silent ə e)	ēt'
8	Ը	ը	ə e	at'
9	Թ	թ	t'	t'o
10	Ժ	ժ	ž	že
11	Ի	ի	i	ini
12	Լ	լ	l	liun
13	Խ	խ	ḫ x (Scott. ch)	hē
14	Ծ	ծ	ts z	tsa
15	Կ	կ	k–g	ken
16	Հ	հ	h	ho
17	Ձ	ձ	d–z	dza
18	Ղ	ղ	ł gh	ład
19	Ճ	ճ	č	čē
20	Մ	մ	m	men
21	Յ	յ	y, j, h,	hi
22	Ն	ն	n	nu
23	Շ	շ	š	ša
24	Ո	ո	o	o
25	Չ	չ	č̣, č̌, ch	ča
26	Պ	պ	p–b	pe
27	Ջ	ջ	ǧ ǰ, dž	dže
28	Ռ	ռ	ṙ	řa
29	Ս	ս	s	sē
30	Վ	վ	v	vev
31	Տ	տ	t–d	tiun
32	Ր	ր	r	rē
33	Ց	ց	c, t's	t'so co
34	Ւ	ւ	u, w	hiun
35	Փ	փ	p, p', ph	p'iur
36	Ք	ք	k, k', x	k'ē
37	Օ	օ	o	ō
38	Ֆ	ֆ	f	fē
39	Ձ	ձ	ʒ	ev

16.12. The Armenian Alphabet.

16.13*b*. Page from 'Arithmetic', by Anania Shirakatsi, 7th century.

16.13*a*. Page from the earliest extant Armenian Gospel, A.D. 887.

16.14. *a* Armenian codex in
majuscule script. (Chester
Beatty Library, Dublin). *b*
Armenian scribe, from an
illuminated Gospel-book.
(National Library, Paris,
Armén. 18).

a

b

16.15*a*. Miniature: The entry into Jerusalem. Matthew 21, 12–16. (Freer Gallery of Art, Washington, D.C.).

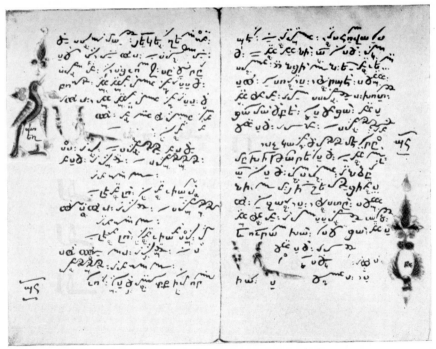

16.15*b*. Armenian manuscript with church melodies, 1352.

16.16b. 15th century manuscript on vellum. (John Rylands Library, *Arm. MS. 3*).

16.16a. Armenian. Title page of *History of Armenians* by Moses Khorewatsi (5th century). Manuscript of the 14th century (Matena-daran, Armenian S.S.R.).

NO.	KHUTSURI MAJUSC.	KHUTSURI MINUSC.	MKHE-DRULI	NAMES OF LETTERS	PHON. VALUE	NUM. VALUE
1				an	a	1
2				ban	b	2
3				gan	g (hard)	3
4				don	d	4
5				en	e	5
6				vin	v	6
7				zen	z	7
8				he	h (weak)	8
9				t'an	t'	9
10				in	i	10
11				kan	k	20
12				las	l	30
13				man	m	40
14				nar	n	50
15				hie	i (ie, y)	60
16				on	o	70
17				par	p	80
18				žan	ž (zh)	90
19				rae	r	100
20				san	s (hard)	200
21				tar	t	300
22				un	u	400
23				wi	wi	500
24				p'ar	p' (ph)	600
25				k'an	k' (kh)	700
26				ghan	ł (gh)	800
27				ķar	ķ (q)	900
28				šin	š (sh)	1,000
29				čin	č	2,000
30				tzan	t z (ś)	3,000
31				dzil	dz	4,000
32				tsil	t s, ds	5,000
33				tšar	t š, dš	6,000
34				xan	x	7,000
35				xhar	x h, x	8,000
36				džan	dz	9,000
37				hae	h (asp)	10,000
38				hoe	hŏ, ŏ	
39				fa	f	
40					ə	

16.17. The Georgian Alphabet.

243

a

b

c

d

16.18. Most Ancient Georgian Inscriptions, from Palestine: (a) *c.* A.D. 433; (b) Bolnisi inscription, A.D. 492; (c) 532–555. (d) Inscription of Bakur and Giri-Ormizd.

16.19b. Oldest dated Georgian MS. (Sinai MS., A.D. 864). (Courtesy Acad. George Tseret'eli).

16.19a. Georgian manuscript: Khanmeti palimpsest, 5th–7th centuries A.D.

16.20b. Hymn cycles of Mik'el Modrekili (late 10th century).
(a and b Courtesy, Acad. George Tseret'eli).

16.20a. Adishi Four Gospels, A.D. 897.

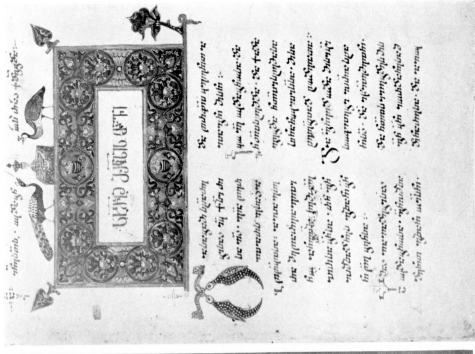

16.21b. Vani Four Gospels, early 13th century. (*a* and *b* Courtesy, Acad. George Tsereteli).

16.21a. Page from John Chrysostom, A.D. 969.

247

16.22b. *Man in Tiger's Skin*, 1680 (*a* and *b* Courtesy, Acad. George Tsereteli).

16.22a. Patericon of John the Monk, late 11th century.

16.23b. Autograph of poet Ilia Cavcavadse (1837–1909), *The Ghost*. (*a* and *b* Courtsey, Acad. George Tseret'eli).

16.23a. Georgian MS. from Mt. Athos, 1074.

16.24a. Page from Psalms, A.D. 974.

16.24b. Autograph of poet Nikoloz Barat'ashvili, 1817–45. (a and b Courtesy, Acad. George Tseret'eli).

250

16.25b. Modern Verse. (*a* and *b* Courtesy, Acad. George Tseret'eli).

16.25a. Autograph of poet Akaki Tseret'eli, 1840–1915.

a

16.26. *a* The 'Alban alphabet' according to Karamianz. *b* The Alban alphabet together with miscellaneous Greek, Syriac, Latin, Georgian, Albanian and Coptic alphabets, contained in a 15th century Armenian manuscript.

b

252

PHONETIC VALUE	BRAHMI					NORTH-INDIAN PROTOTYPE & CENTRAL ASIAN VARIETIES					SOUTH-INDIAN PROTOTYPES					EARLY SOUTH-INDIAN					MODERN NORTH INDIAN				
	AŚOKA	BHATTIPRŌLU	ŚUŊGA	KUṢĀNA	KṢATRAPA	GUPTA	BOWER M.S.	STEIN COLL.	EARLY TIBETAN	KUṬILA	TAMIL CAVES	KALIŊGA	SĀTAVĀHANA	KADAMBA	PALLAVA	EARLY WEST. CĀLUKYA	EARLY EAST. CĀLUKYA	COLA	PĀNDYA	LATE WEST. CĀLUKYA	DEVA-NĀGARĪ	GURMUKHI	GUJARATI	SINDHI	MULTANI
a																								m	
ā																									
i																									
u																									
e																									
o																									
ka																									
kha																									
ga																									
gha																									
ča																									
cha																									
ja																									
jha																									
ña																									
ṭa																									
ṭha																									
ḍa																									
ḍha																									
ṇa																									
ta																									
tha																									
da																									
dha																									
na																									
pa																									
pha																									
ba																									
bha																									
ma																									
ya																									
ra																									
la																									
va																									
śa																									
ṣa																									
sa																									
ha																									

17.1 and 2. Alphabet Chart: Indian and Further-Indian scripts.

MAIN N.-E.-INDIAN			SOUTH-INDIAN						(FURTHER INDIAN) SINHALESE				FURTHER-INDIAN		FURTHER INDIAN									
KRSNA KIRTANA M.S.	BENGALI	ORIYA	VIJAYANAGAR	TELUGU	KANARESE	GRANTHA	TAMIL	VATTELUTTU	VESSAGIRI (A)	MAHARATMALE	VESSAGIRI (B)	MODERN	VÕ-CANH	PŪRNAVARMA	MON	PYU	(BURMESE) KYOK CHA	(BURMESE) PALI	(BURMESE) CHA LÕNH	PATIMOKHA	MODERN SIAMESE	AHOM	ERLANGA	MODERN JAVANESE

b

a

c

d

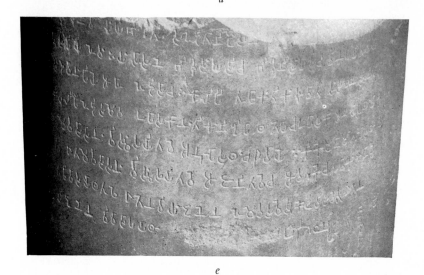

e

17.3. *a* Sohgaura copper plate (4th century B.C.). *b* Eran coin inscription (4th–3rd century B.C.). *c* Mahasthan inscription (4th–3rd century B.C.). *d* Inscription from Sarnath, Benares (Courtesy of A. Master). *e* Asoka inscription from South India.

256

17.4. Aśoka inscription. The Delhi-Toprā pillar,
c. 242 B.C.

a	ai	ca	ḍha	pa	va	-ḥ	ṣa	the
ā	au	cha	ṇa	pha	śa	kä	ṣä	tho
i	ṛ	ja	ta	ba	ṣa	wa	tha	thai
ī	ka	jha	tha	bha	sa	rä	thā	thou
u	kha	ña	da	ma	ha	lä	thi	thǫ
ū	ga	ṭa	dha	ya	-ṃ	pä	thī	thǭ
e	gha	ṭha	na	ṛa	-ḥ	mä	thu	
c	ṅa	ḍa	nä	la	-ḥ	śä	thū	

17.5. The Central Asian Slanting Gupta.

a	kh	ṇd	bh
ā	g	dh	m
i	gh	ṇ	y
ī	n	nt	r
u	č	th	l
ū	ch	d	v
e	ǧ	dh	ś
ai	ǧh	n	ṣ
o	ñ	p	s
au	ṭ	ph	h
ṛ	ṭh	b	kṣ

a

c

b

259

VOWELS

1	2	3	4	5	6	7	8	9	10	11	12
A	₁Ā	₂Ā	I	₁Ī	₂Ī	U	Ū	Ṛ	E	O	AU

SYLLABLES

13	14	15	16	17	18	19	20	21	22	23	24
ka	kha	ga	gga	gha	ṅga	ca	₁cha	₂cha	ja	₁ña	₂ña

25	26	27	28	29	30	31	32	33	34	35	36
ṭa	ṭha	ṭhṭha	ḍa	ṇḍa	ṇa	ta	tta	tha	da	dha	na

37	38	39	40	41	42	43	44	45	46	47	48
pa	pha	ba	₁bha	₂bha	ma	ya	ra	la	va	drai	m̐

49	50	51	52	53	54	55	56	57	58	59 & 60	
śa	sa	ṣa	ha	rddha	rṣṭa	khā	₁lyśa	rvā	mā	tā–ndi	

61	62	63	64	65	66	67	68	69	70	71	72
sṭā	hvā	jā	jyā	jā	jā	ttra	₂lyṣā	ñi	hi	₁lyṣi	lī

73	74	75	76 ṣku	77	78	79	80	81	82	83	84
jsī	spṛ	ḍu	ḍū	ṭu	nu	pu	₁rru	₂rru	rrū	₂rrū	rū

85	86	87	88	89	90	91	92	93	94	95	96
bū	hū	ysmu	gu	śśu	śu	₁tu	₂ttu	pyu'	pyū	grū	brū

97	98	99	100	101	102	103	104	105	106	107	108
₁sṭū	₂ttū	rvṛ	kye	kiai	tcei	ysno	khyāu	lo	dām	biṃ	ṣṣiṃ

109	110	111	112	113	114	115	116	117	118	119	120
rtha	dda	nna	kkra	sde	tva	yyo	dye	ttye	₂pyu	gya	jva

121	122										
ryau	crrā										

NUMERALS

123	124	125	126	127	128	129	130	131	132	133	134
1	2	3	4	5	6	7	8	9	10	20	30

135	136	137	138	139	140	141	142	143	144		
40	50	60	70	80	90	100	200	300	400		

17.7. Khotanese characters, according to Leumann.

260

a

0མི་ ཞིག་ལ་ བུ་ གཉིས་ ཡོད་པ་རེད། དེ་དག་ ལས་

ཆུང་བ་ དེས་ རང་གི་ ཕ་ལ་ ཞུས་པ། འན་ཡབ་ ངས་ ཕྱིན་པའི་

b

c

d

17.8. Tibetan character *a* Tibetan manuscript (Chester Beatty MS. 28). *b* Specimen of *dbu chan*. *c* Specimen of a current hand; a variety of *dbu med*. *d* Tibetan manuscript (India Office Library).

[Lepcha script specimens]

17.9a. Specimens of Lepcha script.

ka	k(la)	kha	ga	gla	ng(a)	cha	chha	ja	nya	t(a)	tꞮa	da
n(a)	pa	p(la)	pha	fa	fla	ba	bla	ma	mla	m	tsa	tsha
za	ya	y	r(a)		l(a)		ha	hla	va	sa	sha	wa

â	á	a	i	í	u	e	o	ó

17.9b. The Lepcha character.

Two (or four, when marked *) signs are given for each *akshara*, the first being employed in print, the second being used in current hand. In the *akshara* thus marked *, the final signs are also shown, which are very much abbreviated, and generally consist of little dashes, commas, circles, etc.

17.9c. Lepcha manuscript, c. 1800 (India Office Library).

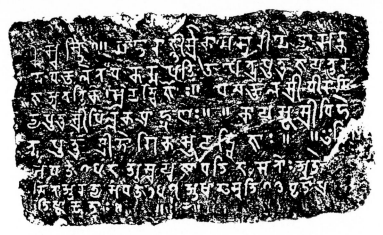

17.10*a*. Deva-nagari inscription dated A.D. 1064 (published by K. N. Dikshit).

	B.C. 250	A.D. 100	200	400	A.D.	400	500	600	750	800–1200	Present day
a					NORTH						(west) (east)
					SOUTH						
					TAMIL						
ka					NORTH						
					SOUTH						
					TAMIL						

17.10*b*. Evolution of the northern and southern Deva-nagari and Tamil *asksharas a* and *ka* from the early Brahmi type of *c.* 250 B.C. to the present day (Courtesy, A. Master).

17.10*c*. Sarada inscription from Hund, 8th century A.D. (Published by R. B. D. Ram Sahri).

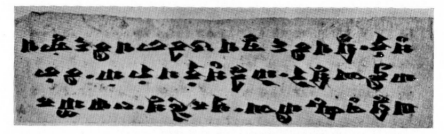

17.11*a*. Kuchean (Indian Office Library).

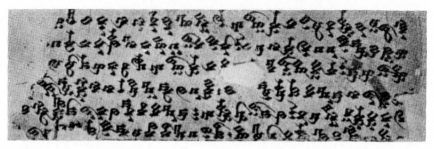

17.11*b*. Khotanese (India Office Library).

17.11*c*. Sanskrit Brahmi (India Office Library).

এতক্ষন বড় ভাই মাঠে ছেল। যখন সে
বাডীর কাছে এল, তখন নাচ গাওনা শুনতে পেলে

a

কোন এক ব্যক্তির মূর্তি সুর তিল। তু মধ্যে কিন্তু থ টা ণ আহার
পিতাকে করিপ পিতঃ কিঅ্যের ন অংশ আমার আপ্

b

ଚେତକ ବେଲେ ଡାହାର ବଡ଼ ପୁଥ ଶେଢରେ ଥ୍ଲ।
ପୁଣି ଅ ସ୍ର କଢରେ ପ୍ରବେଶ ହୋଇ ନାଠ ଓ ବାଦ୍ୟର

c

ଡଥକୁ ପାହାର ଡକର ବ୍ୟଙ୍କା ବେଠା ଖେଢଲ ଯ
ରହସ୍ । ଓ ଘର ଲୁଲିଲ ଅଯ୍ସ ଡ ବାସ୍ସା ଯମ୍ଧା ହୋଚ ରହୁ

d

ଏକ ଆଦ୍‌ମକା ଦୋ ଲଟକା ଥା,
ଆଓର ଓ ଲେଗ୍‌କେ ବିର୍‌ସେ ଛୋଠା ବାଡ଼୍ଘାରୁ

e

17.12. *a* Bengali script: as employed in print. *b* Bengali script: current hand.
c Oriya script: standard variety (Kalahandi state). *d* Oriya script: Chatisgarhi
(Patna State). *e* Oriya script: Hindustani, used by the Orissa Moslems.

17.12*f*. Oriya 'illuminated' manuscript of palm leaf, *Gītagovinda* by Yayadeva (India
Office Library).

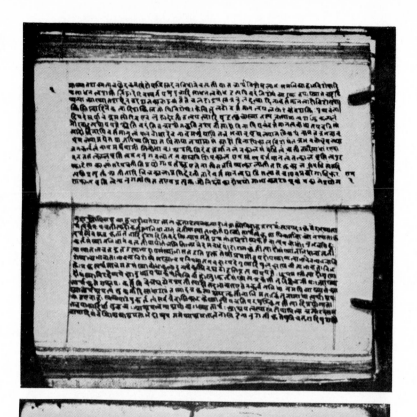

17.13. Sanskrit manuscripts, written in Devānāgarī, Śāradā, and Nepālī scripts: *top*, Devānāgarī (*Alamkaraparisekara*), *c.* 1800 (India Office Library, *E.2042*); *middle*, treatise on ritual in Śāradā script, A.D. 1781 (ibidem, *E.3326 a*); *bottom*, *Pañca Mahāraksa sūtrānī*, in Nepālī script, A.D. 1677 (ibidem, *K.7754*).

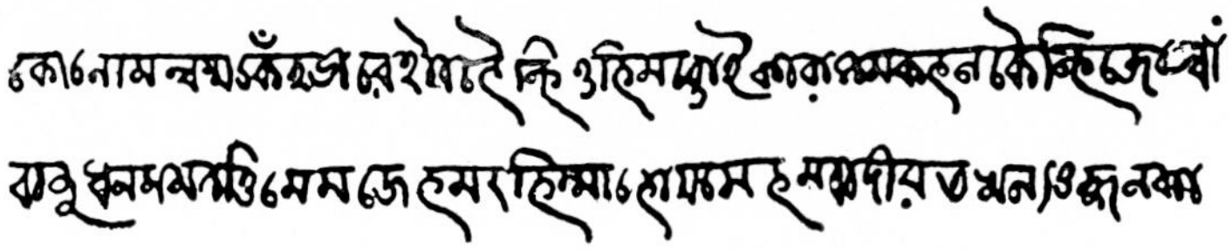

a

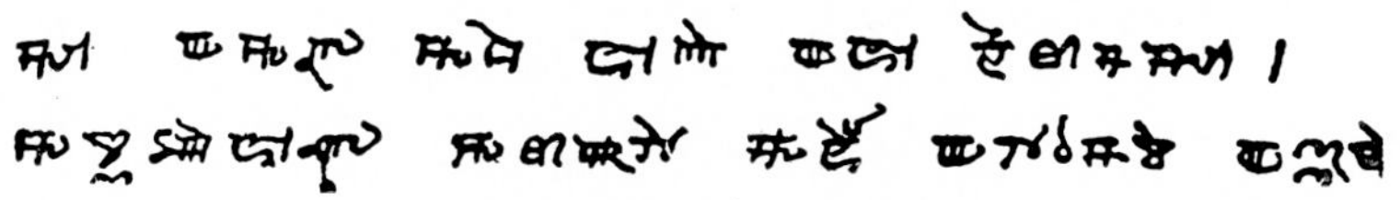

b

17.14. *a* Maithili script. *b* Manipuri script.

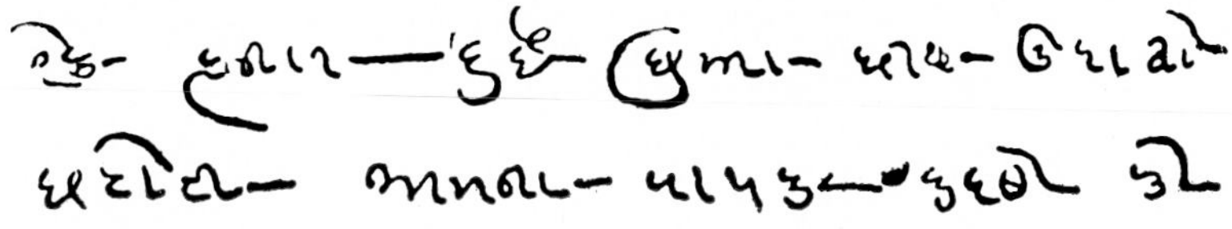

c

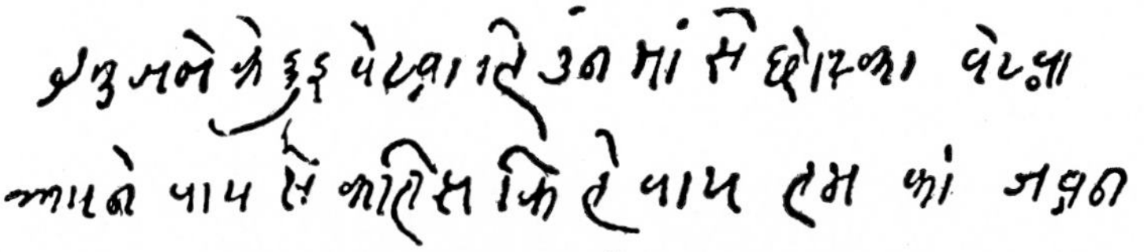

d

17.14. *c* Kaithi script from East Purnea. *d* Kaithi script, Awadhi variant (Eastern Hindi) from Gonda district.

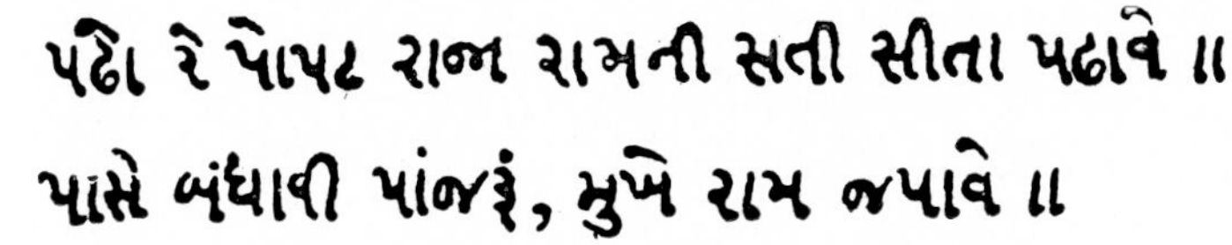

પઢો રે પોપટ રાજા રામની સતી સીતા પઢાવે ॥
પાસે બંધાવી પાંજરૂં, મુખે રામ જપાવે ॥

e

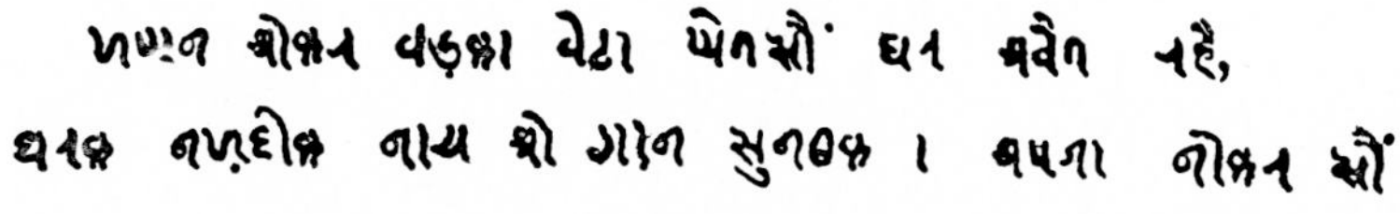

f

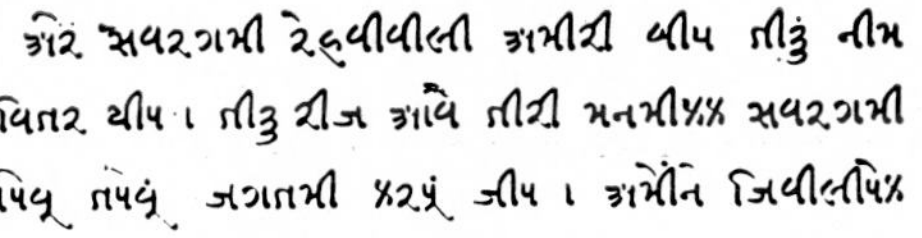

g

17.14. *e, f, g* Specimens of Gujarathi script.

17.15*a*. Marathī manuscript in Modi script, *Notes on Nagpur*, *c.* 1800 (India Office Library, *Mar. B.15*).

17.15*b*. Gurumukhī manuscript, *Janam Sākhī*, 1750 (India Office Library *Panj. B.40*).

प्रिय ड्र दिरिंगर,

आप की लिपि पुस्तक के
लिये मैं हिन्दी-वर्णमाला का
नमूना भेज रहा हूं। आशा
करता हूं यह आप के काम
के लिये काफी होगा।

आप का—
परमेश्वर दयाल.
आरा कॉलेज,
(पटना विश्व-विद्यालय)

17.16a. Modern Indian script: Hindi.

॥ श्री ॥

श्रीयुत डॉ॰ दिरिंगर यांस

मराठी लिपीचा नमुना म्हणून,
तुमच्या मूळाक्षरांचें पुस्तकामध्यें
प्रसिद्ध करण्यासाठीं, हीं एकदोन वाक्यें
लिहिण्यांत मला आनंद होत आहे,
आणि या एवढ्याशा लेखनानेंहि
तुमचा कार्यभाग साधेल अशी
आशा वाटते. कळावें.

आपला स्नेहांकित
मा॰ गो॰ दाभाडे

17.16b. Modern Indian script: Marathi.

প্রিয় ডা: দিরিংশর

আপনার লিপিপুস্তকে প্রকাশের নিমিত্ত
বর্ণমালার নমুনা পাঠাইলাম। আশা করি ইহদ্বারা
আপনার উদ্দেশ্য সিদ্ধ হইবে।
ইতি—
শ্রীতারকনাথবাগচী
তৃতত্ত্ব বিভাগ
কাশী হিন্দু বিশ্ববিদ্যালয়
৺ কাশীধাম।

17.17a. Modern Indian script: Bengali.

প্রিয় ডা: দিরিংশর

আপনার বর্ণমালার কিতাপখনত প্রকাশর
কারণে বর্তমান সময়ীয়ন আসামর আধুনিককালের
এই লিপিন লিখি পঠালোঁ। এই লিপিন আপনার সমত
পাঠাতে সক্ষম হম

ইতি
আপনার—
শ্রীসত্যব্রত ঘোষ
(ঘরগয়া)
আসাম

17.17b Modern Indian script: Assamese.

17.18 Specimens of Bihari scripts. *a*, Maithili. *b*, Southern Maithili. *c*, *d*, Bhojpuri. *e*, Balasore District. *f*, Eastern Masahi. *g*, Midnapore District.

17.19. Bengāli and Kannada manuscripts. (*Above*) Bengāli: *Svarodaya, c.* 1780 (India Office Library, *MSS. Ben. F.3*); (*below*) Kannada: *Viveka Chintamanya, c.* 1790 (ibidem *MSS. Kan.C.1*).

17.20. *a* Limbū manuscript: alphabet, *c.* 1800 (India Office Library *Hodgson Coll. 87*). *b* Hindī manuscript in Kaithi script: *Santasagara*, 1794 (ibidem. *M.S. Hin. B.55*). *c* Gujarātī manuscript: *Pavagadhano garabo*, 1750 (ibidem, *MSS. Guj. 17*).

17.21. *a* Modi script. *b, c* Mahajani script. *d* Multani script. *e* Sindhi script.

PHON. VALUE	GUR-MUKHĪ	LANDĀ	ṬĀKRĪ	ŚĀRADĀ	PHON. VALUE	GUR-MUKHĪ	LANDĀ	ṬĀKRĪ	ŚĀRADĀ
ṛa					ṭha				
va					ṭa				
la					ña				
ra					jha				
ya					ja				
ma					cha				
bha					ça				
ba					ṅa				
pha					gha				
pa					ga				
na					kha				
dha					ka				
da					ha				
tha					sa				
ta					ō				
ṇa					'ûrâ'				(u)
ḍha					'îrî'				(i)
ḍa					'airâ'				(a)

17.22. The four main local scripts of north-western India.

17.23*a*. Sanskrit inscription in 'box-headed' characters, early 6th century A.D. (published by Mirashi in 1935).

17.23*b*. Part of the earliest Kanarese inscription, from Halmidi. Attributed to 5th century A.D., by A. Master.

17.24a. Jaina Kanarese from Kopbal.

c

17.24. *b* Part of a Telugu inscription from Koikonda. *c* Rock inscription in 'Shell' character, from Ci-Arutön (Java), attributed to the 4th–5th century A.D. It may be considered to be the early Grantha lithic style.

b

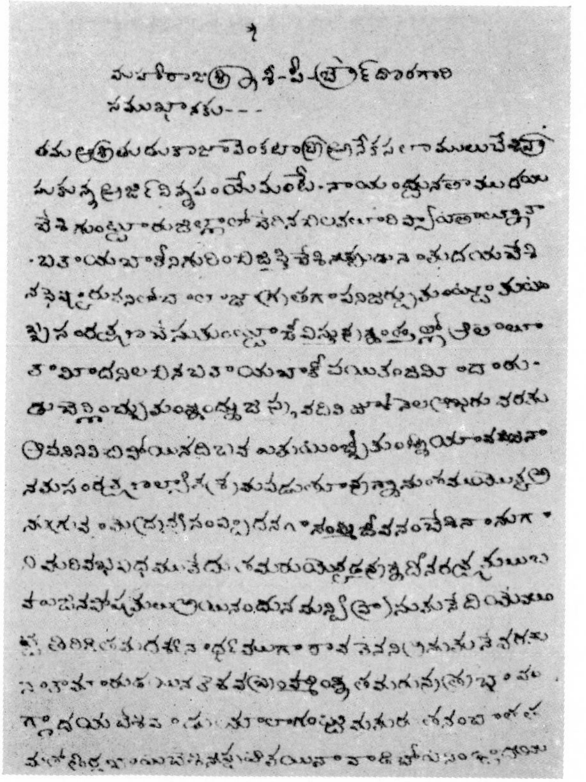

17.25*a*. Telugu manuscript, *Urzees*, 1820 (India Office Library *Tel. D.6*).

ಇಬ್ಬರು ಹಾದಿಕಾರರು ಕೂಡಿ ಹೋಗುತ್ತಿದ್ದರು ।
ಅವರಲ್ಲಿ ಒಬ್ಬನಿಗೆ ಹಾದಿಯಲ್ಲಿ ಬಿದ್ದಿರುವ ಹಣದ ಚೀಲವು ಸಿಕ್ಕಿತು ।

b

ఒక మనుష్యునికి యిద్దరు కుమారులు వుండిరి.—
వారిలో చిన్నవాడు, ఓ తండ్రీ ఆస్తిలో నాకు వచ్చే

c

ಎಕಾ ಗೃಹಸ್ಥಾಕ ದೋಗ್-ಜಾಣ ಪೂತ ಆಶಿಲ್ಲೆ ।
ತಾಂತುಲೆ ಪೈಕಿಂ ಸಾನು ಆಪ್ಣಾಗೆಲ್ಯಾ ಬಾಪ್ಸು ಕಡೆ

d

17.25. Modern specimens, *b* Kanarese, *c* Marathi written in Kanarese character, *d* Telugu.

ഒരു മനുഷ്യന്നു രണ്ടു മക്കൾ ഉണ്ടായിരുന്നു.
അതിൽ ഇളയവൻ അപ്പനോടു, അപ്പാ,

a

அவனுடைய மூத்தகுமாரன் வயலிலிருந்தான்.
அவன் திரும்பி வீடுகெடுச்சமீபமாய் வருகிறபோது,

b

17.26. *a* Malayalam script. *b* Tamil script.

17.26*c*. Part of an inscription written in a kind of Vattelutu mixed with Grantha, attributed to the 9th century A.D.

17.26*d*. Part of a grant to Jews at Kochin, attributed by Burnell to the middle of the 8th century, and by Buehler, to the 10th or 11th century.

MAIN PĀLI SCRIPTS

PHONETIC VALUE	SINHALESE	BURMESE	THAI	KHMER	
				AKS. CHRI.	AKS. MŪL
a					
ā					
i					
ī					
u					
ū					
e					
o					or
ya					
ra					
la					
va					
sa					
ha					
ḷa					
ka					
kha					
ga					
gha					
ña					

17.27. The Main Pāli scripts.

PHONETIC VALUE	SINHALESE	BURMESE	THAI	KHMER	
				AKS. CHRI.	AKS. MÜL

MAIN PĀLI SCRIPTS

PHONETIC VALUE	SINHALESE	BURMESE	THAI	AKS. CHRI.	AKS. MÜL
ca					
cha					
ja					
jha					
ña					
ṭa					
ṭha					
ḍa					
ḍha					
ṇa					
ta					
tha					
da					
dha					
na					
pa					
pha					
ba					
bha					
ma					

17.28. The Main Pāli scripts.

281

b

PHONETIC VALUE	MALDIVIAN DIVES AKURU	GABULI TANA
h		
th		
ṅ		
r		
b		
l		
k		
a		
w		
m		
ph		
dh		
t		
ḷ		
g		
n		
s		
ḍ		

17.29. *a* Specimen of modern Sinhalese script. *b* Letter written in modern Sinhalese. *c* The Maldivian Dives Akuru and Gabuli Tana.

c

nī   yal   baranō'   pago'p

18.3*a*. Akhar Srah or Thrah.

18.3*b*. Two lines of the 'Song of Kadhar.'

ni ti–k–u–ḥ k–u–ba–v ri–o–m–n

18.3*c*. Akhar Rik.

nī   s–va–t–ti k   harĕi   adit

18.3*d*. Akhar Atuo'l.

n – i – m   t – i – k – u – ḥ   k – u – ba – v

18.3*e*. Akhar Yok.

18.1. Specimens of Cham characters.

VOWELS		CONSONANTS		CONSONANTS	
a	𐑴	ka	𐑴	pha	𐑴
ā	𐑴	kha	𐑴	ba	𐑴
i	𐑴	ga	𐑴	bha	𐑴
i	𐑴	gha	𐑴	m o'	𐑴
u	𐑴	ṅo'	𐑴	ya	𐑴
ū	𐑴	cha	𐑴	ra	𐑴
ṛo'	𐑴	chha	𐑴	la	𐑴
ṛō'	𐑴	ja	𐑴	va	𐑴
ḷo'	𐑴	jha	𐑴	s'a	𐑴
ḷō'	𐑴	ño'	𐑴	sa	𐑴
e	𐑴	ta	𐑴	ha	𐑴
ai	𐑴	tha	𐑴	ṇa	𐑴
o	𐑴	da	𐑴	ḍa	𐑴
au	𐑴	dha	𐑴	ḅa	𐑴
am	𐑴	no'	𐑴	(ṅa)	𐑴
akh	𐑴	pa	𐑴	(ña)	𐑴
		(na)	𐑴	(ma)	𐑴

18.2. The Cham character as employed in Vietnam.

VOWELS		CONSONANTS		CONSONANTS		CONSONANTS	
a	ᝋ	gha	ᝋ	dha	ᝋ	va	ᝋ
i	ᝋ	no'	ᝋ	no'	ᝋ	sa	ᝋ
u	ᝋ	cha	ᝋ	pa	ᝋ	ha	ᝋ
e	ᝋ	chha	ᝋ	pha	ᝋ	ṇa	ᝋ
ai	ᝋ	ja	ᝋ	ba	ᝋ	da	ᝋ

CONSONANTS		jha	ᝋ	bha	ᝋ	ba	ᝋ
ka	ᝋ	ño'	ᝋ	mo'	ᝋ	(ña)	ᝋ
kha	ᝋ	ta	ᝋ	ya	ᝋ	(ṅa)	ᝋ
ga	ᝋ	tha	ᝋ	ra	ᝋ	(na)	ᝋ
		da	ᝋ	la	ᝋ	(ma)	ᝋ

18.3. The Cham character as employed in Cambodia.

285

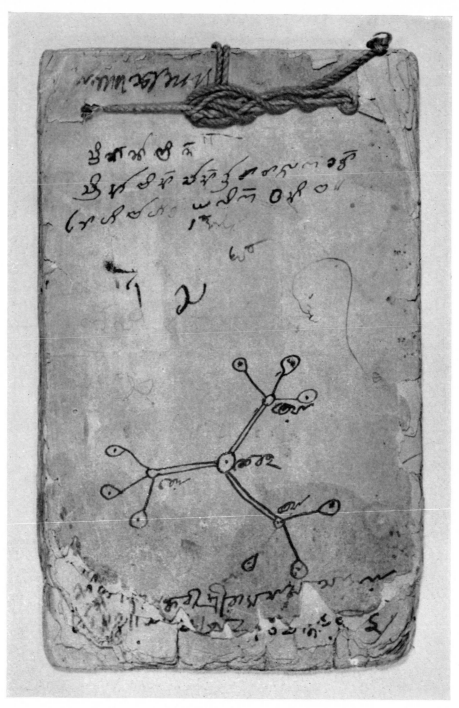

18.4. Title page from a Chakma manuscript (in the author's possession).

18.5. Page from a Chakma manuscript (in the author's possession).

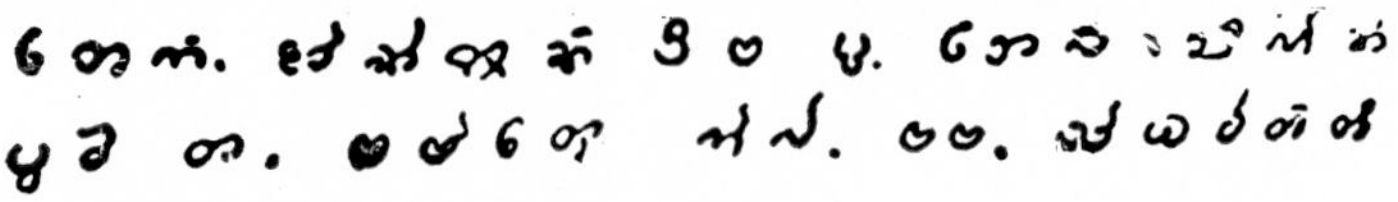

[Chakma script text]

18.6a. Chakma.

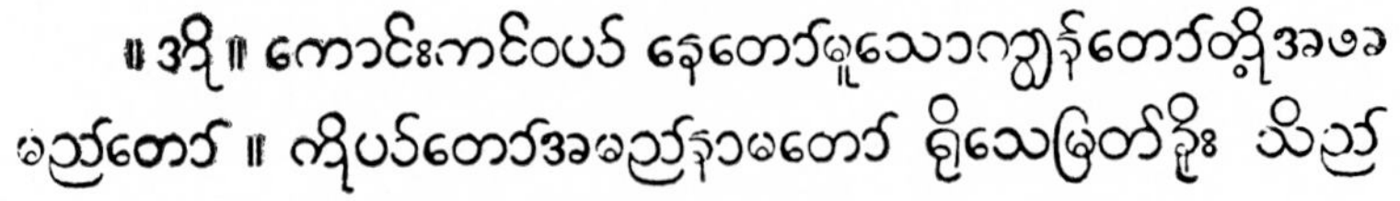

။ ၃ရို ။ ကောင်းကင်ဝယ် နေတော်မူသောကျွန်တော်တို့အဖခ
မည်တော် ။ ကိုပယ်တော်အခည်ဒာမတော် ရှိသေမြတ်ဦး သိည်

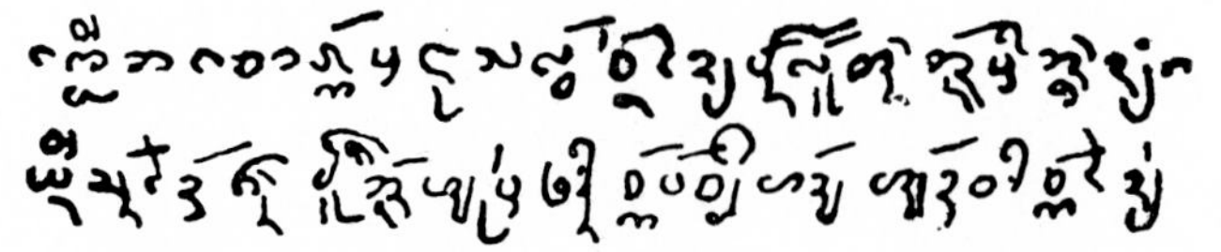

18.6b. Burmese.

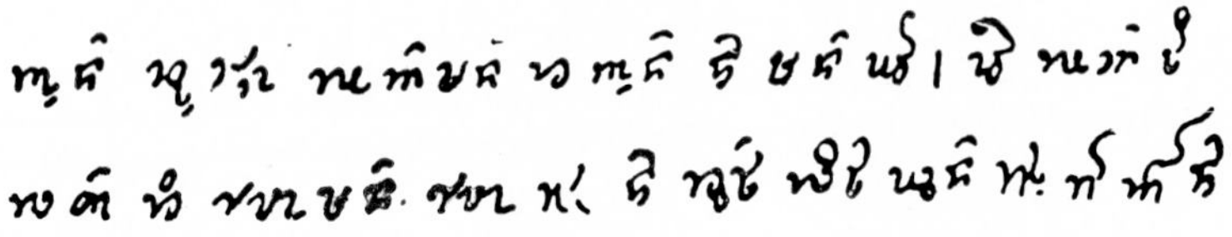

[Hkün script text]

18.6c. Hkün.

[Ahom script text]

18.6d. Ahom.

[Patimokkha script text]

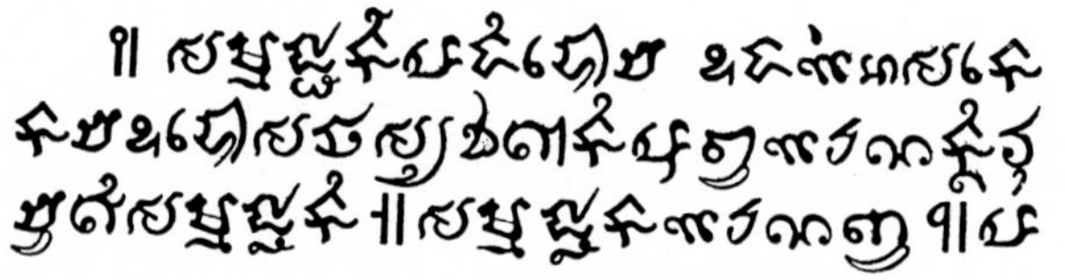

18.6e. Patimokkha.

18.6. Further Indian scripts.

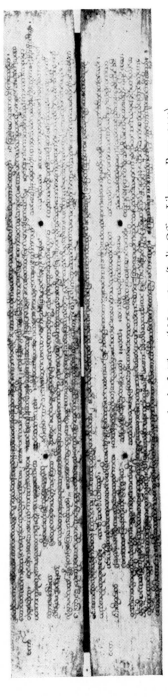

18.7a. Burmese manuscript on palm-leaf; *The evil Nats*, 1805 (India Office Library, *Burm. 3449*).

18.7b. Siamese manuscript; *Thao Sawatthi racha* (ibidem, *Siam. 14*).

18.8a. Manual for the Ordination of a Buddhist Priest: mother of pearl on wood, written in Burmese Pali. (Cambridge University Library Or. *783*).

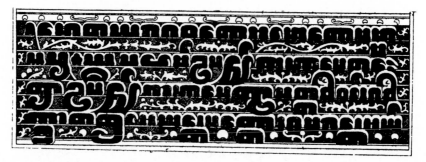

18.8*b. Kammuwa,* a sacred Buddhist book. Specimen of Pali script.

18.8*c.* Burmese manuscript on copper (Chester Beatty Library, *MS. 60*).

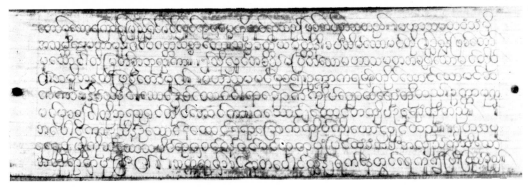

18.9*a*. Burmese: last leaf of the Abhui: rājapuṃ manuscript on the lineage of kings. 'Written on the 5th day of the waxing moon of the month of Tabaung 1164 B.E.' (AD 1798)

18.9*b*. Thai manuscript on cats (Chester Beatty Library, *M.S. 1304*).

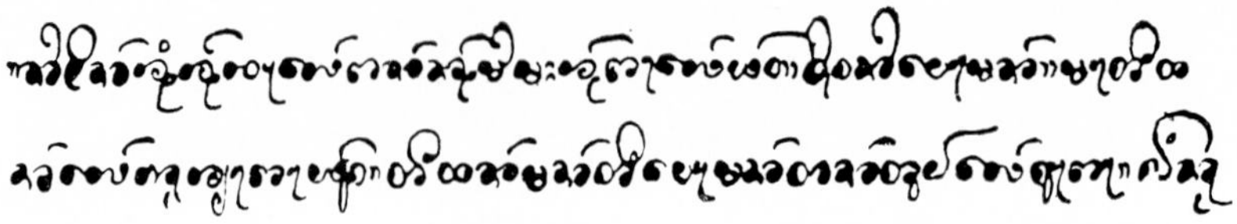

18.10a. Khamti current hand.

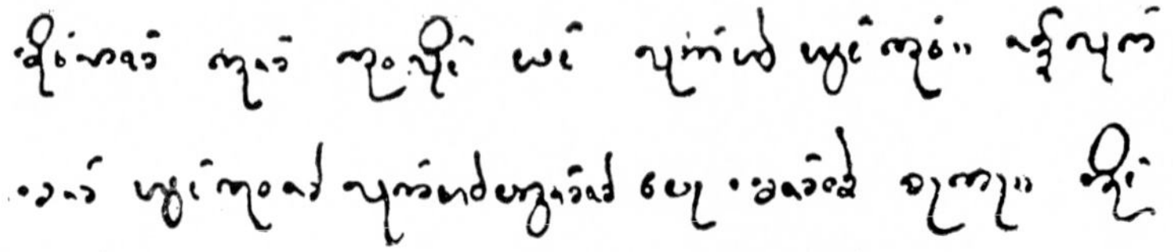

18.10b. Khamti printed script.

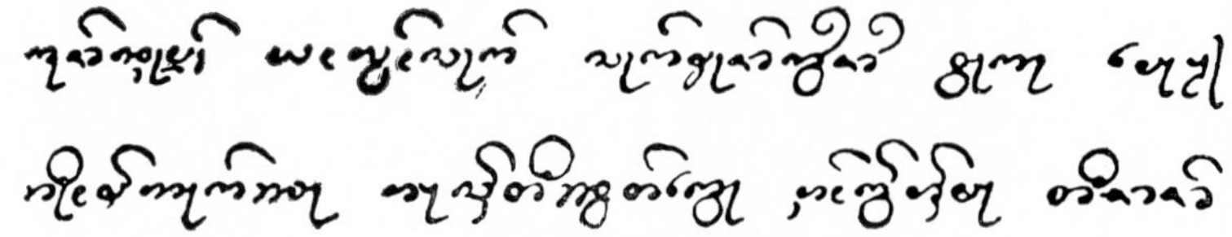

18.10c. Tairong Khamti.

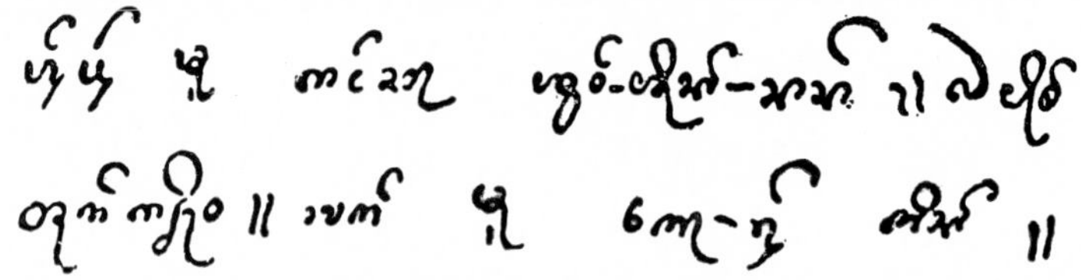

18.10d. Aitonia character.

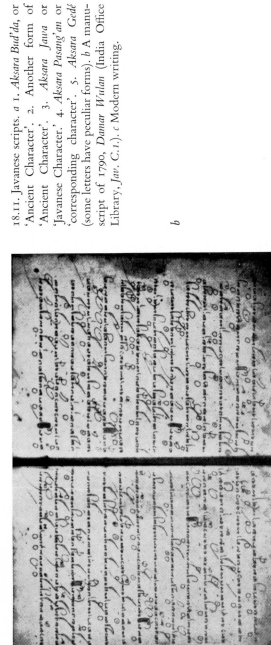

18.11. Javanese scripts. *a* 1. *Aksara Bud'da*, or 'Ancient Character'. 2. Another form of 'Ancient Character'. 3. *Aksara Jawa* or 'Javanese Character'. 4. *Aksara Pasang'an* or 'Javanese Character'. 5. *Aksara Gedé* 'corresponding character' (some letters have peculiar forms). *b* A manuscript of 1790, *Damar Wulan* (India Office Library, *Jav. C.1*). *c* Modern writing.

18.12. Kalasan inscription from Java, in Sanskrit AD 778.

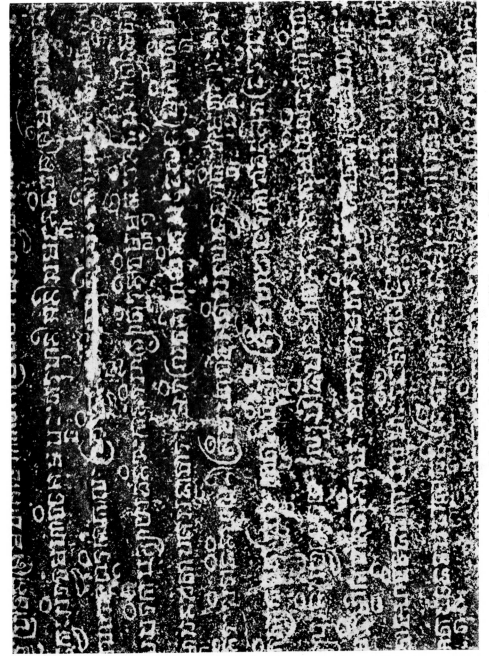

18.13. Calcutta incription of Erlangga (Old Javanese part) AD 1041.

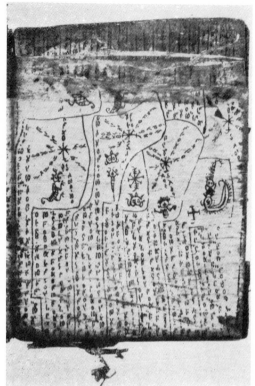

18.14a. Written page of a Batak manuscript.

18.14b. Cover of the manuscript above, both written on the inner bark of *terap* tree (Cambridge University Library *Or. 930*).

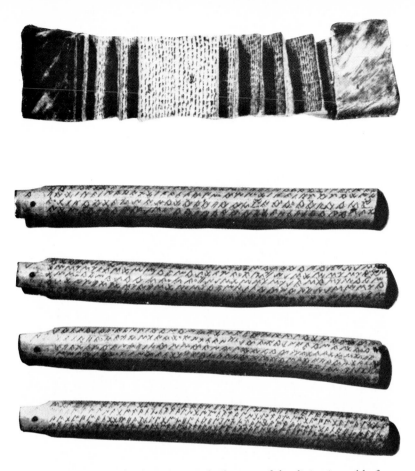

18.15. (Above) Batak book written on bark: part of the divination table for the 30 days of the month (below) portion of a *Story of Creation*, written on bamboo in Malay language using the Rèndjang characters of the Palembang and Benkulen districts of South Sumatra. The four sticks are 'numbered' (left) *ta, pa, la, sa*. (Explanation by P. Voorhoeve, University Library, Leyden).

a	e-i	o-u	ka	ga	nga	ta	da	na	pa	ba	ma	ya	la	wa	sa	ha	

18.16. The main alphabets of Further India, particularly of the Philippine Islands (based on F. Gardner, *Philippine Indic Studies*, 1943). 1–6, Old Javanese or Kavi. 7–8, Early Sumatra. 9, Batak character. 10, Buginese. 11–14, Tagalog. 15–16, Iloco. 17–18, Bisaya. 19, Pangasinan. 20, Pampangan. 21, Tagbanua. 22–26, Mangyan varieties. 27–30, Buhil.

A
E-I
OU
BA
CA
DA
GA
YA
LA
MA
NA
PA
SA
TA
I
UA
?

(b)

(a)

a

c

d

e

| a | ya | o, ú | yo | o | | yo | u | yu | ü | | i | a |

| k | n | t | r(l) | m | p | s(d) | (ng) | tj | ch | kh | th | ph | h |

f

18.17. *a* Specimen of Bisaya writing. *b* Tagbanua characters (*a* if read upwards according to Dr. Gardner; *b*, in Professor Kroeber's opinion it should be read downwards). *c Belarmino*, re-edited in 1895 by P. Lopez. *d* Buhil writing, 1941, copied from bamboo (F. Gardner, *Philippine Indic Studies*, 1943). *e* Specimen of Mangyan writing: it reads *Pagpunsion ti namatay no nakutkut ye ti but-ol*, meaning 'A feast is given to the dead, when his bones are dug up.' (F. Gardner and I. Maliwang, *Indic Writings*, etc., 2, pp. 17–18). *f* The Korean alphabet.

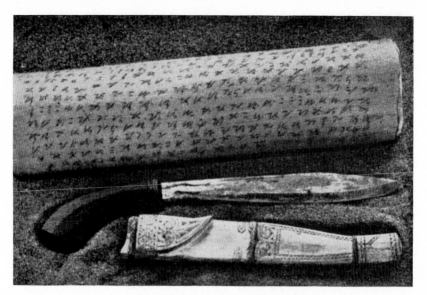

a

18.18. *a* Philippine bamboo manuscript, with writing knife and its container. *b* Left-handed boy 'writing' with a knife on a bamboo tube.

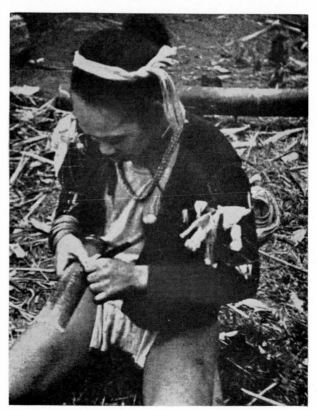

b

Letters	Phon. Value	Letters	Phon. Value	Letters	Phon. Value
ㅈ	ć (fr. tch)	ㄱ	k	ㅏ	a
ㅊ	ćʻ	ㄴ	n	ㅑ	ya
ㅌ	tʻ	ㄷ	t	ㅓ	ɔ (ŏ)
ㅋ	kʻ	ㄹ	ṙ – l	ㅕ	yɔ
ㅍ	pʻ	ㅁ	m	ㅗ	o
ㅎ	h	ㅂ	p	ㅛ	yo
ㅇ		ㅅ	s, – t	ㅜ	u (fr. ou)
				ㅠ	yu
				ㅡ	ə
				ㅣ	i
				ㆍ	å (ă)

18.19. The Korean alphabet.

19.1. Early Greek alphabets.

19.2. Early Greek inscriptions written from right to left; *a–f* from Thera; *g* Ionic votive inscription to Apollo; *h–j* inscriptions from Athens; *k* graffito on jug c. 725 B.C.; *l* graffito on pottery c. 7th cent. B.C.; *m* Bronze Aryballos, late 7th cent. B.C.; *n* Bronze lebes rim 600–525 B.C.

a

b

c

d

e

f

g

19.3. Early Greek inscriptions in *boustrophedon* style. *a* Stele from Lemnos, 6th cent. B.C.; *b* Archaic inscription from Corinth. *c,d* Graffiti: names inscribed on rock at Thera, late 8th century B.C.; *e* Inscribed will-block from Temple of Apollo Pythios, Gortyn, 600–615 B.C.; *f* Stone stele with text of sacred law from Magnesia, Thessaly, *c.* 550 B.C.; *g* Part of inscribed marble altar? *c.* 500–480 B.C.; from Attica.

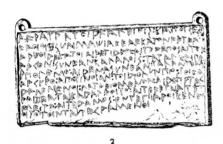

ΣΕΜΑΦΡΑΣΙΚΛΕΙΑΣ
ΚΟΡΕΚΕΚΛΕΣΟΜΑΙ
ΑΙΕΙΑΜΤΙΛΑΜΟ
ΓΑΡΑΘΕΟΝΤΟΥΤΟ
ΣΑΧΟΣΟΝΟΜΑ

1

ΑΘΑΝΑΙΑΣ:ΙΑΡΑ:ΤΑΣΕΜΗΒΣΑΡΟΙ

2

ΝΑΙΡΕΝΑΡΟΝ
ΟΥΔΙΣΤΥΚΑΚΟΣ
ΛΕΣΕΙΟΥΔΕΘΝ
ΝΟΝΤΑΠΟΛΟΣ
ΑΝΘΡΟΠΟΝΛΥ
ΣΑΜΕΝΟΣ
ΚΑΜΑΤΟ

4

3

ΙΙΛΕΣΕΤΟΣΙΤΕΡΑΣΟΛΛΟΓΟΣ
ΝΕΝΑΣΤΑΣΔΑΜΑΤΡΣΤΑΣΘΕΣΜΟΦΟΡΟΣ
ΜΕΝΣΕΡΟΣΕΣΔΥΜΕΝΕΣΕΑΣΑΕΓΕΓΕΡΚΟ
ΣΙΓΧΟΛΟΣΤΥΚΑΟΙΣΣΤΟΤΕΔΑΜΣΟΓΟΡΣΕ
ΣΤΑΣΔΑΡΥΜΑΣΓΟΣΑΚΟΝΤΑΕΣΔΕΜΕΑΦΑΕΤΟΣ
ΑΝΑΣΕΒΕΣΑΝΕΝΕΟΔΕΚΥΡΟΣΔΕΚΟΓΕΤΕΡΕΛΛ
ΟΔΕ

5

19.4. Early Greek inscriptions from left to right.
1 Grave pillar of Phresikkia, Attica, *c.* 540 B.C.
2 Inscription on a silver cup dedicated to the Megarian Athena, from Kozani, *c.* 500 B.C.
3 Bronze plaque with treaty between Elis and Heraea, *c.* 500 B.C.
4 Gravestone of Charon from Teithronion, Phocis, *c.* 500 B.C.
5 Bronze plaque with ritual inscription, Arkadian, *c.* 525 B.C.

Phon. Value	North Semitic	Greek 9th–6th cent. B.C.	Eastern branch		Western branch	Classical	Uncial		
			Ionic	Attic			4th cent. A.D.	7th cent. A.D.	9th cent. A.D.
a	⌐(')	ΔΔ	Δ A	A A	Δ A	A	⋏	⋏	⋏
b	9	99⅂	B	B B	ß B	B	B	B	B
g	7	1⋀	Γ	⋀⋀	⋀ (	Γ	Γ	Γ	Γ
d	△	⊲P	△	△	△ D	△	△	⋏	△
ĕ	(h)⅁	⅂Ϝ	Ɛ Ε	Ϝ Ε	Ϝ Ε	E	ε	ε	ε
u(y)	(w)Ч	ΥϜΥ∨	Y ∨	Y	Y∨Ϝ (w)	Y	∨	Y	Y
z	I I	I	I	I	I	Z	Z	Z	ʒ
ē	H Ɵ (h)	Ɵ H(h)	H	Ɵ H	Ɵ H(h)	H	н	н	H
th	⊕(ṭ)	⊕ ⊙	⊕ ⊙	⊕ ⊙	⊗ ⊙	Θ	⊝	ϑ	ϑ
i	Ɫ	₹ ⸗	I	I	I	I	ı	⟩	ï
k	Ɏ	⅂K	K K	K	K	K	ⅼ<	к	к
l	⌐⌐	Ⴑ⋀	⋀	L	L	⋀	⋏	λ	⋀
m	ʮ	ⱱ⅄	M	M	ⱱM	M	M	M	M
n	Ϥ	Ϥ Ͷ	N N	N	N N	N	N	и	N
x	⅂ ₮(s)		Ξ			Ξ	Ƶ	₹ ȝ	ʒ ʒ
o	o( )	Ο	Ο	Ο	Ο	Ο	o	0	0
p	⅂	⅂ Γ	Γ Π	Γ	Γ Π	Π	⊓	Γ	Π
s	ⱱ(ṣ)	M Υ							
q	Ϙ Ϙ(q)	Ϙ Ϙ		Ϙ	Ϙ				
r	◁	◁P	P	P P	P R	P	P	P	P
s	w(š)	ϟ	⟨	ϟ	ϟ ⟨	Σ	c	c	c
t (y see above)	┼ ×	T	T	T	T	T	T	T	T
ph			Φ ϕ	Φ ϕ	Φ ϕ	Φ	Φ	Φ	Φ
kh			X	X	× ┼(x)	X	X	X	X
ps			Υ ∨		Y Ψ(kh)	Ψ	Ψ	Y ┼	┼
ō		⊙	Ω			Ω	ω	ω	ω

19.5. Development of the Greek alphabet.

Greek cursive script			Greek minuscule			Modern		Modern
2nd cent. B.C	2nd cent. A.D.	7th cent.	9th cent. A.D.	10th–11th cent.	12th– 14th cent	Capitals	small letters	letters in print
ᴀ ᴅ	ᴀ ᴅ	ʋ œ	a	ɑ	ɑ ᴅ	A A	a ᴢ	α
B υ	B	β υ	u	B u	uβ∈c	B	b β	β
ᴦ ᴦ	ᴦᴦ	Y γ	γ	v v	ᴦ ⌐ v	ᵹ	ᶎ	γ
Δ ᴅ	δ ᴄ	ᴅ δ	δ	Δ δ	δ Δ	D	ᴦ	δ
∈ ∈	∈ ℓ	∈ ᴦ c	ϵ	∈ ᴇ	ᴦ∈Ɛ	Ɛ ℓ	Ɛ	ε
Y V	Y ᴦ	V u	υ	v	u ᴗ	V	ʋ	υ
Z	ᴢᴢ	ℓ3 3	Z 3	3 ᴢ	ℓℓᴢᴢ	Z	ᴊᴊℓ	ᴢ ᴣ
ʜ	ᴀ	h ᴢ	h	h ʟ ʜ	ʜ ʜ ᴢ ʜ	H	n ᴦ	η
θ	θ ᴅ	θ ᴅ ℓ	θ	θ ᴅ	θ ℓ ℓ	ᴜ	ᴅ	θ θ
ᴉ	ᴉ	ᴉ Ï ᴢ	ᴉ ᴢ	ᴉ ᴛ	ï ᴢ	ᴊ ᴊ	ᴊ	ᴊ
ᴋ	k u	k ᴦ	u	K k	Ku x	K	u κ	κ
λ	ᴦ	ᴊ ℓ	ᴦ	ᴦ λ	λ λ	ᴀ	ᴌᴌᴌ	λ
ᴦ u	u u	ᴀ u	μ	μ u	u u	M	μ	μ
N	ᴍ ᴍ	υ ᴌ	ᴦᴦ	ᴦ N	N ᴦ γ υ	N	ᴌ	ν
ᴦ ᴢ	ᴢᴢ	ᴣ ᴣ	ᴣ	ᴣ ᴣ	ᴣ ᴣ Ɛ	ᴢ	ᴣ ᴣ	ξ
o	o	o	o	o	o	O	σ	o
ᴨ	π	π ᴜ	ϖ	π ϖ	π ϖ	π	ϖ	ϖ
P	ℓᴢᴢ	ℓ ℓ	ℓ	Pℓᴣ	ᴦℓᴨᴢ	ᴨ	ρ	ℓ
c	c c	c ᴢ ᴇ	σ ℓ	σ (c	σ ℓ c	ℓ ℓ	σ ᴅ	ᴦ c
ᴦ ᴊ	ᴊ	ᴊ ᴛ ᴛ	ᴛ	ᴛ ᴛ	ᴛ ᴛ ᴊ	ᴊ	ᴛ ℓ	ᴦ ᴊ
φ	φ	φ	φ	ᴣ φ	φ φ φ	φ	ᴦ ᴦ	φ
X	X	X	x	X	X	X	x ᴛ	z
ᴦ	ᴦ	ᴛ	ᴛ	ᴛ ᴨ	ψ	ᴨ ᴨ	ᴦ	ψ
ω	ω	ω	∞	∞	ω	ᴜ	w	ω

19.6. Development of the Greek alphabet.

19.7. Greek monumental inscriptions of the Roman Imperial period.

a

b

c

19.8. Greek monumental funerary inscriptions of the Roman Imperial period.

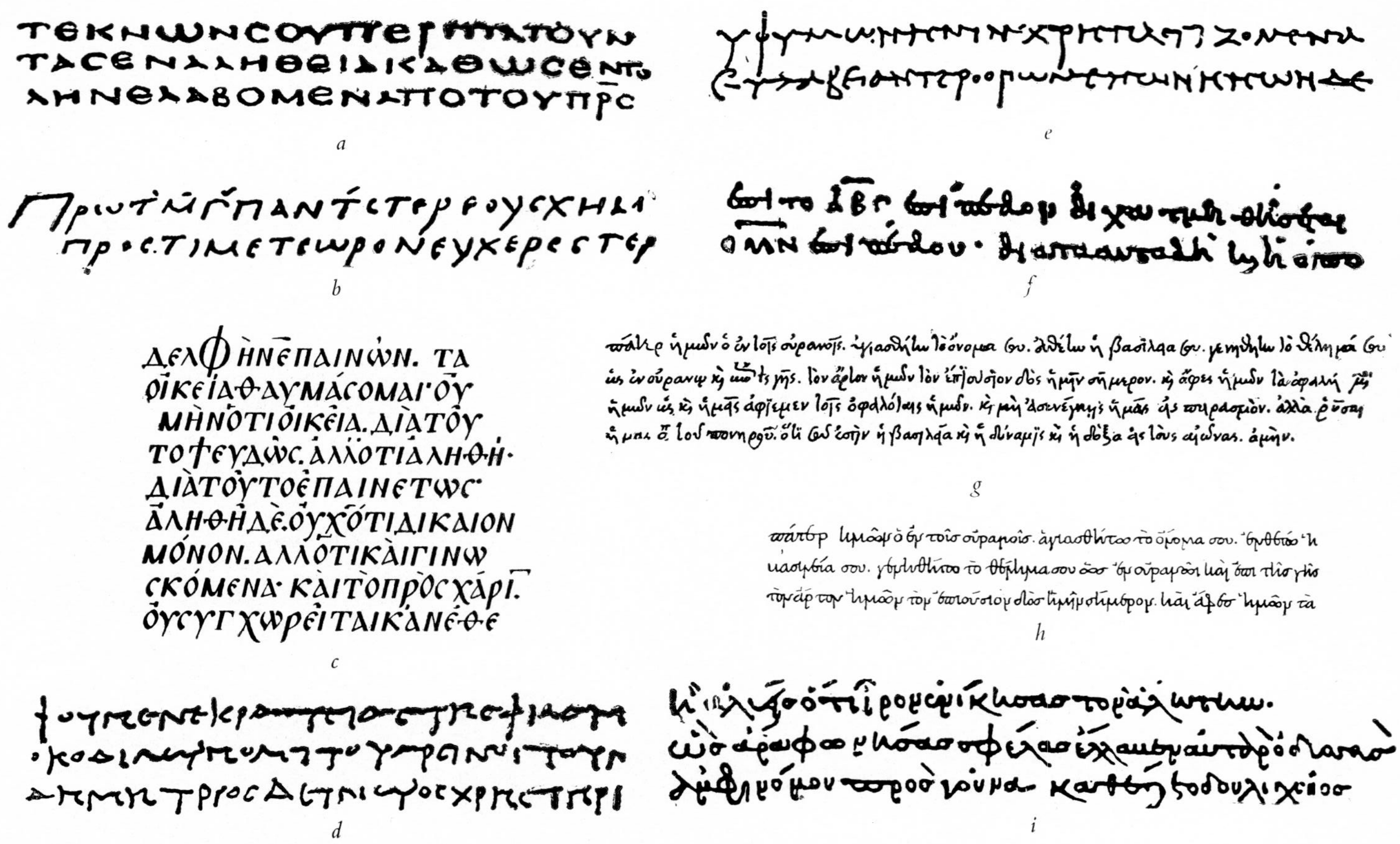

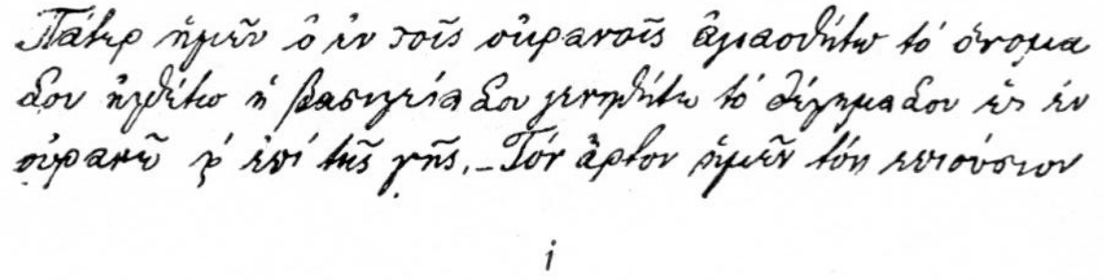

ΔΕΛΦ ΗΝ ΕΠΑΙΝΩΝ. ΤΑ
ΟΙΚΕΙΑ Δ ΑΥΜΑϹΟΜΑΙ ΟΥ
ΜΗΝΟΤΙ ΟΙΚΕΙΑ. ΔΙΑΤΟΥ
ΤΟ ΓΕΥΔΩϹ. ΑΛΛΟΤΙ ΔΛΗΘΗ.
ΔΙΑΤΟΥΤΟ ΕΠΑΙΝΕΤΩϹ
ΑΛΗΘΗ ΔΕ, ΟΥ ϹΟΤΙ ΔΙΚΑΙΟΝ
ΜΟΝΟΝ. ΑΛΛΟΤΙ ΚΑΙ ΓΙΝΩ
ϹΚΟΜΕΝΑ· ΚΑΙ ΤΟ ΠΡΟϹΧΑΡΙ.
ΟΥ ΓΥΓΧΩΡΕΙΤΑΙ ΚΑΝ Ε Θ Ε

19.9. Specimens showing the development of Greek script, from uncial style to modern current hand. a Fifth century A.D.; b seventh century A.D.; c ninth century A.D.; d 237 B.C.; e 163–162 B.C.; f A.D. 888; g fifteenth century A.D.; h tenth century A.D.; i thirteenth century A.D.; j nineteenth century A.D.

ΤΟΥΤΩΝΤΡΙΩΝ
ΠΛΗCΙΟΝΔΟΚΕΙ
CΟΙΓΕΓΟΝΕΝΑΙΤΙ
ΕΜΠΕCΟΝΤΟCΕΙ
ΤΟΥCΛΗCΤΑCΟΔΕ
ΕΙΠΕΝΟΠΟΙΗCΑ
ΤΟΕΛΕΟCΜΕΤΑΤΤ
ΕΙΠΕΝΔΕΑΥΤΩΟϹ
ΠΟΡΕΥΟΥΚΑΙCΟΙ
ΠΟΙΕΙΟΜΟΙΩCΕΝ
ΔΕΤΩΠΟΡΕΥΕCΟΝ
ΑΥΤΟΥCΑΥΤΟCΕΗΛ
ΘΕΝΕΙCΚΩΜΗΝ·
ΤΙΝΑ
ΓΥΝΗΔΕΤΙCΟΝΟΜΑ
ΤΙΜΑΡΘΑΥΠΕΔΕ
ΞΑΤΟΑΥΤΟΝΕΙC
ΤΗΝΟΙΚΙΑΝΚΑΙ
ΤΗΔΕΗΝΑΔΕΛΦΗ
ΚΑΛΟΥΜΕΝΗΜΑ
ΡΙΑΜΚΑΙΠΑΡΑΚΑ
ΘΕCΟΙCΑΠΡΟCΤ
ΠΟΔΑCΤΟΥΚ̄ῩΗ
ΚΟΥΕΤΟΝΛΟΓΟΝ
ΑΥΤΟΥ·ΗΔΕΜΑ
ΘΑΠΕΡΙΕCΠΑΤΟΠ
ΡΙΠΟΛΛΗΝΔΙΑΚ
ΝΙΑΝ
ΕΠΙCΤΑCΑΔΕΕΙΠ
Κ̄Ε̄ΟΥΜΕΛΙCΟΙΟ
ΤΙΗΑΔΕΛΦΗΜΟΥ
ΜΟΝΗΝΜΕΚΑΤ
ΛΙΠΕΝΔΙΑΚΟΝΙΝ
ΕΙΠΕΟΥΝΑΥΤΗΙ
ΝΑΜΟΙCΥΝΑΝΤΙ
ΛΑΚΗΤΕ
ΑΠΟΚΡΙΘΕΙCΔΕΕΙ
ΠΕΝΑΥΤΗΟΚ̄C̄
ΡΟΑΜΑΡΘΑΜ
ΗΜΝΑCΚΑΙΘΟΡΥ

ΝΕΤΟΕΝΙΩΕΙΝΑΙ
ΑΥΤΟΝΕΝΤΟΠΩ
ΤΙΝΙΠΡΟCΕΥΧΟΜϹ
ΝΟΝΩCΕΠΑΥCΑ
ΤΟΕΙΠΕΝΤΙCΤΩΝ
ΜΑΘΗΤΩΝΑΥΤΟΥ
ΠΡΟCΑΥΤΟΝΚ̄Ε̄ΔΙ
ΔΑΞΟΝΗΜΑCΠΡϹ
ΕΥΧΕCΘΑΙΚΑΘΩϹ
ΕΔΙΔΑΞΕΝΤΟΥC
ΜΑΘΗΤΑCΑΥΤΟΥ
ΕΙΠΕΝΔΕΑΥΤΟΙCϹ
ΤΑΝΠΡΟCΕΥΧΗCΘϹ
ΛΕΓΕΤΕ·
ΠΑΤΕΡΑΓΙΑCΘΗΤϹ
ΤΟΟΝΟΜΑCΟΥ·
ΕΛΘΑΤΩΗΒΑCΙΛ
ΑCΟΥΓΕΝΗΘΗΤϹ
ΤΟΘΕΛΗΜΑCΟΥΩϹ
ΕΝΟΥΡΑΝΩΟΥΤϹ
ΚΑΙΕΠΙΓΗCΤΟΝ
ΑΡΤΟΝΗΜΩΝΤΟΝ
ΕΠΙΟΥCΙΟΝΔΟCΗ
ΜΙΝΚΑΘΗΜΕΡΑΝ
ΚΑΙΑΦΕCΗΜΙΝΤΑ
ΑΜΑΡΤΙΑCΗΜΩΝ
ΩCΚΑΙΑΥΤΟΙΑΦΙϹ
ΜΕΝΠΑΝΤΙΟΦΙ
ΛΟΝΤΙΗΜΙΝΚΑΙ
ΜΗΕΙCΕΝΕΓΚΗϹ
ΗΜΑCΕΙCΠΙΡΑCΜϹ
ΚΑΙΕΙΠΕΝΠΡΟCΑ
ΤΟΥCΤΙCΕΞΥΜΩΝ
ΕΞΕΙΦΙΛΟΝΚΑΙΠϹ
ΡΕΥCΕΤΑΙΠΡΟCΑ
ΤΟΝΜΕCΟΝΥΚΤΙ
ΟΥΚΑΙΕΙΠΗΑΥΤΩ
ΦΙΛΕΧΡΗCΟΝΜΟΙ
ΤΡΙCΑΡΤΟΥCΕΠΙ
ΦΙΛΟCΜΟΥΠΑΡΕ
ΝΕΤΟΕΞΟΔΟΥΠΡ

19.10 Greek uncial script: a page from the famous *Codex Sinaiticus* (fourth century A.D.).

This is perhaps the earliest Greek vellum codex extant. In 1933 it was purchased by the British Museum from the Soviet Government for £100,000.

19.11. Earliest preserved Greek manuscripts of the Bible: *a* Fragment of papyrus roll from Dervein. Height 7 cm. *b* Fragment of *Deuteronomy*, 2nd cent. B.C. (*Rylands Papyrus No. 458*).

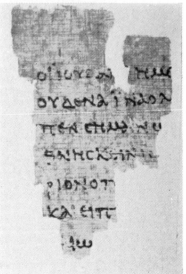

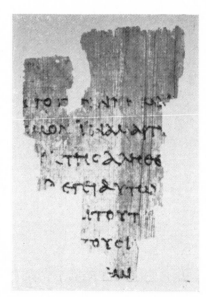

19.11. *c, d* St. John's Gospel, Ch. 18, first half 2nd cent. A.D. (*Rylands Papyrus No. 457*).

19.12. *Papyrus Mimaut*, 3rd–5th century A.D. (Louvre *Pap 1.2391*).

19.13a. *Deuteronomy* 2, 30–34 (Col. 1) and 2, 34–3, 1 (Col. 2). Fine literaay 19.13b. *Numbers* 7, 1–15. Fine Greek literary hand of late 1st or early 2nd hand of late 1st or early 2nd century, (Chester Beatty Pap. VI, fol. 10 century, (Chester Beatty Pap. VI, fol. 10 recto). verso).

19.14a. *Romans* 11, 3–12, c A.D. 200 (Chester Beatty Pap. II, fol. 14 recto).

19.14b. *Revelation* 13, 16–14, 4. Rough Greek hand of the late 3rd century (Chester Beatty Pap. III, fol. 7 recto).

19.15a. Ezekiel 16, 57–17, 1. First half of 3rd century (Chester Beatty Pap. IV, fol. 16 recto). 19.15b Genesis 42, 27–35. Documentary Greek hand of the 3rd century (Chester Beatty Pap. V, fol. 20 recto).

19.16*a*. Portion of a poem by Bacchylides, variously attributed to the first century
B.C. or A.D. (British Museum, *Pap. 733*).

19.16*b*. Portion of the three speeches by Hyperides against Demosthenes and for
Lycophron and Euxenippus, 1st century A.D. (British Museum, *Pap. 108, 115*).

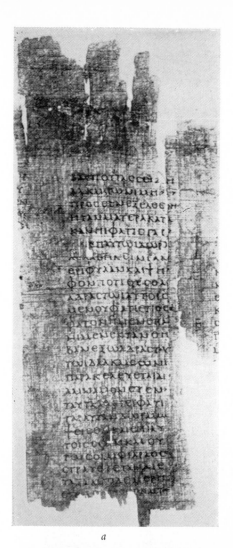

a

b

19.17. *a* One of the few extant documents in the Doric dialect. *b* fragment of a lost Greek tragedy, 3rd century A.D. (British Museum, *Pap. 695*). *c* fragment dating from the seventh year of Nero.

c

19.18. The *Sayings of Jesus*, fragment of a papyrus codex found at Oxyrhynchus, attributed to the third century A.D. (Bodleian Library, Oxford).

19.19*a*. Earliest extant Greek literary document on parchment: *Oration* by Demosthenes; late 1st century A.D. (British Museum, *Add. MS. 34473*).

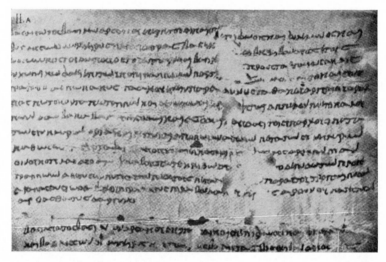

19.19*b*. Second earliest Greek document written on parchment. It is dated to 22–21 B.C., and was found with two other documents near Avromān (British Museum, *Add. MS. 38895B*).

19.20. Greek palimpsest; lower script, *Codex Z* (*Gospel of St. Matthew*), written in Greek uncials of the sixth century A.D. (Trinity College, Dublin, *MS. K.3.4.A., No. 28*).

a   b

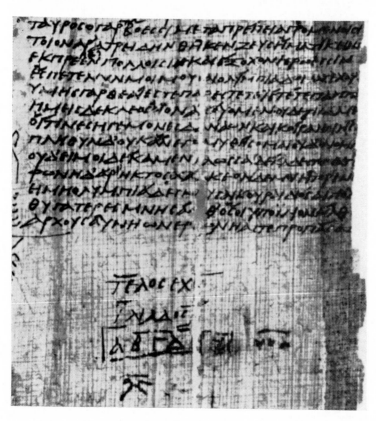

c

19.21. Homer manuscripts written on papyrus. *a* Berlin *Pap. 6869* (first century B.C.); *b* Fayyûm, No. 6 (period of Augustus); *c* British Museum *Pap. 126* (fourth century A.D.).

a

b

19.22. *a* The *Ambrosian Iliad* variously attributed to the third to fifth centuries A.D. (Ambrosian Library, Milan, *Codex F.205, inf.*), *b* Alcman (Louvre Museum, Paris, *Pap. E. 3320*).

323

a

b

19.23. *a* Parts of four poems by Alcaeus (flourished late 7th and early 6th centuries B.C.) written on papyrus in the 2nd century A.D. (Bodleian Library, MS. *Class. b.18* (P.)). *b* Timotheus, *Persae* (col. 5, v. 187–247), the earliest preserved literary papyrus, 4th century B.C.

19.24. Aristotle, *Constitution of Athens* (British Museum, *Pap. 131*).

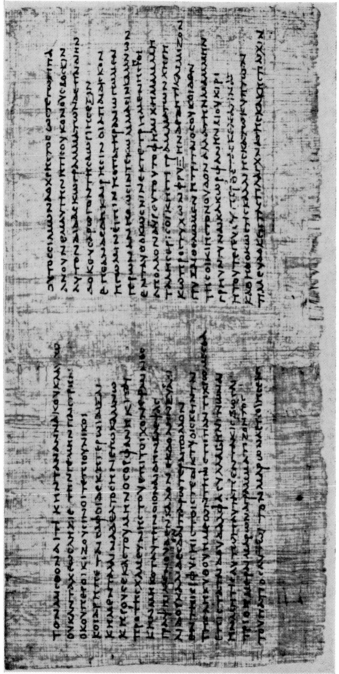

19.25. Herodas, *Mimes* (British Museum, *Pap. 135–3*).

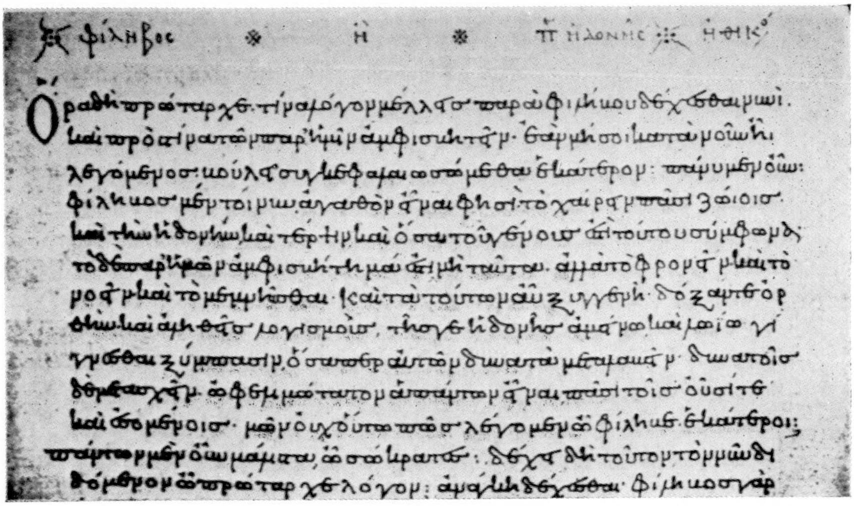

a

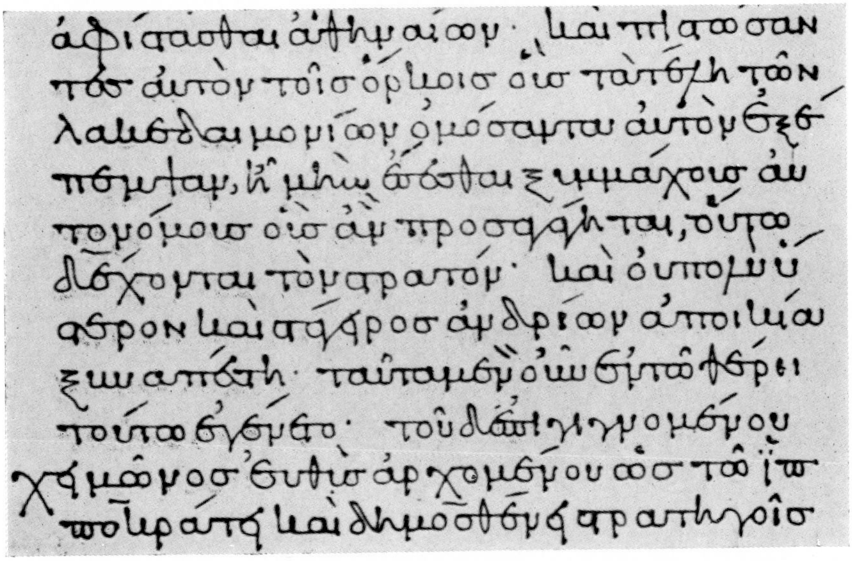

b

19.26. *a Dialogues* by Plato written for Arethas of Patras in A.D. 896 (Bodleian Library, Oxford, *Clarke MS. 39*); *b* Thucydides, tenth-century copy (Laurentian Library, Florence, *Plut. 59.2*).

19.27a. Aristophanes (Vatican Library *Pal. Gr. 67*).

19.27b. Aeschylus (Laurentian Library, Florence, *Cod. 31.8*).

19.27c. Demosthenes, early 11th century A.D. (Laurentian Library, *Plut. 59.9*).

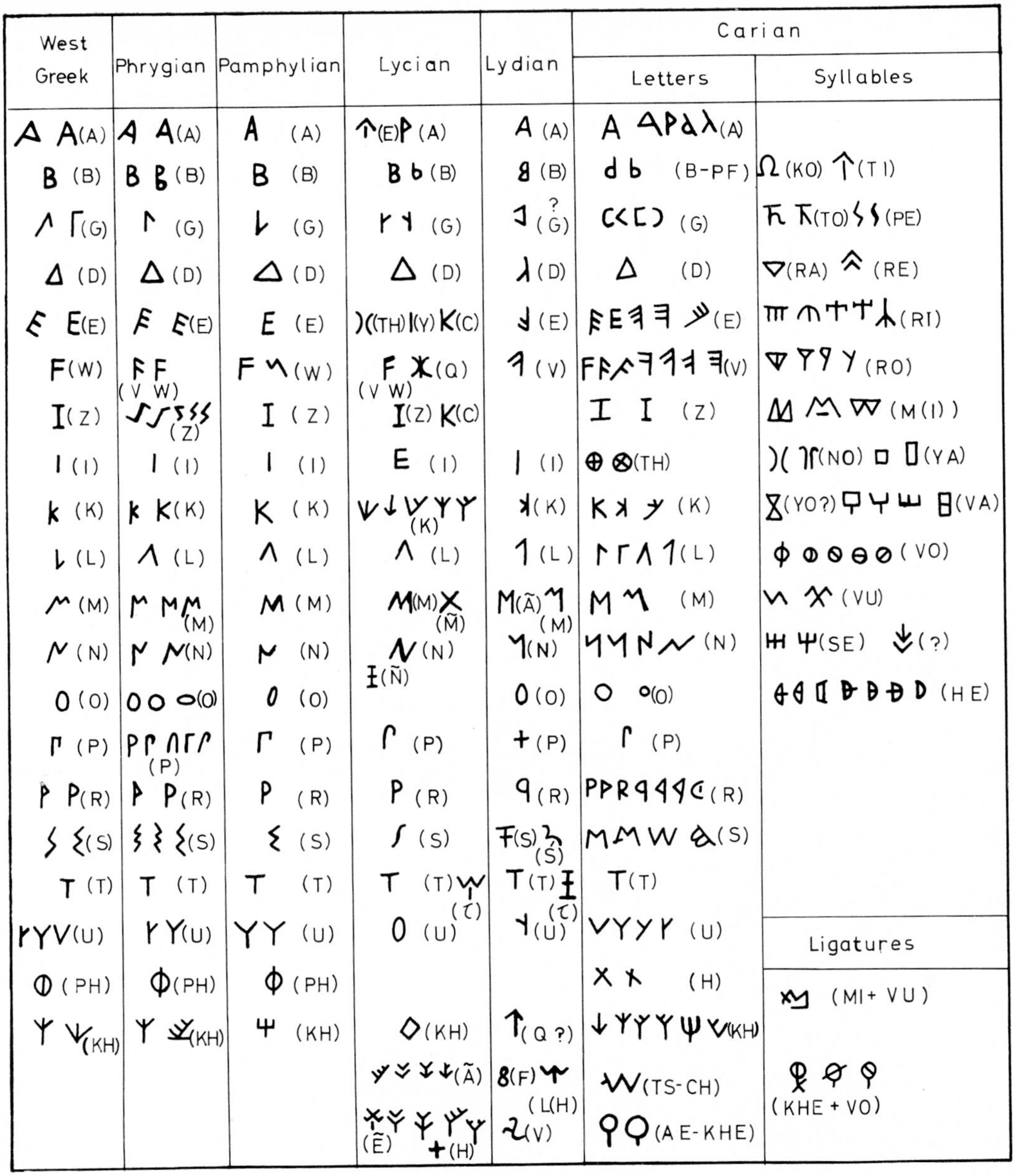

West Greek	Phrygian	Pamphylian	Lycian	Lydian	Carian	
					Letters	Syllables
Δ A(A)	Δ A(A)	A (A)	↑(E)P(A)	A (A)	A ΔPδλ(A)	
B (B)	B B(B)	B (B)	B b(B)	8 (B)	d b (B-PF)	Ω (KO) ↑(TI)
Λ Γ(G)	Γ (G)	↳ (G)	Γꓭ(G)	コ(G)?	C(C)(G)	Ŧ Ŧ(TO) ϟϟ(PE)
Δ (D)	Δ (D)	△ (D)	Δ (D)	λ(D)	Δ (D)	▽(RA) ⌃(RE)
Ɛ E(E)	Ƒ Ƒ(E)	E (E)	)(TH)I(Y)K(C)	ꓭ(E)	ϝEꓯƎ �(E)	⯬ ∧⧻⫟木(RI)
F(W)	ϜF (V W)	F ꓦ(W)	F Ҳ(Q) (V W)	ꓯ(V)	FⱤ⅄ƗꓯꓯƎ(V)	▽ ꓬꓳꓬ(RO)
I(Z)	ϟϟ ϟϟϟ(Z)	I (Z)	I(Z) K(C)		I I (Z)	ﻌM Mꟽꟽ(M(I))
I (I)	I (I)	I (I)	E (I)	I (I)	⊕⊗(TH)	)((NO) ▢ ⊓(YA)
k (K)	k K(K)	K (K)	Ⅴ↓ⱽꓬꓬ(K)	ꓮ(K)	Kꓮꓨꟻ(K)	Ⅹ(YO?) ⊓ⱶⱼⱶ Ɵ(VA)
↳ (L)	ꓥ (L)	ꓥ (L)	ꓥ (L)	↿(L)	⌐Гꓥꓶ(L)	φ ⊕⊝Ɵ(VO)
↗ (M)	ꓯ ꟽꟽ(M)	M (M)	M(M)Ҳ(M̃)	M(Ã)ꟼ(M)	M ꟽ (M)	ꓦ Ⅹ (VU)
ꓠ (N)	ꓦ ꟽ(N)	ꓦ (N)	ꓠ(N) Ɨ(Ñ)	ꓬ(N)	ꓯꓳꓠ⌁(N)	₩ Ψ(SE) ⩒(?)
O (O)	OO ◠(O)	Ɵ (O)		O (O)	O ◦(O)	ꓛꓛꓑ ℔ꓓꓒꓓ(HE)
Γ (P)	PꟼꓟГΓ(P)	Γ (P)	ℾ (P)	✛ (P)	ℾ (P)	
P P(R)	P P(R)	P (R)	P (R)	ꟼ (R)	ℙ℟ꓘ⅂⅂⅃(R)	
ϟ ⧣(S)	ϟϟ ⧣ϟ(S)	⧣ (S)	ʃ (S)	Ⅎ(S)₂(S)	M ꟽⱲⱾ(S)	
T (T)	T (T)	T (T)	T(T)ꟽ(T̃)	T(T)Ɨ(T̃)	T(T)	
ꓨꓬꓦ(U)	ꓨꓬ(U)	ꓨꓬ(U)	Ɵ (U)	ꓬ(U)	ꓦꓬꓬꓨ (U)	
Φ (PH)	Φ(PH)	φ (PH)			Ⅹ ꓘ (H)	Ligatures
ꓬ ꓦ(KH)	ꓬ ⩒(KH)	Ψ (KH)	◇(KH)	↑(Q?)	↓ꓬꓯꓯ Ψꓦ(KH)	ꓮꓞ (MI+VU)
			ⱷⱱⱶⱶ(Ã)	8(F)ꓩ(L(H))	ꟽ(TS-CH)	𝝓 𝝓 𝝓
			⩗ꓬⱱꓥ(Ẽ) ✛(H)	ꓩ(V)	φφ(AE-KHE)	(KHE+VO)

19.28. The Asianic alphabets.

329

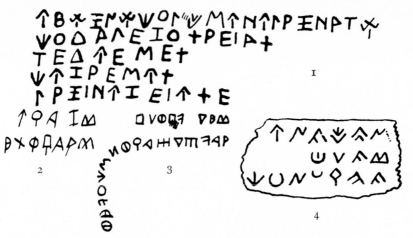

19.29a. (1) Lycian inscription, (2)–(4) Carian inscriptions.

19.29b. Carian inscriptions.

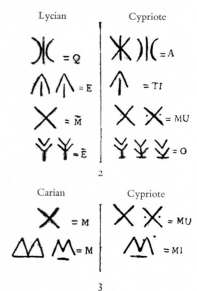

19.29c. (1) Lycian and Carian signs compared with Cretan signs, (2) and (3) and with Cypriote syllables.

| LETTERS | | NAME | PHON. VALUE | LETTERS | | NAME | PHON. VALUE | |
MAJUSCULES	MINUSCULES			MAJUSCULES	MINUSCULES			
Ⲁ	ⲁ	alpha	a	Ⲣ	ⲣ	ro	r	
Ⲃ	ⲃ	vita	v (b)	Ⲥ	ⲥ	sima	s	
Ⲅ	ⲅ	gamma	g	Ⲧ	ⲧ	tau	t	
Ⲇ	ⲇ	delta	d	Ⲩ	ⲩ	ypsilon	y, u	
Ⲉ	ⲉ	epsilon	ĕ	Ⲫ	ⲫ	phi	ph	
Ⲍ	ⲍ	zita	z	Ⲭ	ⲭ	khi	ch=kh	
Ⲏ	ⲏ	ita	i, ē	Ⲯ	ⲯ	psi	ps	
Ⲑ	ⲑ	ṭita	ṭ	Ⲱ	ⲱ	omega	omega	
Ⲓ	ⲓ	iōta	i	Ϣ	ϣ	šei	š	
Ⲕ	ⲕ	kappa	k	Ϥ	ϥ	fai	f	
Ⲗ	ⲗ	laula	l	Ϧ	ϧ	khai	ḥ	
Ⲙ	ⲙ	mi	m	Ϩ	ϩ	hori	h	
Ⲛ	ⲛ	ni	n	Ϫ	ϫ	djandja	ǧ	
Ⲝ	ⲝ	xi	x	Ϭ	ϭ	chima	č (ancient)	
Ⲟ	ⲟ	omicron	ŏ					
Ⲡ	ⲡ	pi	p	Ϯ	ϯ	ti	ti	

19.30. The Coptic alphabet.

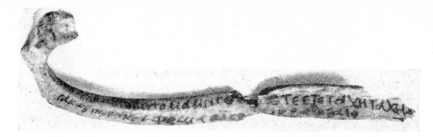

19.31*a*. Coptic imprecation written on a rib.

19.31*b*. *Papyrus* Q: Oldest Coptic Gospel (St. John), 4th century A.D. (Bible House Library, London).

19.32b. *Pistis Sophia*, a treatise of Valentinus. Vellum MS. Late 4th or early 5th century (B.M.).

19.32a. Deuteronomy, Jonah and Acts, Coptic. Sa'idic Dialect. Papyrus, early 14th century (B.M.).

333

19.33. Specimens of Coptic books. *a* New Testament in Sahidic, on vellum, 5th or 6th century; *b Psalm 118*, v. 124–51; *c* Bohairic liturgical hymns, on paper, 14th or 15th century; *d* Arabic text written in Coptic Bohairic hand, 14th century.

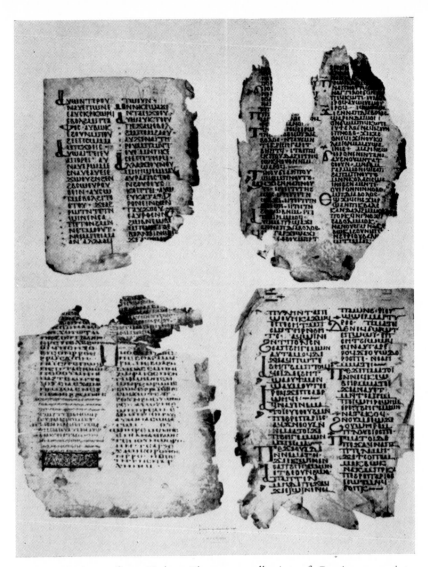

19.34. Specimens from Herbert Thompson collection of Coptic manuscripts (University Library, Cambridge, *MS. Or. 1699*). *Above (left)*, Apocryphal book on *Resurrection; (right)*, *Homilies* by Shenūte. *Below*, *Martyrology* and *Homilies*.

19.35. Leaf of a papyrus codex of the 4th–5th century A.D. containing the conclusion of a Manichean homily written in the Subachmimic dialect of Coptic (Chester Beatty Library).

19.36. Encomium of St. Menas dated A.D. 892/3 (from the Coptic MS. 590 in the Pierpont Morgan Collection). (*By permission of the Société d'Archéologie Copte, Cairo*).

19.37. Various Messapian inscriptions.

Phonetic value	Symbols	Numerical value
a, â	𐌀 𐌰 𐌰	1
b (b?)	𐌱 𐌱 𐌱	2
g, γ	𐌲 𐌲	3
d, (d?)	𐌳 𐌳	4
e	𐌴 𐌴	5
q	𐌵 𐌵 𐌵	6
z	𐌶 𐌶	7
h	𐌷 𐌷	8
p (θ)	𐌸 𐌸	9
i	𐌹 𐌹 𐌹	10
k	𐌺 𐌺	20
l	𐌻 𐌻	30
m	𐌼 𐌼	40
n	𐌽 𐌽	50
j	𐌾 𐌾	60
u	𐌿 𐌿	70
p	𐍀 𐍀	80
—	𐍁	90
r	𐍂 𐍂𐍂	100
s	𐍃 𐍃	200
t	𐍄 𐍄	300
w, ü	𐍅 𐍅	400
f	𐍆 𐍆	500
χ (kh)	𐍇 𐍇	600
hv (hw)	𐍈 𐍈	700
o	𐍉 𐍉	800
(sampi)	↑ ↑	900

a

b

c

19.38. *a* The Gothic alphabet. *b* Page from the *Codex Argenteus*. *c* The *Paternoster* according to the same *codex*.

Uncial Greek	Cyrillic	Bulgarian Glagolitsa	Croat. Glagolitsa	Names of the letters	Phonetic value	Num.
A	Ⰰ Ⰰ	(glyphs)	(glyphs)	az	a	1
Ь B	Б Б	(glyphs)	(glyphs)	buky	b	2
		(glyphs)	(glyphs)	vedi	v	3
Γ	Г	(glyphs)	(glyphs)	glagol	g	4
Δ	Δ	(glyphs)	(glyphs)	dobro	d	5
Є	Є	(glyphs)	(glyphs)	est', yest'	e – ye	6
T (τθ) ϛ	Ж Ж	(glyphs)	(glyphs)	zhivete	zh	7
ϛ (ϰ: δϛ)	S S	(glyphs)	(glyphs)	zelo	z – dz	8
Z	Z	(glyphs)	(glyphs)	zemlya	z	9
H	H	(glyphs)	(glyphs)	izhe (ije)	$\bar{\imath}$	10
I Ï	Ï I	(glyphs)	(glyphs)	i	i	20
Tϲ (τϲ)	ħ	(glyphs)	(glyphs)	dew' yerv' dyerv'	d'–d^g t'–t^g y	30
K	K	(glyphs)	(glyphs)	kako	k	40
Λ	Λ Λ	(glyphs)	(glyphs)	lyudy	l	50
M	M M	(glyphs)	(glyphs)	myslite	m	60
N	N N	(glyphs)	(glyphs)	nash	n	70
O	O	(glyphs)	(glyphs)	on	o	80
Π	Π	(glyphs)	(glyphs)	pokoy	p	90
P	P	(glyphs)	(glyphs)	r'tsi	r	100
C	C	(glyphs)	(glyphs)	slovo	s	200

19.39. The Early Slavonic alphabets.

Uncial Greek	Cyrillic	Bulgarian Glagolitsa	Croat.	Names of the letters	Phonet. Value	Num.
T	T			tv'rdo	t	300
8 or ου	ογ			uk	u	400
φ / θ	φ		φ	fert / thita	f / th	500 / 9
X	X			kher	kh	600
ω	ω			ot	ō	700
ω (σσ) Sem. sh?	Ш			sha	sh	—
↯ (σσ?)	ШТЧ			shta	sht	800
(Ç,Ç Z,σσ) Sem ts?	Ч			tsi	ts	900
(Ç, τσ?) T sem. ts?	Y			ch'rv	ch	1000
℧ (οε)	Ъ			yer	ŭ-y	—
℧ι (οειι)	ЪІ ЪН		—	yery	y	—
б (ε)	ь		ТІ	yerek	ĭ	—
Gт	Ѣ, Ѩ			yat'-yet'	ya-ye	800
10	Ю			yu	yu	—
Iε	ѥ		—	ye	ye	—
î ĩ (ιν)	A↑î		—	e^n s	eng	900
о / î о+ιν	Ѫ		—	o^n s	ong	—
I+A	Ѩ		—	ye^n s	yeng	—
I+Ѫ	Ѭ		—	yo^n s	yong	—
ξ ξ	ξ ξ	—	—	ksi	ks	60
Ψ Ψ	Ψ	—	—	psi	ps	700
V	v Y		—	izhitsa	y-v-i / ü	—

19.40. The Early Slavonic alphabets (continued).

PHON. VALUE	CYRILL.	RUSSIAN		BULGAR.	SERBIAN	UKRAIN	OLD RUM.
		PRINT	CURSIVE				
a	Ꙗ Д	А А		А	А	А	д
b	Б	Б Б		Б	Б	Б	Б
v	В	В В		В	В	В	В
g	Г	Г Г		Г	Г	Г (Т)	Г Д
d	Д	Д Д		Д	Д	Д	Д
ye	Є	Е Ѥ		Е	Е	Е (Є)	Е Ѣ
zh (j)	Ж Җ	Ж Ж		Ж	Ж	Ж	Ж Ж
z	З	З З		З	З	З	Ѕ Ꙁ
i	Н	И И		И	И	И	Н
i	І	І Ꙉ				І (Ї)	І (Ї)
y		(Й й)		(Й)	Ј	(Й)	
k	К	К К		К	К	К	К
l	Ҹ л	Л Л		Л	Л ҿ	Л	Ҹ
m	Ѧ м	М М		М	М	М	М
n	N N	Н Ж		Н	Н ҈	Н	N
o	О	О О		О	О	О	О (ѡ)
p	П	П Ҥ		П	П	П	П
r	Р	Р Ҏ		Р	Р	Р	Р
s	С	С Ҫ		С	С	С	С
t	Т	Т Ҭ		Т	Т	Т	Т

19.41. The main Slavonic alphabets of today.

342

PHON. VALUE	CYRILL.	RUSSIAN		BULGAR.	SERBIAN	UKRAIN.	OLD RUM.
		PRINT	CURSIVE				
ty	ħ				Ћ		
u (oo)	ȣ or	У у		У	У	У	ȣ or
f	ф	Ф ₤		Ф	Ф	Ф	ф
kh	х	Х х		Х	Х	Х	х
ts	ц	Ц ц		Ц	Ц	Ц	ц
ch	ч	ч ч		ч	ч	(Џ) ч	ч ц
sh	ш	Ш ш		ш	ш	ш	ш
shch	ц ш ͭ	Ш ц		щ		щ	ψ
mute	ъ	Ъ ъ		ъ	ъ		ъ
y	ⲓ	Ы ы					ы
mute	ь	Ь ь		ь	ь	ь	ь
ye	ѣ	ѣ ₤		ѣ			ѣ
e	э	Э э					(IE)
yu	ю	Ю ю		Ю	Ю		ю
ya	я ꙗ	Я я		Я	Я		ꙗ
ph	ѳ	ѳ ѳ					ѳ (ft)
y	ѵ	ѵ ѵ					ѵ у
ú	ѫ			Х			ѫ
iu	ꙙ ͭ			IX			ꙙ ↑↑ ia in Ѯ Ѱ ks ps

19.42. The main Slavonic alphabets of today (continued).

a

ZHTKШHHTZHPГ
ШYƁШYΛЄXШYM
CXHKYΠЄ:YNЄ:TШ
YΛCXH:ФM:ЄCTPШ
ГHNKYΠЄ:YKƧ:TШ
YΛCXH:ထONΔ:TШYPT
ШYNAΠHΛЄƧШΠAN
ЄCTPYГHNKYΠЄ:K:
TШYΛCXH:M:AΛXACH
KYΠЄ:A:XΛШ YƁPH N:A:

b

19.43. Cyrillic. *a* Traces of graffiti on the right column near the main entrance of the round church in Preslav. *b* Old Bulgarian inscription from the church in Bjal-Brjag, in the district of Preslav (Courtesy Acad. I. Goshev).

344

ΚΕΒΟΗΘΗΤΟΝΔΥΛΟCΥΒΛΗϘΤΗΝ
CΤΡϘΤΕΛϘΤΗΝ

a

ДѢЛИТѪРАЗГѢ·ВЫЖЕ
ВРАЗН·ВРАЗНГНИСѢЛ
ГАШАКМЛОУ·ПОПНСАНОУ
ОУМОУ·ІАКОСОУШТАА
ГОЖСТЪСТВОМЬСНАБЖН
ІА·ПОЛОЖЕННІЕМЬНЕБЛА
ГОДАТНЖНАРНУОУТ·
ОБЖЕНА·НЗНЖАНТАЛ
ЗЬДАНИІЕ·НПРНСМІЕСХ
ШТААГОВЪЦН·ПОѢЖ
ДЕНЕБЫБѢША·НБЫБѢ
ШААГООТЪБЫТНІА·ПЛ
РНУОУШЕОТЪНЕБЫТН·
ІА·БЫБѢ·НЕТЪХЖ
ЖЕНАБА·Н·ГАЛѪЖОУ
ТЬ·КОУСАВЪРАЩАЖШЕ·

b   *c*

19.44. Old Bulgarian inscriptions. *a* Inscription of Aliates Stratelat, commander of the Byzantine garrison, in the round church of Preslav (A.D. 972). *b* Inscription of 'Črgubilja Mostič' after its reconstruction, 11th–13th century (Archaeological Museum, Sofia). *c* Sviatoslav-Izbornic, fol. 4 (A.D. 1073) (Courtesy Acad. I. Goshev).

ⳍⰲⰸⵌⰿⰰⰍⵒⵓⰵⰰⱈⵒⵈⵗ

(The image a shows a funerary inscription in Cyrillic script)

19.45. Development of the Cyrillic monumental scripts. *a* Funerary inscription in Cyrillic script of A.D. 993 (dedicated by Tzar Samuel to his parents and brother); *b* manuscript of A.D. 1073; *c* manuscript of A.D. 1284; *d* prayer book of A.D. 1400; *e* manuscript of 15th century; *f* manuscript of 1561.

а Б в г д е ж ѕ з ꙁ н ї і к л м н н о ѡ п р с т ꙋ ȣ ф ф х ѿ ѿ ц ч ч ш
ψ ъ ꙑ ь ѣ ѣ ѥ ѩ ю ꙗ ꙗ ꙗ ꙗ ѣ ѫ ѭ ꙉ а ꙁ ю ю ꙟ ꙋ ꙋ ꙑ ꙋ ꙗ ꙋ ш

a

а Б в г д е ж з з з н ї і к л м н о о о п р с т ꙋ ꙋ ф х х ѿ ц
ꙋ ꙗ ш ψ ъ ꙁ ꙑ ь ѣ ѣ ю ꙗ ꙝ ꙟ ꙗ з ꙳ ѣ ꙋ р о ф Т Ꙉ ѱ

b

а ꙁ ꙁ Б в г д е ꙉ е ж з з н ї і к л м н о ѳ п р с т ꙋ ꙋ ф х ѿ ц
ꙋ ꙗ ш ψ ꙑ ъ Ꙍ ꙑ Ꙍ ꙋ ѣ ю ꙗ ꙗ з ѥ з з ꙉ ꙉꙗ ꙉꙑ ꙉꙑ ꙋ

c

а Б в г д е ж з з н ї і к л м н о о п р с т о ꙋ ф х ѿ ц ꙋ ш ψ
ꙑ Ꙍ ꙑ ь ѣ ю ꙗ ꙗ з ꙋ ꙉꙋ ꙉꙑ ꙉꙑꙉ ꙉꙑ ꙉꙑꙋ

d

ꙋ ꙗ ꙗꙗ Б в г д е ж з з з з ꙁ з н ї к л м н н о ѡ ѡ ꙋ п р с т ꙋ ꙋ ꙋ ф х ѿ ч ш ψ ъ ꙑ
ꙑ ꙗ ꙑ ѣ ꙗ ю ꙗ ꙗ ꙗꙗ ꙗ ꙗ з з ꙉ ꙋ ꙓ ꙋ ꙋ ꙋ ꙋ ꙉ ꙋ ꙋ ꙋ ꙑ є є ꙋ ꙋꙋ

e

Татѣль нострꙋ, кареле ещй ѫ черюрй,
сфйцаскъсе нꙋмеле тъꙋ: Вїе ѫпрърꙏцїа
тꙗ: фїе бо́ꙗ та, пре кꙋмь ѫчерю, шй пре

f

19.46. *a–e* Varieties of early Cyrillic alphabets. *f* Roumanian in Cyrillic character.

19.47*a*. Cryptic annotation in a manuscript of the 16th century.

19.47*b*. Cursive writing, 1555.

19.47*c*. Cursive variety of 1562.

19.47*d*. Manuscript of 1668.

19.47. Specimens of Cyrillic cursive writing.

Language	Special letters
Moldavian	ё, щ, ъ,
Tajiki	ӣ, ӯ, ғ, ķ, х, ч, аз, дар,
Kurdish	ә, ö, h, г', ә', к', п', р', т', h', ч', ё, ц, ъ, ы, ю, я,
Ossetic	æ,
Abkhasian	ц, к, х, ч, ә, ҙ, ҕ, дә, цҙ, жҙ, жә, зә, ҕ, кҙ, ҡ, тә, та, хҙ, хә, цҙ, цә, шҙ, шә, ҷ, шә, ё, й, щ, ҙ, з, ю, я, е, ҙ, з, ҡ, ҩ, ҭ, т,
Abasinian	г1, г1в, к1, к1в, п1, т1, ф1, х1, х1в, ц1, ч1, ч1в, ш1, ы1, ъ, I, гъь, г1в, джь, джв, къь, къв, к1ь, х1в, х1в, гъв,
Adigen	к1, п1, п1, т1, ф1, ц1, ч1, ш1, щ1, ы1, I1, Iу, гъ, жь, къ, лъ, хъ, чъ, шъ,
Kabardian-Circassian (Cherkessian)	к1, к1у, п1, п1, т1, ф1, ц1, щ1, Iу, жь, хъ, кхъ, кхъу, хъу, Iу,
Chechen	г1, к1, п1, т1, ц1, ч1, ы1, I1, аь, йо, оь, уь, юь, яь,
Komi-Permian	і, ö,
Udmurt (Votyak)	ӝ, ӟ, ӥ, ӵ, ӧ,
Mari (Cheremiss)	ä, ö, ÿ,
Mordvine-Erzya	-сь, -нь,
Mordvine-Moksha	-сь, -нь, лх, рх,
Nenets (Yurak)	нг, и,
Selkup (Ostyako-Samoyed)	е', к', н', у',
Chuvash	ă, ĕ, ç, ÿ,
Turkmenian (Turkoman)	җ, ң, ө, ү, ә,

19.49. Cyrillic (Russian) alphabet adapted to non-Slavonic languages.

Ingush	гӏ, кӏ, пӏ, тӏ, хӏ, цӏ, чӏ, бӏ, лӏ, аь, яь,
Avarian	гӏ, кӏ, тӏ, хӏ, цӏ, чӏ, бӏ, г, к, т, х, ч, ч.
Darghi	гӏ, кӏ, тӏ, хӏ, цӏ, чӏ, бӏ.
Lesghian	кӏ, пӏ, тӏ, цӏ, чӏ, l.
Lakh	кӏ, пӏ, тӏ, цӏ, чӏ, бӏ, аь, жв, уь, шв,
Tabasaran	кӏ, пӏ, тӏ, хӏ, цӏ, чӏ, l, аь, оь,
Vogul(Mansi)	нг,
Ostyak (Khantian)	қ, ӧ, ӓ, н, ӧ, ө, ӱ, э,
Komi (Zyryan) (Syryan)	i, ö,

Azerbaijani	к, ч, в, ғ, ә, ј, ө, ү, h, ё, ӥ, ц, щ, ъ, ь, э, ю, я,
Tatar	ө, ү, ж, н, ә,
Bashkir	ө, ү, h, ә, з, (з), ж, ç, (ç), ғ, н,
Kumyk	гъ, гь, къ, нг, оъ, уъ,
Kara-Kalpak	ғ, қ, х,
Nogai	нъ, оъ, уъ, з, м,
Kazakh	ғ, қ, н, ө, ү, h, i, ә,
Kirghiz	н, ө, ү,
Altaic	j, н, ö, ÿ,

19.50. Cyrillic (Russian) alphabet adapted to non-Slavonic languages (continued).

Language	Letters	Language	Letters
Karachai	ў,	Tungus Proper (Evenki)	нг,
Balkar	нъ, нг, ў	Lamut (Even)	з, ь, п, э, и,
Uzbek	ў, қ, ғ,	Gold (Nanai)	нг,
Uighur	к, н, ғ, ү, ө, җ, ә, h,	Chukcha (Luoravetian)	ӄ, ӈ,
Yakut	ҕ, ҥ, ө, h, ү.	Koryak (Nymylan)	ӄ, ӈ,
Tuva (Soyot or Uryankhai)	ҥ, ө, ү,	Nivkh (Gilyak)	'frequently used
Khakas	и, ч, ӌ, ғ, і, ö, ÿ,	Siberian Eskimo (Yuit)	г, к, н, х,
Buryat	ө, ү, h, оо, өө, үү, үу, зз,	Dungan	ә, ж, н, ү,
Kalmyk (Kalmuck)	ә, h, җ, ң, ө, ү, ä, гъ, дж, нъ, ö, ÿ,	Mongolian Proper	ө, ү, аа, оо, өө, үү, үу, зз,

19.51. The Cyrillic alphabets.

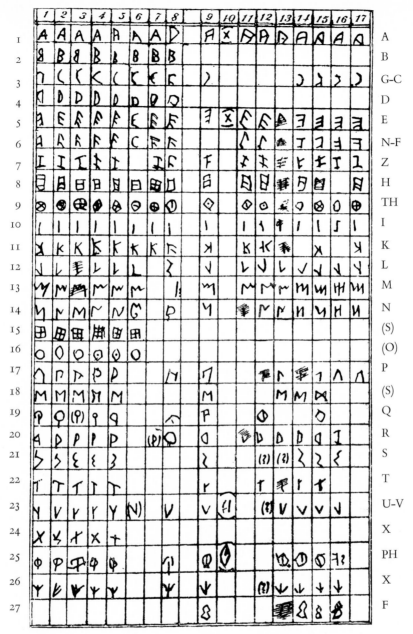

20.1. Etruscan sample alphabets (in columns). 1, Marsiliana. 2, Viterbo, 3, Cære.
4–5, Formello. 6, Colle. 7, Narce. 8, Leprignano. 9, Rusellæ. 10–13, Chiusi. 14,
Bomarzo. 15–17 Nola.

20.2 Etruscan inscription. *a* Marsiliana tablet. *b* The *stele* from Vetulonia. *c* The Perugia *Cippus*.

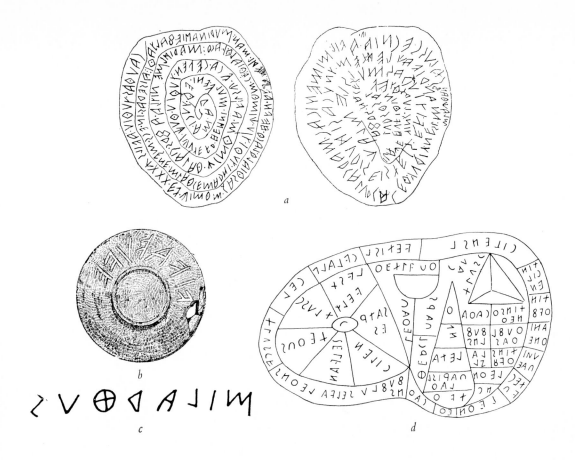

a

e

20.3. *a* The Magliano leaden tablet (left, obverse, right, reverse). *b* Etruscan partial syllabary from Orbetello. *c* Inscription on a vase. *d* The *Templum* of Piacenza. *e* The Etruscan 'classical' alphabet in all but final form. *f* Etruscan inscriptions from a 3rd century B.C. ossuary, from Chiusi (Vatican Museum).

	Lepontic	Sondrio	Bolzano	Magrè	Venetic
A					
B					
C					
D					
E					
V-W					
Z					
H					
Θ					
I					
K					
L					
M					
N					
×S					
O					
P					
Ś					
R					
S					
T					
U					
Φ					
X					
?					

20.4. North Etruscan and allied alphabets.

Phon. Value	Messapian	Picenian	Oscan	Umbrian	Siculan	Faliscan
a						
b						
g						(k)
d						
e						
v (f)						
z (ts)						
h						
θ (th)				(t)		
i		(? ie)	(? ie)			
k						
l						
m		?				
n						
s						
o			(v̆ v̆=o) (y̆ y̆=u)			
p						
s		? ? ? ?				
q						
r				(q=r̆)		
s	(sh x)?			(sh d)?		
t						
u						
ks / ps	(ks) (ps)		(ks x)			

20.5. Pre-Italic and Italic alphabets.

357

20.6a. The Picenian inscription of the 'Warrior' from Capestrano.

20.6b. Oscan inscriptions.

20.6c. The famous Faliscan inscription in two copies.

20.7. Noviliara funeral stele, written in Picenian, *c.* 550 B.C.

20.8. Eugubine tablet, table 5. Upper part is written in Umbrian script, lower part in Roman character.

			SCANDINAVIAN			DOTTED
PHON. VALUE	GERMANIC	ANGLO-SAXON	EARLY SIGNS	DANISH	SWED. NORW.	
				LATE SIGNS		
	LETTERS	LETTERS	LETTERS	LETTERS	LETTERS	LETTERS

21.1. Main branches of the Runic script.

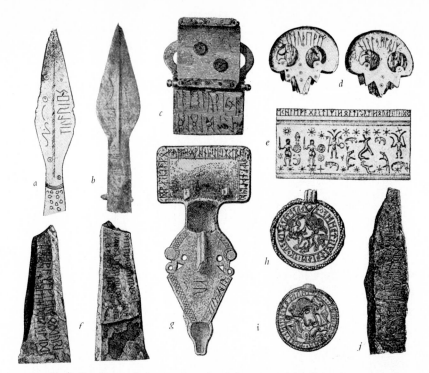

21.2. Early Runic inscriptions. *a* Spearhead from Kovel (Volhynia), attributed to the fourth century A.D.; *b* Spearhead from Dahmsdorf near Muencheberg (Brandenburg). *c* Clasp from Vi-mose in Fyn (S.-W. Denmark), attributed to the middle of the third century A.D.; *d* The end–clasp of a sword-sheath from Torsbjerg, attributed to *ca.* 300; *e* The 'Golden Horn' from Gallehus (northern Schleswig), of *ca.* A.D. 400. *f* The stone from Tune (S.-E. Norway), of the fifth century A.D.; *g* The brooch from Charnay (French Department of Saône and Loire; old Burgundian kingdom) of the fifth century A.D.; *h–i Bracteates* from Vadstena (Sweden) and Tjorkœ (Sweden) of the sixth–seventh centuries A.D. *j* Funerary inscription written from right to left, from Kyœlevig, or Strand (Ryfylke, Norway) of the sixth century A.D.

21.3. Metal and whale's bone used as writing material in England; (*below*) the *scramasax* or sword-knife, found in the Thames in 1857, and now in the British Museum; it probably belongs to about A.D. 800; (*above*) one side of the 'Franks Casket', attributed to about A.D. 650 or A.D. 700; the runes have been translated: 'The fish-flood (sea) lifted the whale's bones on to the mainland; the ocean became turbid where he swam aground on the shingle.'

a

b

21.4. *a* Sepulchral stone from Kallerup, Denmark, 9th century A.D. *b* Stone from the Odense region, Denmark, 9th century A.D. *c* Inscription from Nœrrenaerå, late 9th century A.D.

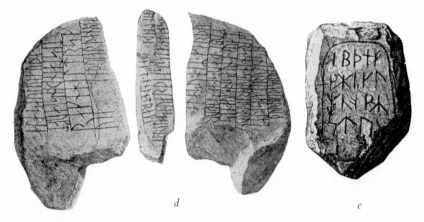

21.4. *d* The longest early Danish inscription from Glavendrup. *e* Alphabetic inscription, partly dotted, from Oestermarie Sogn (Bornholm).

21.4*f.* Funerary inscription from Aºs, Sweden, of the 11th century.

21.4 Scandinavian Runic inscriptions

4. R 5. < 6. X 7. P 8. N
   r   k   g   w   h

12. � 13. ⌐ 14. Y 15. ⟨ 16. ↑
    p   (z)   R(ř)   s   t

20. Γ 21. ◇ 22. ⊗ 23. ⋈ 24. Y
    l   ŋ(ng)   o   d   f

a

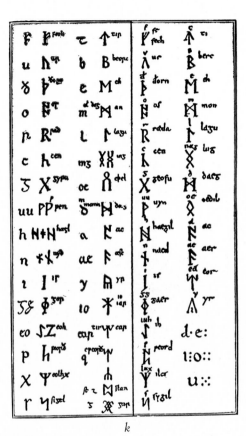

k

g Τ Υ ' \ (↓↑ .|·|·.
   f u þ a r k h n i a s t b m l R

h f u th r k h n i a s t b l m n.

i (X X X X X X)

j (Ψ symbols) þ i s a r r u n a r

a |IIIII .ıı. IIIII. .III. ı.II.ıı.III   :·: ...:·:·. .:·. :·. .·: *a*

b (runic symbols) (tree-like symbols) *a*

l

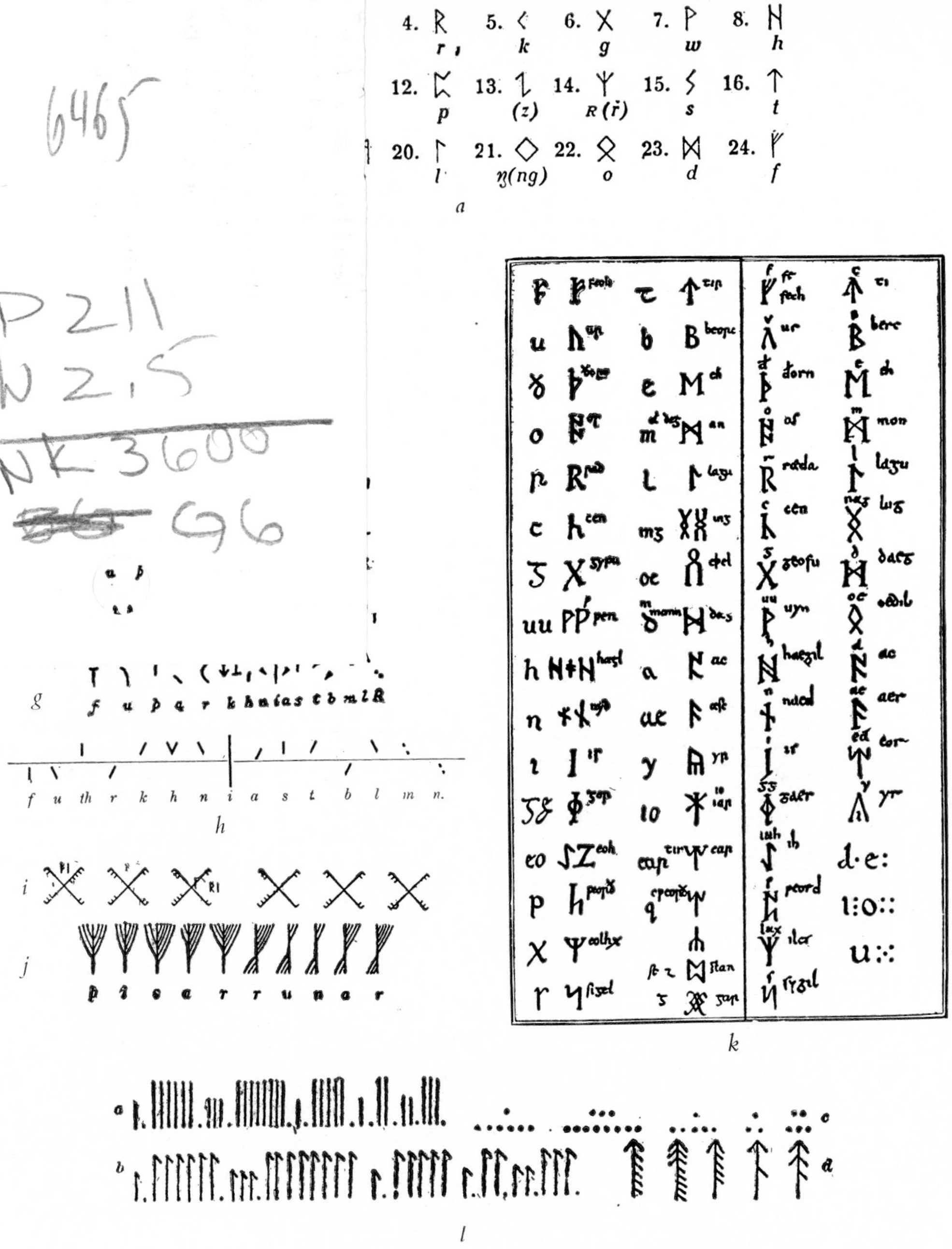

21.5. *a* The Runic 'alphabet' according to Agrell; *b* Negau inscription, 2nd century B.C.? *c* Maria Saalerberg inscription, 1st century B.C.? Scandinavian varieities, *d* Roek; *e* Forsa; *f* Jæderen, Norway and Isle of Man; *g, h* Hælsinge, *i* Tjaldrunir (Roek inscription); *j* Kvistrunir (Maeshowe, Orkney) *k*; Anglo-Saxon Runic alphabet (*Codex Salisburgensis* 140); *l Corui* (Lat. Corvi) in (a) üsruna, (b) lagoruna, (c) stofruna, (d) hahalruna (St. Gallen MS. 270).

21.6a. Runic 'alphabet' of a manuscript of about A.D. 1300.

21.6b. Runic–oghamic inscription (Manx Museum).

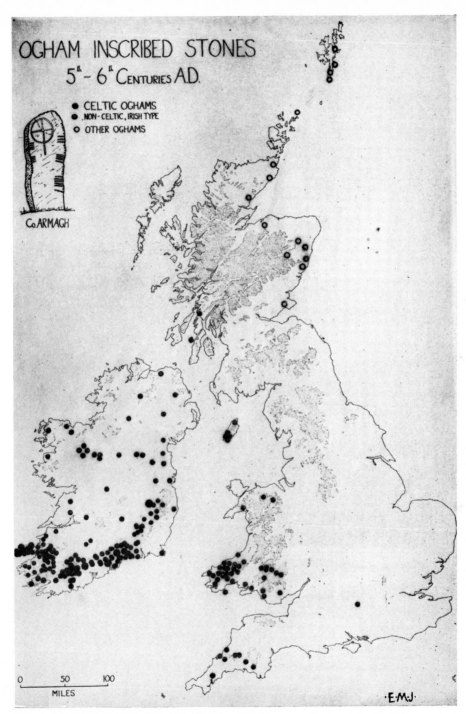

OGHAM INSCRIBED STONES
5ᵗʰ – 6ᵗʰ CENTURIES A.D.

● CELTIC OGHAMS
◉ NON-CELTIC, IRISH TYPE
○ OTHER OGHAMS

Co.ARMAGH

0   50   100
MILES

·E·M·J·

21.7. Map showing the distribution of Ogham inscribed stones in Britain.

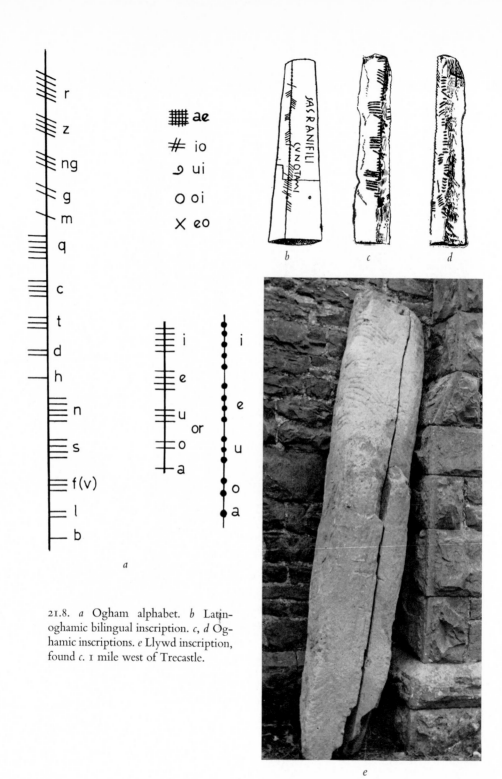

21.8. *a* Ogham alphabet. *b* Latin-oghamic bilingual inscription. *c, d* Oghamic inscriptions. *e* Llywd inscription, found *c.* 1 mile west of Trecastle.

21.9. Silchester stone.

21.10. Left, Oghamic inscription. Right, Oghamic–Latin digraphic inscription (British Museum).

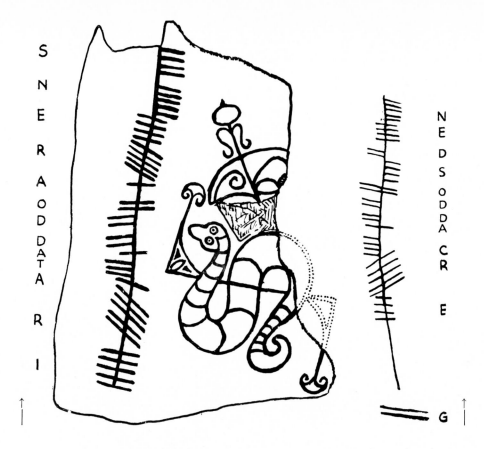

21.11*a*. Pictish Ogham.   21.11*b*. Pictish Ogham.

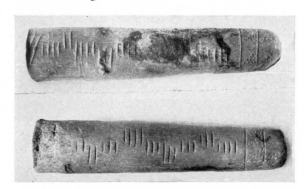

21.11*c*. Germanic Oghams.

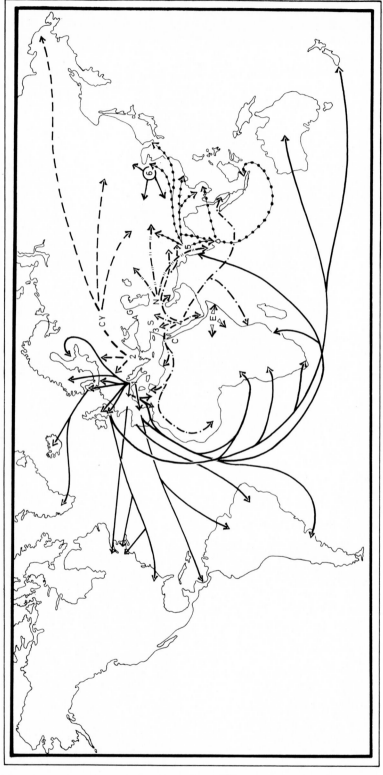

1 —————— Western Christianity: Latin. 2 Eastern Christianity: ━ ━ ━ CY-Cyrillic (including Russian); S-Syriac; ·········· N-Nestorian; A-Armenian; G-Georgian; C-Coptic; E-Ethiopic. 3 Judaism: Hebrew. 4 —··—··— Islām: Arabic. 5 •—•—•—• Buddhism: Pāli and other scripts. 6 Confucianism: Chinese.

Map 3. Alphabet follows religion.

NORTH-SEMITIC				GREEK				ETRUSCAN		LATIN			MODERN CAPS.		
Early Phoenician	Early Hebrew (cursive)	Moabite	Phoenician	Early	Eastern	Western	Classical	Early	Classical	Early	Early Monumental	Classical	Gothic	Italic	Roman

Legend:

(1) = '
(2) = g
(3) = k
(4) = h
(5) = w
(6) = z
(7) = ṭ
(8) = th
(9) = y
(10) = s
(11) = ks
(12) = ʿ
(13) = ṣ
(14) = š
(15) = kh
(16) = ph
(17) = ps
(18) = ō

22.1. From North Semitic to Modern caps.

373

I—Monumental script II—Uncial III—Cursive and minuscule

22.2. Development of the Latin alphabet.

I—1, 4th cent. B.C. 2, 3rd cent. B.C. 3, 4th cent. A.D. 4, Later variants of the Latin monumental script. 5, Rustic capitals, 3rd cent. A.D. 6, Modern capitals.

II—1, Inscriptional uncial, 3rd cent. A.D. 2, Roman monumental uncials, 3rd cent. A.D. 3, Gallic uncials, 5th cent. A.D. 4, Roman uncials, 7th cent. A.D. 5, Irish semi-uncials, 7th cent.

III—1, Cursive writing, 2nd cent. A.D. 2, Current hand, 3rd cent. 3, Gallic cursive, 6th cent. 4, Caroline hand (8th–9th cent.). 5, Early 'black letter' or Gothic, 13th cent. 6, Irish minuscule. 7, Anglo-Saxon minuscule. 8, Italic type. 9, Roman type.

374

MANIOS : MED FHE FHAKED : NUMASIOI

MA NIOS:MED:FHEFHAKED:NUMASIOI

Manius me made (for) Numasius

22.3*a*. The Præneste fibula, 7th century B.C.

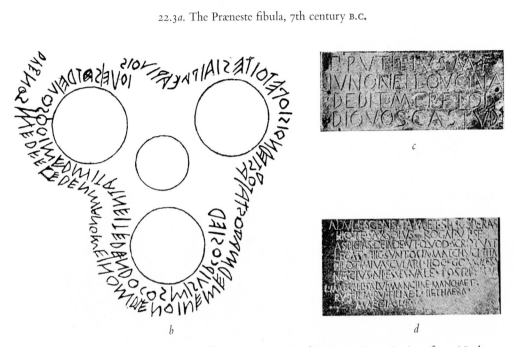

c

b

d

22.3. *b* The inscription of Duenos, 6th century B.C. *c* Dedication to Juno Lucina; from Norba, 4th century B.C. *d* Roman funerary *carmen*, of the period of Silla.

MATRE
MATVTA
DONODIIDRO
MATRONA

e

CORNELIOLFSCIPIO
IDILES·COSOL·CESOR
HONCOINO·PLOIRVME·COSENTIONT·R
DVONORO·OPTVMOFVISE·VIRO
LVCIOM·SCIPIONE·FILIOS·BARBATI
CONSOL·CENSOR·AIDILIS·HIC·FVET·A
HEC·CEPIT·CORSICA·ALERIAQVE·VRBE
DEDET·TEMPESTATEBVS·AIDE·MERETO

f

FERONIA
STATETIO
DEDE

g

22.3. *e* Dedication to Juno; from Pisaurum, 4th century B.C. *f* Funerary inscription of Consul L. Cornelius Scipio, 259 B.C. *g* Dedication to Feronia, 4th century B.C.

22.3. Early Latin inscriptions.

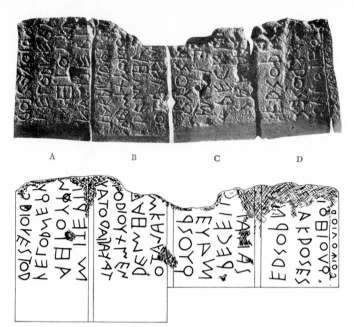

22.4a. Oldest preserved Latin text: photograph and transcription of the *cippus* from the Roman forum. Late 7th or early 6th century B.C.

22.4b. Funerary inscription of Consul Lucius Mummius, the conquerer of Corinth. 146 B.C.

22.5. One of the four faces of the *cippus* from the Roman forum (see also 22.4*a* c).

22.6. Specimens of Roman lapidary capitals.

22.7a. Bilingual Latin–Umbrian text from Todi, Vatican Museum (C.I.L. I, 1408).

22.7b. Marble slab from Arch of Claudius, Capitoline Museum, Rome (C.I.L. VI, 921).

22.8b. Roman monumental script, Tombstone of Agrippina the Elder (C.I.L. VI, 886) who died in A.D. 33, and was buried by her son Caligula in A.D. 37 (Museo Nuovo Capitolino) Courtesy E. Wasmuth Verlag and F. Nash)

22.8a. Roman monumental script of the 1st century A.D.: dedication to C. Antonius Rufus, from Alexandria Troas (British Museum).

22.9a. Roman inscribed wooden tablet.

	Pompeii	Alburnus Major
A		
B		
C		
D		
E		
F		
G		
H		
I		
K		
L		
M		
N		
O		
P		
Q		
R		
S		
T		
U-V		
X		
Y		
Z		

22.9b. Varieties of the early Roman cursive script (wax tablets from Pompeii and Alburnus Major).

22.10. Two pages from a 'book' (codex) of wax tablets, from Pompeii, A.D. 58.

22.11. Roman wooden diptych (6 inches by 4¾ inches): waxed tablets, dated to the seventh year of Septimius Severus (A.D. 198). The text, in Latin cursive, and a woman's signature, written for her, in incorrect Greek, occupy the two sides of the interior of the diptych, which are here represented (*above*, page 2 of the diptych; *below*, page 3). Bodleian Library, at Oxford, MS. *Lat. Class.*, f. 9–10.

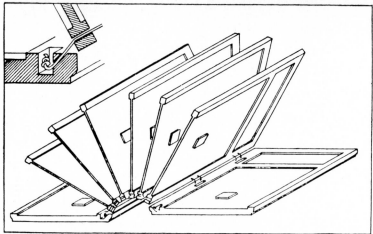

22.12. (*Above*) 'Page' from a *heptaptych* (British Museum, *Add. MS.* 33270); (*below*) *Octoptych* from Herculaneum, as reconstructed by M. Paolini.

22.13a. Triptych from Pompeii, dated A.D., 10.5.54.

22.13b. Latin papyrus, belonging to the 1st century A.D.

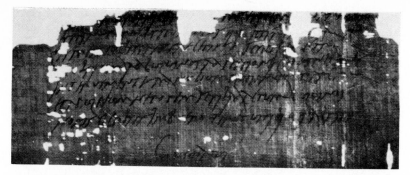

22.14*a*. Latin letter dated 7th October, A.D. 167 (British Museum, Pap. 730).

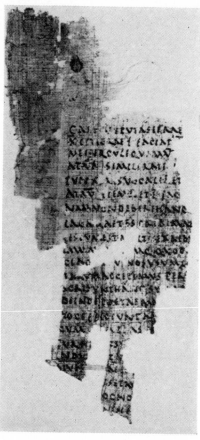

22.14*b*. Latin papyrus written on both sides: (left) obverse, military document of A.D. 163–72; (right) reverse, fragment of an unknown grammatical treatise, early 3rd century A.D. (Archaeology Museum, Michigan University).

22.15 Inscription of Pupus Torquatianns. Roman cursive script, 3rd century A.D. (Vatican Museum).

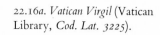

22.16a. *Vatican Virgil* (Vatican Library, *Cod. Lat. 3225*).

22.16b. *Codex Vaticanus Vergilius*, folio 17r.

UTCUMTEGRÊMI CATCCIPIETLAE ISSIPANDI DO
REGALISINTERMENSASLATICEMQVELACHVM
CVMDABITAMPLEXVSADQVEOSCVLADVLCIXH
OCCVLTVMINSPIRES IGNEMFALLASQVEVENE
PARETAMORDICTISCARAEGENETRICISETALÊX

22.17a. *St. Gall Virgil*, in an elegant capital book hand of the 4th century A.D.
(St. Gall, *Cod. no. 1394*).

ETIAM SVA ATQ: PROCVLILLARVMCVLAVNATVMANI
MAIORES ONECADVN·ALTIS·DEAIONTIBVSVMBRAE ·A

POETA   CORYDON

IO: FORMON SVAMCORYDONPASTORARDEBATALEXIN
DELICIAS·DOALINI·NECQVIDSPERAREThABEBAT
TANTVAAINTERDENSASVMBROSACACVMINAFAGOS
ADSIDVAEVENIEBATIBIHAECINCONDITASOLVS

22.17b. *Roman Virgil* (Vatican Library, *Cod. Lat. 3867*, fol. *3 verso*).

22.18. a (left) Palimpsest of Cicero's *De Republica*. Primary script, uncials of 4th or 5th century A.D., written in Italy. Re-written in 7th century, in Bobbio, to copy Augustine, *In Psalmos*. (Vatican Library, *Cod. Lat. 5757*). b (above) *Livius Lateranensis* (Livy, XXXIV), portion of a fragment consisting of seven pieces of parchment, forming a leaf and a half. 4th or 5th century A.D. In 1906 it was found in a cypress box made for Pope Leo III. 795–816. (Vatican Library, *Cod. Lat. 10696*).

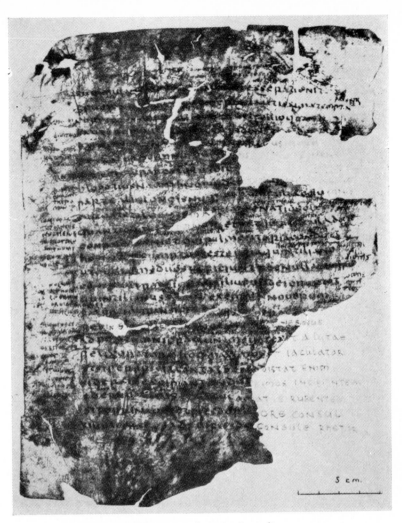

22.19 Fragment from Antinopolis.

22.20. (*Above*) Virgil, Aeneid; fragment from a papyrus codex, written in half-uncial of the 5th century A.D. (University Library, Cambridge, *Add. MS. 4031*); (*insert*) *Latin-Greek lexicon for Aeneid* (University Library, Cambridge, *Add. MS. 5869*). Incomplete folio from a parchment codex written in uncials of the 6th century A.D. Both from Oxyrhynchus.

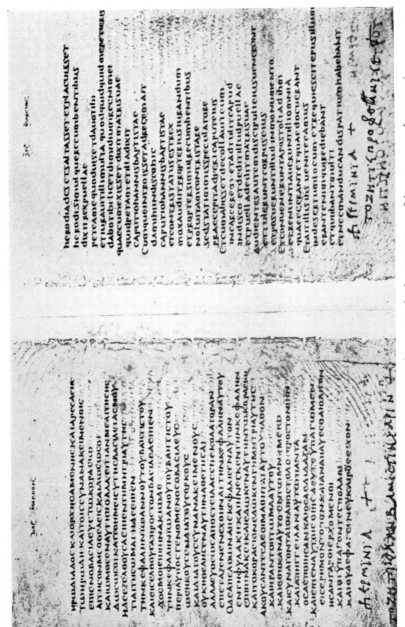

22.21. *Codex Bezae* (University Library, Cambridge, Nn. II, 41; fol. *304 verso* and *305 recto*).

393

22.22. *a* (above) The earliest Christian *Chronicle*. Jerome's Latin version of the *Chronicle* of Eusebius. The oldest known manuscript written in uncials, chiefly in three hands of the 5th and 6th centuries. (Bodleian Library, Oxford. MS. *Auct. T. II, 26*, fol. 121). *b* (left) *Codex Laudianus*, uncials, 6th century, probably written in Sardinia.

22.23. Primasius, *in Apocalypsium*, half-uncial of the 7th or 8th century (Bodleian Library, Oxford, *MS. Douce 140*).

22.24. *Codex Vercellensis* or *Eusebianus*, assigned to St. Eusebius, bishop of Vercelli, who died in 371 A.D. It is apparently the earliest preserved *Vetus Latina* codex (Capitulary Archives, Vercelli, North Italy).

22.25. *Codex Brixianus*, 418 folios of 20 lines. Uncials of the first half of the 6th century. Written in silver on purple stained vellum, the opening lines of the chapters being in gold. Contains Eusebius Caesariensis, *Canones evangeliorum* and the *Four Gospels* in the order of the *Vetus Latina* (Queriniana Library, Brescia, North Italy).

22.26. *Codex Palatinus*: (230 folios are preserved). The manuscript shown here is written in two columns of 20 lines, in silver on well prepared and deeply dyed parchment, the opening lines of *St. John* and *St. Luke* being in gold. Attributed to the 5th century A.D., and apparently the earliest preserved purple *Gospel* of the *Vetus Latina* (Trinity College, Dublin, *N. iv. 18*).

22.27. Codex Amiatinus, *c.* A.D. 700.

ecaelo.filius
hominisqui
estincaelo.
etsicutmoses
exaltauitser
pentemInde
serto itaexal
tarioportet
filiumhomi
nis. utomnis
quicreditin
ipsononpe
reat.sedha
beatuitamae
ternam.sic
enimdilexit
dsmundum
utfiliumsu
umuniceni
tumdaret. ut
utomnisquicreditineum
crediTineum
nonpereat:

sedhabeat)
uitamaeter
nam.nonent
misitds filiu
suuminmun
dumutiudicet
mundum. sed
utsaluetur
mundusper
ipsum.quicre
ditineum non
iudicatur.
quiautemnon
crediTiamiu
dicatusest.
quinoncre
ditinnomine
unigeniti
filioi.hoc
estautem
iudicium quia
luxuenit
inmundum.

22.28. *Codex Claromontanus*, written in uncials of the 7th century, contains the Vulgate version (Vatican Library, *Cod. Lat. 7223*, fol. 230 *recto*).

22.29. *a* Codex Ottobonianus, contains the *Pentateuch* in Vulgate version with parts in *Vetus Latina*. N. Italy, 7th or 8th century A.D. (Vatican Library, *Off. Lat. 66*, fol. 52 *recto*). *b* Oldest complete copy of *Hexameron* by Ambrose. Written in 8th century minuscule at Corbie (Corpus Christi College, Cambridge, MS. 193).

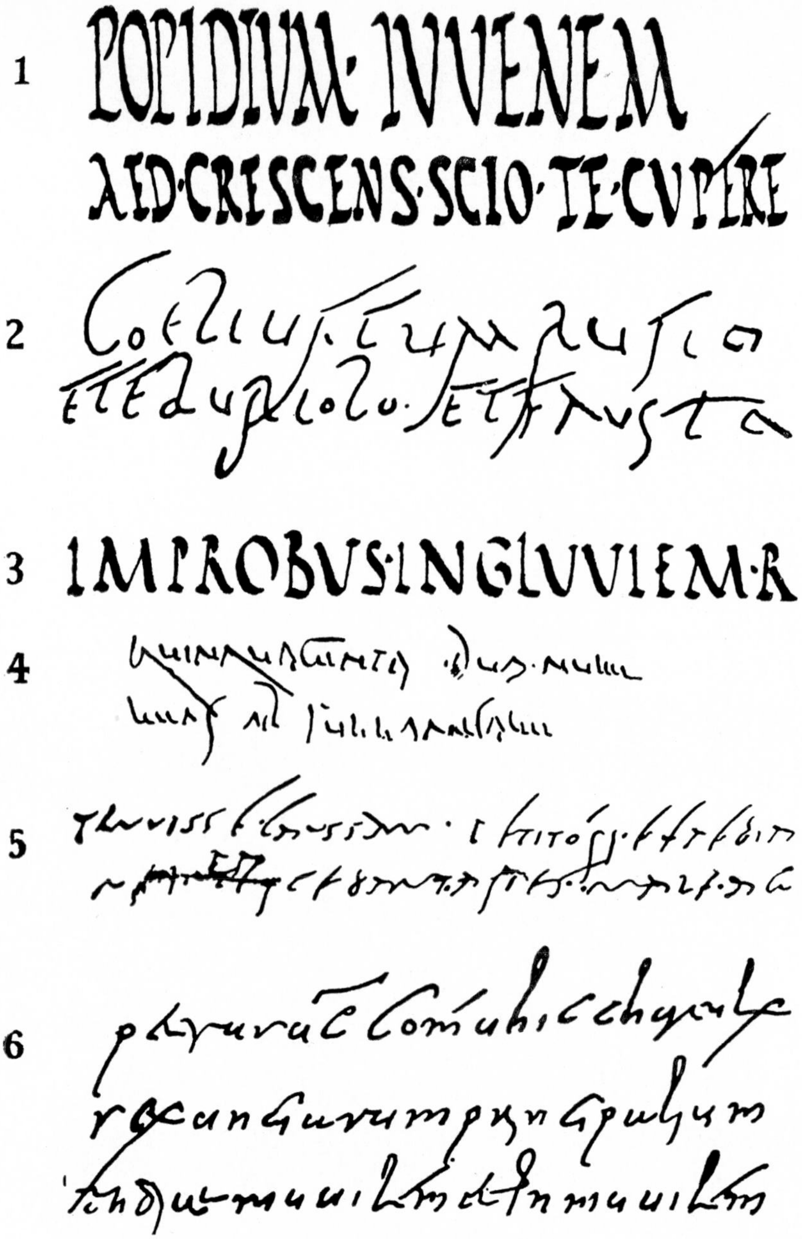

1. POPIDIVM·IVVENEM
AED·CRESCENS·SCIO·TE·CVPERE

2. *(cursive script)*

3. IMPROBVSINGLVVIEM·R

4. *(cursive script)*

5. *(cursive script)*

6. *(cursive script)*

22.30. Specimens of Latin scripts, I (G. Battelli, *Lezioni di Paleografia*, Città del Vaticano, 1936).

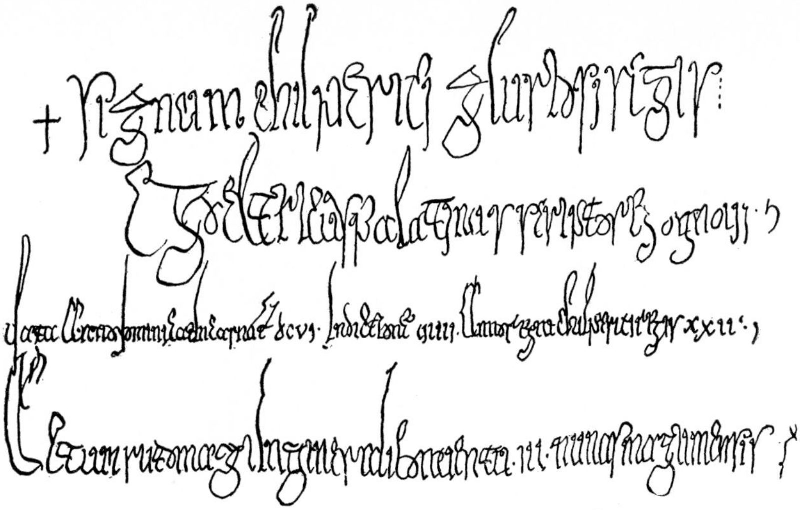

22.31*a*. The end of a Merovingian document of A.D. 583.

A athair fil hi nimib, Noemthar thainm. Tost do flaithius. Did do toil i tálmain amail ata in nim. Tab ·ar dun indiu ar sasad lathi. Ocus log dun ar fiachu amail

22.31*b*. Specimen of Irish script, 9th century A.D.

1, Rustic capitals, A.D. 79 (Pompeii, painted wall-inscription)	*Popidium . iuvenem* *aed [ilem] . Crescens . scio . te . cupere*
2, Majuscule cursive, A.D. 79 (Pompeii, graffito)	*Coelius . cum Rufio* *et Eburiolo . et Fausto*
3, Rustic capitals (MS., fifth century A.D., Vergil; *Cod. Vat. Lat. 3867*)	*improbus . ingluviem . r[anisque]*
4, Majuscule cursive, A.D. 57 (Wax tablet, Naples)	*quinquaginta . dua . num [=]* *mos ob fullonicam*
5, Majuscule cursive, A.D. 51–54 (*Papyrus Claudius*, Berlin)	*tenuisse . caussam . petitori . expedia [t]* *ne procedant* [corrected from *intercedant*] *artes . male . ag [entibus]*
6, Minuscule cursive, seventh century A.D. (*Papyrus Marini XC*; document from Ravenna)	*Petrus vir clarissimus com. uhic chartule* *sex unciarum principalium* *[subs] tantiae muvilem et inmuvilem*

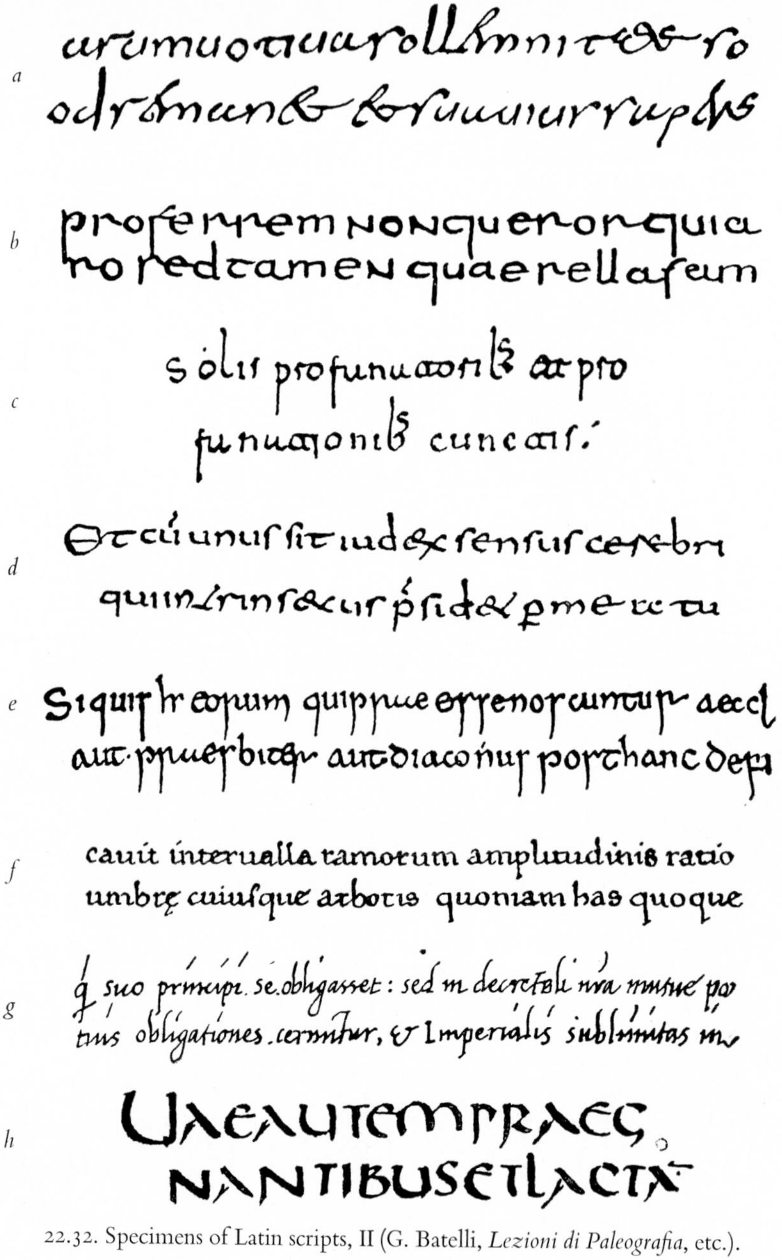

a

b

c

d

e

f

g

h

22.32. Specimens of Latin scripts, II (G. Batelli, *Lezioni di Paleografia*, etc.).

ue·uolumtatte·di pra

22.33*a*. Anglo-Irish semi-uncials of the 7th century A.D. Gospel of St. Chad, now at Lichfield.

& predicatione uof faciat implere digna con

22.33*b*. Winchester School hand, 11th century (Bibliothéque National, Paris).

a b c d e f g h i k l m n o p q r s s t u w x y z

22.33*c*. The 'black letter' or Gothic hand.

---

a, Minuscule semi-cursive, eighth century A.D.
(St. Maximus, Milan, Bibl. Ambros.)

b, Semi-uncials, prior to A.D. 509–510
(St. Hilarius; Rome, Arch. Cap. di S. Pietro)

c, Visigothic, A.D. 954
(Escorial, Madrid)

d, Germanic pre-Caroline, eighth–ninth century A.D.
(St. Gregory, Bibl. Ap. Vatic.)

e, Anglo-Saxon minuscule as employed on the continent; Mainz, Germany, eighth–ninth century A.D.
(Bibl. Ap. Vatic.)

f, Round humanistic or renaissance hand, fifteenth century A.D.
(Plinius, Bibl. Ap. Vatic.)

g, Cursive humanistic, fifteenth century A.D.
(M. Salamonio, Bibl. Ap. Vatic.)

h, Uncials, fourth century A.D.
(St. Gallen)

. . . arum votiva solemnitate so [let]
[*qu*]*od remanet et suavius sapere*
proferrem non queror quia
[*igno*]*ro sed tamen quærella fam*[*osa*]

solis profanatoribus et pro[—]
fanationibus cunctis
Et cum unus sit iudex sensus cerebri
qui intrinsecus presidet permeatu[*s*]

si quis autem eorum qui præesse noscuntur.
æccl[*esiae*]
aut . praesbiter . aut . diaconus post hanc defi-
[*nitionem*]
[*diiudi*]*cavit intervalla ramorum*
amplitudinis ratio
umbræ cuiusque arboris . quoniam has quoque
quam suo principi se. obligasset: sed in decretali
nostra mutue po[—]
tius obligationes . cernuntur. et imperialis
sublimitas in-
Vae autem praeg[—]
nantibus et lactan[—]

1

2

3

4

5

6

7

8

9

10

11

22.35. *Sacramentary* by Gelasius written at Corbie in the 8th century (Vatican Library, *Reg. Lat. 316*, fol. *46 recto*).

22.34. Specimens of manuscripts written in 'national' hands. (*1*) Merovingian (in France), 7th century A.D.; (*2*) Merovingian, 8th century; (*3*) Visigothic minuscule (in Spain), 945; (*4*) Visigothic cursive script, before 779; (*5*) Visigothic, 11th century; (*6*) Roman minuscule, 9th century (*Vitae Sanctorum: Farfa codex*); (*7*) North Italian pre-Caroline minuscule (*Codex 490*, Capitulary Library, Lucca); (*8*) Idem, late 8th century; (*9*) Idem, 8th–9th century (upper part, uncial script); (*10*) Beneventan script, from Cassino, 8th century; (*11*) Idem, 11th century.

22.36. Priscian manuscript written in England, presumably at Canterbury, 'in a very fine hand' of the 8th century (Corpus Christi College, Cambridge, MS. 144).

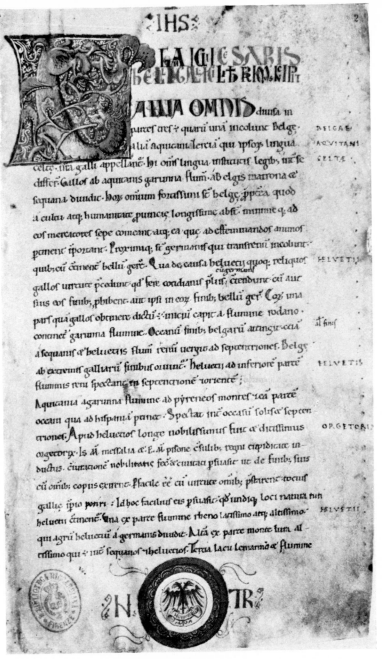

22.37. Caesar C.V. *Commentaria* 11th century (Bibl. Ricc. Florence).

22.38. (*Above*) A 12th-century codex of Terence, from south-west France (Vatican Library, *Vat. Lat. 3305*); (*below*) Plautus (British Museum, *Royal MS. 15, C. xi*, fol. 56).

22.39. Codex Palatinus, 8th century A.D. (Trinity College Library, Dublin).

22.40. *a Book of Kells.* St. Matthew's Gospel Folio 12r (Trinity College Library, Dublin). *b Book of Dimma,* p. 31 (Trinity College Library, Dublin).

22.41. (*Above*) Origines, *Homiliae in Lucam*, 8th- or 9th-century minuscule (Corpus Christi College, Cambridge, MS. 334). (*below*) *Varia Medica*, including Hippocrates and Galenus (University Library, Glasgow, *Hunterian MS. T.4.13*, fol. 99 *recto*; it is written in 'a curious and awkward mixed minuscule (Visigothic, Beneventan, Caroline . . . . .') (Lowe)).

22.42. St. Cyril of Alexandria (d. 444), *Thesaurus adversus haereticos*, transl. by Alphonsus Jorge of Trebizonda. The illuminated border shows in the upper part the Catalan royal arms, and in the lower part those of Naples. The codex, written in Italy, belonged to Alfonso V the Magnanimous (1416–58), king of Aragon, Sicily and Naples (Central Library, Barcelona, MS. 561, fol. 1).

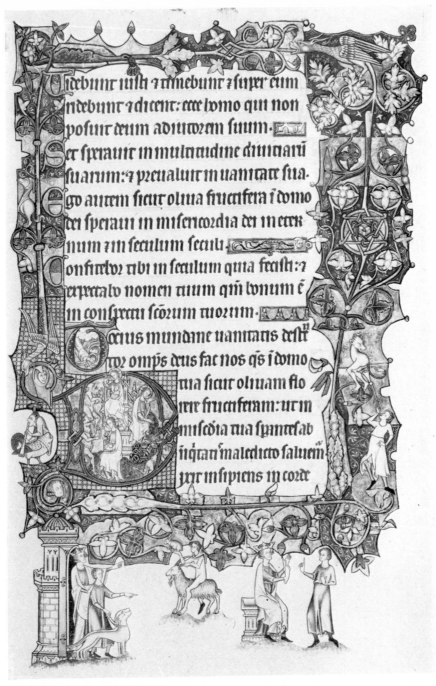

22.43. *Ormesby Psalter*, psalm 52, v. 8–11, *c*. 1300–25.

22.44a. Luttrell Psalter: Gothic 'liturgical hand', *c.* 1340.

22.44b. A Book containing divers Sortes of Hands, by John de Beauchesne and John Basildon, 1571.

22.45. English Court hands: note the Saxon letters surviving.

BASKERVILLE

ABCDEFGHIJKLMNOPQRSTUVW *ABCDEFGHIJKLM*
abcdefghijklmnopqrstuvwxyz *abcdefghijklmnopqrstuv*

BEMBO

ABCDEFGHIJKLMNOPQRSTUVWXYZ *ABCDEFGHIJKLMN*
abcdefghijklmnopqrstuvwxyz *abcdefghijklmnopqrstuvwx*

CLARENDON

ABCDEFGHIJKLMNOPQRSTUVWXYZ
abcdefghijklmnopqrstuvwxyz

FOURNIER

ABCDEFGHIJKLMNOPQRSTUVWXYZ *ABCDEFGHIJKLM*
abcdefghijklmnopqrstuvwxyz *abcdefghijklmnopqrstuvw*

GARAMOND

ABCDEFGHIJKLMNOPQRSTUVWX *ABCDEFGHIJKLM*
abcdefghijklmnopqrstuvwxyz *abcdefghijklmnopqrstuvw*

GILL

ABCDEFGHIJKLMNOPQRSTUVWXYZ *ABCDEFGHIJKLMNOP*
abcdefghijklmnopqrstuvwxyz *abcdefghijklmnopqrstu*

SCOTCH

ABCDEFGHIJKLMNOPQRSTUVW *ABCDEFGHIJKL*
abcdefghijklmnopqrstuvwxyz *abcdefghijklmnopqrst*

SPECTRUM

ABCDEFGHIJKLMNOPQRSTUVWXYZ *ABCDEFGHIJKLMNO*
abcdefghijklmnopqrstuvwxyz *abcdefghijklmnopqrstuvwxy*

TIMES

ABCDEFGHIJKLMNOPQRSTUV *ABCDEFGHIJKLM*
abcdefghijklmnopqrstuvwxyz *abcdefghijklmnopqrst*

22.46. Mid 20th century type. Text faces.

ABCDEFGHIJKLMN
OPQRSTUVWXYZ
abcdefghijklmnopqrs
tuvwxyz

BODONI ULTRA ITALIC

ABCDEFGHIJKLM
NOPQRSTUVWXY
abcdefghijklmnopq
rstuvwxyz

CASTELLAR

ABCDEFGHIJKL
MNOPQRSTUV
WXYZ

22.47. Mid 20th century type. Display and title faces.

MISTRAL

ABCDEFGHIJKLMNOPQ
RSTUVWXYZ
abcdefghijklmnopqrstuvwx

ASHLEY

ABCDEFGHIJKLMNOPQRSTUVWX
YZ
abcdefghijklmnopqrstuvwxyz

PEPITA

ABCDEFGHIJKLMNOP
QRSTUVWXYZ
abcdefghijklmnopqrstuvwxyz

FRANCESCA RONDE

ABCDEFGHIJK
LMNOPQRSTUV
abcdeefghijklmnopqrstuvwxyz

22.48. Mid 20th century type. Script faces.

ABCDEFGHIJKLM
NOPQRSTUVWX
abcdefghijklmnop
qrstuvwxyz

ABCDEFGHIJKLM
NOPQRSTUVWXY
abcdefghijklmnop
qrstuvwxyz

22.49. Mid 20th century type. Script faces.

Roman Cursive Majuscule	Roman Cursive Minuscule	Roman Uncials	Roman Semi-Uncials	Anglo-Saxon Majuscule	Caroline Minuscule	"Gothic"	Venetian Min.(Italic)	N.Italian Min.Roman	Mod. Lower Case		
									Gothic	Italic	Roman

22.50. Development of lower case.

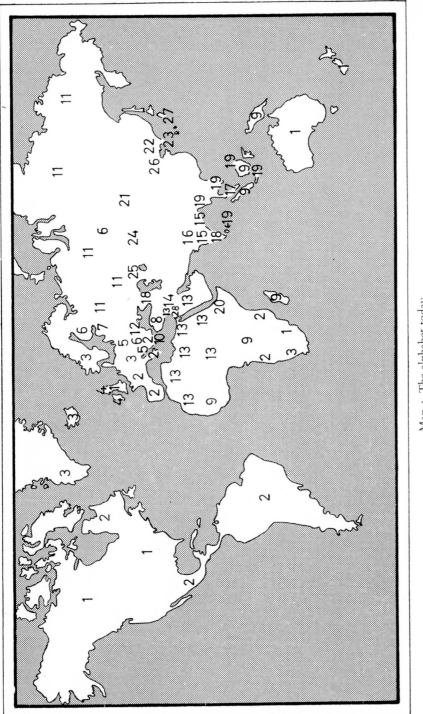

Map 4. The alphabet today.

1. English
2. Romance Branch
3. Germanic Branch (excl. English)
4. Celtic Branch
5. W.-Slavonic Branch
6. Finno-Ugrian Branch
7. Baltic Branch
8. Modern Turkish

9. Recent Adaptations of Latin Alphabet
10. Greek Alphabet
11. Cyrillic: Russian Alphabets
12. Cyrillic: Serbian and Bulgarian Alphabets
13. Arabic Alphabet
14. Persian-Arabic Alphabet

15. Urdu Alphabet
16. Pashtu Alphabet
17. Malay-Arabic Alphabet
18. Armenian and Georgian Alphabets
19. Indian and Further Indian Branch
20. Ethiopic Script
21. Mongolian Alphabet
22. Manchurian Alphabet

23. Korean Alphabet
24. Turco-Tatar Languages in Arabic Characters
25. Turco-Tatar Languages in Russian characters
26. Chinese Scripts
27. Japanese Scripts
28. Hebrew Alphabet.

III. The Alphabet by rote
42 characters§

1.	æ	ae		25.	ţh	ith
2.	b	bee		26.	ɟh	thee
3.	ɕh	chee		27.	ʃh	ish
		(see)		28.	ʒ	zhee
4.	d	dee		29.	ŋ	ing
5.	ee	ee		30.	ɑɑ	ahv
6.	f	ef		31.	a	at
7.	g	gae		32.	e	et
8.	h	hae		33.	i	it
9.	ie	ie		34.	o	ot
10.	j	jae		35.	u	ut
11.	k	kae		36.	au	aul
12.	l	el		37.	ω	foot
13.	m	em		38.	ꭒ	brood
14.	n	en		39.	ou	owl
15.	œ	oe		40.	oi	oil
16.	p	pee				
		(kue)			───	
17.	r	rae				
18.	s	ess		41.	ʑ	zess
19.	t	tee		42.	wh	whae
20.	ue	ue				
21.	v	vee				
22.	w	wae				
		(eks)				
23.	y	yae				
24.	z	zed or zee				

22.51. Augmented Roman alphabet.

424

helpiŋ ſhe bliend man

loŋ agœ ſhær livd a
bliend man. hee livd whær
treeʒ and flouerʒ grœ; but
ſhe bliend man cœd not see
ſhe treeʒ or flouerʒ.

ſhe pœr man had tœ feel
ſhe wæ to gœ wiſh hiʒ stick.
tap-tap-tap went hiʒ stick on
ſhe rœd. hee waukt slœly.

22.52. Specimen of writing in the INITIAL TEACHING
ALPHABET.

hamlet

bie William ſhækspeer

from act ſhree, Seen wun

hamlet: tw bee, or not tw bee: ſhat is ſhe kwestion:

Wheſher 'tis nœbler in ſhe miend tw suffer

ſhe sliŋs and arrœs ov outræjus fortuen,

. Or tw tæk arms agænst a see ov trubls,

and bie oppœsiŋ end them. Tw die: tw sleep;

Nœ mor; and bie a sleep tw sæ wee end

ſhe hart-æc, and ſhe ſhousand natueral ſhocks

ſhat fleſh is ær tw, 'tis a consummæſhon

devoutly tw bee wiſht. Tw die, tw sleep;

tw sleep: perchans tw dreem; ie, ſhær's ſhe rub;

for in ſhat sleep ov deſh whot dreems mæ cum,

When wee hav ſhuffld off ſhis mortal coil,

Must giv us paus: ſhær's ſhe respect

ſhat mæks calamity ov sœ loŋ lief;

for hw wœd bær ſhe whips and scorns ov tiem,

ſhe oppressor's roŋ, ſhe proud man's contuemly,

ſhe paŋs ov dispieſed luv, ſhe lau's delæ,

ſhe insolens ov offis, and ſhe spurns

ſhat pæſhient merit ov ſhe unwurſhy tæks,

22.53. Hamlet in INITIAL TEACHING ALPHABET.

CONSONANTS

	Bi-labial	Labio-dental	Dental and Alveolar	Retroflex	Palato-alveolar	Alveolo-palatal	Palatal	Velar	Uvular	Pharyngal	Glottal
Plosive	p b		t d	ʈ ɖ			c ɟ	k g	q ɢ		ʔ
Nasal	m	ɱ	n	ɳ			ɲ	ŋ	N		
Lateral Fricative			ɬ ɮ								
Lateral Non-fricative			l	ɭ			ʎ				
Rolled			r						ʀ		
Flapped			ɾ	ɽ					ʀ		
Fricative	ɸ β	f v	θ ð s z	ʂ ʐ	ʃ ʒ	ɕ ʑ	ç ʝ	x ɣ	χ ʁ	ħ ʕ	h ɦ
Frictionless Continuants and Semi-vowels	w ɥ	ʋ	r				j (ɥ)	(w)	ʁ		

VOWELS

	Front	Central	Back
Close	i y (y ʉ u)	ɨ ʉ	ɯ u
Half-close	e ø (ø o)	ə	ɤ o
Half-open	ɛ œ (œ ɔ)	œ ɜ	ʌ ɔ
Open	a (ɒ)	æ	ɑ ɒ

(Secondary articulations are shown by symbols in brackets.)

OTHER SOUNDS.—Palatalized consonants: ţ, đ, etc.; palatalized ʃ, ʒ : ɕ, ʑ. Velarized or pharyngalized consonants: ł, đ, z, etc. Ejective consonants (with simultaneous glottal stop): p', t', etc. Implosive voiced consonants: ɓ, ɗ, etc. ɼ fricative trill. σ, ʓ (labialized θ, ð, or s, z). ʆ, ʓ (labialized ʃ, ʒ). ʇ, ʗ, ʖ (clicks, Zulu c, q, x). ɺ (a sound between r and l). ŋ Japanese syllabic nasal. ƫ (combination of x and ʃ). ʍ (voiceless w). ɩ, ʏ, ɵ (lowered varieties of i, y, u). ə (a vowel between ø and o).

Affricates are normally represented by groups of two consonants (ts, tʃ, dʒ, etc.), but, when necessary, ligatures are used (ʦ, ʧ, ʤ, etc.), or the marks ͡ or ‿ (t͡s or t‿s, etc.). ͡ also denote synchronic articulation (m͡ŋ = simultaneous m and ŋ). ɔ, ʃ may occasionally be used in place of tʃ, dʒ, etc., and ƾ, ƻ for ts, dz. Aspirated plosives: ph, th, etc. r-coloured vowels: eɹ, aɹ, ɔɹ, etc., or eᴿ, aᴿ, ɔᴿ, etc., or ɚ, ɑ, ɔ, etc.; r-coloured ə: aɹ or ɚ or ɹ or ɑ or ɔ, or ɔ.

LENGTH, STRESS, PITCH.— ː (full length). · (half length). ˈ (stress, placed at beginning of the stressed syllable). ˌ (secondary stress). ˉ (high level pitch); ˍ (low level); ˊ (high rising); ˏ (low rising); ˋ (high falling); ˎ (low falling); ˆ (rise-fall); ˇ (fall-rise).

MODIFIERS.— ̃ nasality. ̥ breath (l̥ = breathed l). ̬ voice (s̬ = z). ʻ slight aspiration following p, t, etc. ̫ labialization (n̫ = labialized n). ̪ dental articulation (t̪ = dental t). ̫ palatalization (z̫ = ʒ). · specially close vowel (e̝ = a very close e). ̣ specially open vowel (e̞ = a rather open e). ꜜ tongue raised (e꜑ or i꜑ = ɨ, t꜑ = alveolar t). ꜛ tongue lowered (e꜓ or e̞ = ę). + tongue advanced (u+ or u̟ = an advanced u, t̟ = t̟). - or ˗ tongue retracted (i- or i̠ = ɨ, t̠ = alveolar t). ˑ lips more rounded. ˏ lips more spread. Central vowels: ï (= ɨ), ü (= ʉ), ë (= ə), ë̝, ö̈, ö̈ (= ɵ), ɛ̈, ɔ̈. ̩ (e.g. n̩) syllabic consonant. ̯ consonantal vowel. ʃ variety of ʃ resembling s, etc.

22.54. The INTERNATIONAL ALPHABET. Revised to 1951.

Nyanja

'Nyanja' is a Bantu term; the word is variously spelt ('Nyanza,' 'Nyasa,' 'Nyassa,' etc.). The Nyanja are a Bantu negroid people of eastern central Africa, living mainly in the Nyasaland Protectorate, lying between northern Rhodesia, Portuguese East Africa, Tanganyika Territory and the Lake Nyasa. The Nyanja dialects, spoken by over 1,500,000 people, are the most interesting group of the whole Bantu family of languages. According to Sir Harry H. Johnston, there are 'two hundred and twenty-six distinct Bantu languages of present times.' These are spoken in nearly the whole of the southern third of Africa, and constitute a very distinct type of speech 'which, as contrasted with others amongst the groups of negro tongues, is remarkable as a rule for the Italian melodiousness, simplicity and frequency of its vowel sounds, and the comparative ease with which its exemplars can be acquired and spoken by Europeans' (Johnston).

Tamvelani Bwana Diringer,

Ndikondwera ndí kulola kuti kalatai ífalítsídwe m'bukhu wanu wa A B C, monga

císanzo ca malembedwe a Cinyanja, ndíganiza cifuno canu cidzakwanila.

Ndine wanu,

Bennett E. Malekebu.

Twi

This language is known by many terms: Twi (originally Kwi or Ekwi, Okwi), Oji or Odshi, Tyi, Chwee or Tshi, Amina, Ashanti, etc. It is a Sudanese form of speech, belonging to the great prefix-pronominal group, and is spoken by about 1,000,000 people living in the Gold Coast Colony and in part of the French colony of the Ivory Coast. Twi, like most African languages, is divided into a number of dialects. Indeed, 'Akuapem, Asante, Akyem and Fante as well as other closely related dialects form the Akan group of languages,' but 'the name Twi has been used for the whole of this group excluding Fante.' 'It would be wise now to adopt Twi as the general name, and in making reference to special forms of the language, to call them Akuapem Twi, Asante Twi, Akyem Twi, etc.' (I.C. Ward). Twi has been written for over 100 years.

Ɔdɔfo Dr. Diringer,

Eyɛ me Thomas Boatin a meboa wɔ Asante Kasa kyerɛ mu wɔ "School of Oriental

and African Studies" wɔ London na merekyerɛ wo.

Meda wo ase wɛ wo krataa a woakyerɛ me no ho.

Woabisa me nsa ano krataa sin yi a wopɛ sɛ wode yɔ Twii-ŋkyerɛ ŋhwesɔɔ wɔ wo

ŋwoma a ɛfa ŋkyere-Nsɛnkyerɛnce ho no mu. Mede anigye reyɔ wo adesredeɛ.

na mewɔ andisasɔɔ sɛ eyi bɛkerɛ deɛ wohwehwe.

Mekyia wo.

Conclusion I. Latin Script adapted to African Languages

Yoruba

The Yoruba are a higher grade and commercially-minded negro people speaking a Sudanese language. They number about 3,000,000 and inhabit the south-west corner of Nigeria from the sea to Jebba and from Dahomey to the borders of the Bini State. The Nago of the Dahomey coast region and, partly, the Bini, are related to them. The Yoruba language ranks as one of the three chief languages of Nigeria. The first Yoruba dictionary, compiled by (an ex-slave and afterwards bishop) Samuel Crowther, was published in 1843.

Dr. Diringer,

Alagba,

Mo gbe pe e fe ki nko iwe kekere kan ti e ó tè sinu iwe yin leri 'Alphabet,' lati fi se apere bi àá ti ikowe l'ede Yoruba.

Tayotayo ni mo fí kowe yi ni sókí, mo si rò pe yio bá, l'ona ti e fe lò o si.

Ke epe o!

Emi ni

E. L. Lasebikan.

Efik

This interesting Sudanese language, spoken by some 50,000 people in Calabar, Nigeria, was reduced to writing about the middle of the last century. *See* also p. 29 f., 148 ff., and 564 f.

Edima Ete,

Mmenem esit ndinwam ye ekpri ŋwed emi ndisin ke ŋwed fo emi abaŋade A B C, ndiwut nte ewetde usem Efik, mmodori enyin nte emi eyekem ye udwak fo.

Okuo ke akpanikɔ,

Nyoŋ Ekanem.

Conclusion 2. Latin script adapted to African languages.

a Numerals

1 airi	15 fingo	29 ɛdipikn
2 grɛid	16 tiɛts	30 ɛdipaːriːd
3 sɛːta	17 ʌigɛt	31 ɛditrita
4 aidu	18 kisani	32 ɛdikanapt
5 dʒiti	19 siːtrik	33 ɛdifaigi
6 tarisi	20 ɛdiːtiɔ	34 ɛdifudipt
7 fuda	21 ɛdiari	35 ɛdifingo
8 citia	22 ɛdigreid	36 ɛditiɛtɔ
9 pikn	23 ɛdisɛːtaː	37 ɛdiʌigɛt
10 paːriːd	24 ɛdiaidu	38 ɛdikisaːni
11 trita	25 ɛdidʒitɔ	39 ɛdisiːtriːk
12 kanapt	26 ɛditarisi	40 krɛido
13 faigi	27 ɛdifuda	60 sɛtado
14 fudipt	28 ɛditia	80 aidudo

100 dʒitɔdo

a

b

Here is the Oberi Ɔkaime script reduced to roman type with the addition of ɔ and ŋ. The question-mark represents an unrecognizable symbol.

1. D. ɔksiritues drins fra nimazidiŋ ? umilen ?
2. ? peprit dei wɔkri fra dzjias o, gizin, dei kalikist
3. bolin elimontas pdzjoprim amitriŋ seniɔ vɔida
4. ruzɔrd mium slanint fra dzjas o, gizin,
5. ventaismint gizin atiɛfpts kn riks dzjibreant
6. ? nɔminent badzjba fra kenod duma arien seslin enedium
7. nipdzjin pinstrik anivad (symbol for ' or ') zu rotri kivziɔ
8. bisanetksi b ? eam beda riks futrim (symbol for ' or ') bulo dapori
9. ? alimoti eis kɔlen abel saprivos andea dei
10. kalamiusiŋ eis kɔlen abel dei ? ramuksi fɔŋ
11. nip ? zin snani zu vus kɔruvik diup etuals seraus
12. kɔlenkist pos dzba talimaiŋ liu ? ad dei rituel
13. ksirin dei ? ɔmi ? en kn dei marr due apinkɔri

c

Conclusion 3. Oberi Okaime script. *a* Numerals, *b* a portion of the script, *c* transliterations.

VOWELS				OLD PHONETIC SYMBOLS	WADE SYSTEM	INTER-NATIONAL PHONETIC SYMBOLS	APPROXIMATE ENGLISH SOUND
PRINT		SCRIPT					
A	a	*a*	*a*	Ƴ	a	ɑ'	a (as in ar)
O	o	*o*	*o*	ʊ	o	ɔ'	aw (as in law)
E	e	*ε*	*e*	ɾ	ê,o	ɔ'	er (as in her)
I	i	*g*	*i*	∣	i	i'	ee (as in bee)
U	u	*u*	*u*	X	u	u'	oo (as in too)
Y	y	*y*	*y*	Ц	ü	y'	German ü

CONSONANTS				OLD PHONETIC SYMBOLS	WADE SYSTEM	INTER-NATIONAL PHONETIC SYMBOLS	APPROXIMATE ENGLISH SOUND
PRINT		SCRIPT					
B	b	*B*	*b*	ㄅ	p	p	b (but not voiced)
P	p	*P*	*p*	ㄆ	p'	p'	p (strongly aspirated)
M	m	*m*	*m*	ㄇ	m	m	m
F	f	*F*	*f*	ㄈ	f	f	f
D	d	*D*	*d*	ㄉ	t	t	d (but not voiced)
T	t	*J*	*t*	ㄊ	t'	t'	t (strongly aspirated)
N	n	*n*	*n*	ㄋ	n	n	n
L	l	*L*	*l*	ㄌ	l	l	l
G	g	*G*	*g*	ㄍ	k	k	g (hard, but not voiced)
K	k	*K*	*k*	ㄎ	k'	k'	k (strongly aspirated)
Ŋ	ŋ	*Ŋ*	*ŋ*	ㄫ	ng	ŋ	ng (final)
H	h	*H*	*h*	ㄏ	h	x	h (aspirated, partly like ch in Scottish loch)
Ч	ч	*U*	*u*	ㄐ	ch(i)	tɕ	j
Q	q	*2*	*q*	ㄑ	ch'(i)	tɕ'	ch
X	x	*X*	*x*	ㄒ	hs(i)	ɕ	sh (palatal)
Z	z	*Zp*	*ʒ*	业	ch	tʂ	j or dg'
C̣	c̣	*C̣*	*g*	ㄔ	ch'	tʂ'	ch (strongly aspirated)
S̨	s̨	*S̨*	*ʃ*	ㄕ	sh	ʂ	sh (as in shore)
R	r	*R*	*r*	ㄖ	j	ʐ	r (tending towards the z in azure)
Z	z	*Z*	*z*	ㄗ	ts(tz)	ts	ds (but not voiced)
C	c	*C*	*c*	ㄘ	ts'	ts'	ts (strongly aspirated)
S	s	*S*	*s*	ㄙ	s,ss,sz	s	s
J	j	*g*	*j*	∣	y	j	y
W	w	*W*	*w*	X	w	w	w

Conclusion 4. Adaptation of alphabetic scripts to Chinese.

Final		Old Phonetic Symbols	Wade System	International Phonetic Symbols	Approximate English Sound
a:	ai	ㄞ	ai	aɪ	long i (as in eye)
	au	ㄠ	ao	ɑo	ow (as in how)
	an	ㄢ	an	an	an (as in can)
	aŋ	ㄤ	ang	aŋ	ang (as in sang)
o:	ou	ㄡ	ou	ou	o (as in note)
e:	ei	ㄟ	ei	eɪ	ay (as in way)
	en	ㄣ	en	ɔn	un (as in French)
	eŋ	ㄥ	êng	ɔŋ or ʌŋ	(no exact equivalent)
i:	ia	ㄧㄚ	ia	ia	yah
	ie	ㄧㄝ	ieh	ie	ye (as in yes)
	iau	ㄧㄠ	iao	iao	yow (as in yowl)
	iu	ㄧㄡ	iu	iɔu	u (as in unite)
	ian	ㄧㄢ	ien	iɛn	e en (as in the end
	in	ㄧㄣ	in	in	een (as in keen)
	iaŋ	ㄧㄤ	iang	iaŋ	yan (as in yankee)
	iŋ	ㄧㄥ	ing	iŋ	ing (as in sing)
u:	ua	ㄨㄚ	ua	ua	wah
	uo	ㄨㄛ	uo	uɔ	wa (as in water)
	uai	ㄨㄞ	uai	uaɪ	wi (as in wife)
	ui	ㄨㄟ	ui(uei)	uɔɪ	wee
	uan	ㄨㄢ	uan	uan	oo an
	un	ㄨㄣ	un	uɔn	oo n
	uaŋ	ㄨㄤ	uang	uaŋ	oo ahng
	uŋ	ㄨㄥ	ung	uŋ	oo ng
y:	ye	ㄩㄝ	yüeh	ye	(no equivalent)
	yan	ㄩㄢ	yüan	yan	(no equivalent)
	yn	ㄩㄣ	yün	yɔn	(no equivalent)
	yŋ	ㄩㄥ	yung	iuŋ	yoong

Conclusion 5. Adaptation of alphabetic scripts to Chinese.

written	printed	sounded as	written	printed	sounded as	written	printed	sounded as
A a	A a	a in at	O o	O o	oa in oat	ð d	ð d	th in these
A ǎ	A ǎ	a .. alms	S s	S s	ur .. fur	Z z	Z z	s in so
O o	θ o	a .. all		*Consonants*		Z z	Z z	s .. is
O o	O o	o .. olive	C c	C c	c in cot	Σ ʃ	Σ ʃ	sh .. show
W u	W u	oo .. foot	G g	G g	g .. go	Z ʒ	Z ʒ	s .. pleasure
U u	U u	oo .. food	T t	T t	t .. to	L l	L l	l .. low
I i	I i	i .. ill	D d	D d	d .. do	L l	L l	ll .. welsh
E ɛ	E ɛ	ee .. eel	P p	P p	p .. put	M m	M m	m .. me
E e	E e	e .. ell	B b	B b	b .. but	N n	N n	n .. no
A a	A a	ai .. aim	F f	F f	f .. foe	N n	N n	hn .. almost
† i	† i	i .. isle	V v	V v	v .. vase	ŋ ŋ	ŋ ŋ	ng .. wing
O o	O o	oi .. oil	C ç	C ç	ch .. chin	R r	R r	r - row
U u	U u	u .. us	J j	J j	j .. jade	R r	R r	hr .. welsh
8 8	8 8	ow .. owl	T t	T t	th .. thin	K k	K k	ch .. german

Besides the above letters there are three vowel marks, ´ = h, ` = y, and ¯ = w only found over vowels, hence their name. These marks are quite often found united over vowels, thus uẵ = uhwa, meaning ashes; ūâ = wuhya, meaning a door; and ūẵ = wuhwa, meaning tinder of birds' down. The effect of these marks always precedes the vowels over which they are found.

Conclusion 6. The Yámana (Yahgan) Phonetic Alphabet.

Conclusion 7. Inscriptions written in unknown scripts. *a–c* The so-called proto-Arabic inscriptions from 'Ur of the Chaldees.' *d* Another enigmatic inscription from Mesopotamia. *e* Spurious (?) inscription from Peru. *f–g* Enigmatic inscriptions from Spain.

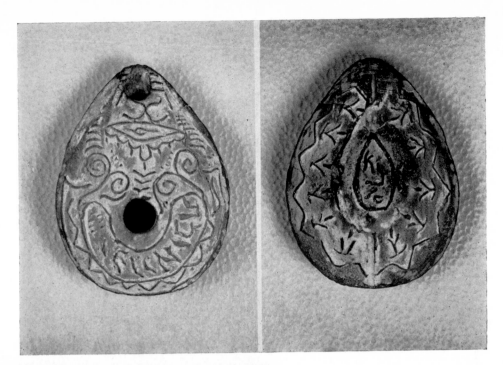

Conclusion 8. *a* (above) obverse and reverse of an 'inscribed' lamp: a forgery. *b* (left) Little bronze lamina inscribed in a script unknown to the excavators, which has actually turned out to be Hebrew. Discovered about 1930 at Minturnae, Italy in the joint excavations of the University of Pennsylvania Museum and the Associazione Internazionale per gli Studi Mediterranei, Rome.

Conclusion 9. The Shapira forgery. Two pages of the line and wash drawing by C. D. Ginsburg, of Shapira's Deuteronomy manuscript (British Museum *Add*. 41294, fol. 35).

SYSTEM	UNITS										100	1000	MISCELL.
	1	2	3	4	5	6	7	8	9	10	100	1000	
CUNEIFORM	𒀸									⟨			10,000
EGYPTIAN HIEROGL. *	I	II	III	IIII						∩	⊚		10,000
HIERAT. *	I	II	III	—			2	=		∧	/		20 40
CHINESE ANCIENT	一	二	三	四	五	六	七	八	九	十	百	千	
CURRENT *				X						+			10,000
PHOENICIAN										—			20
SYRIAC													
PALMYRENE	/												
KHAROSHTHĪ													20
BRAHMĪ	—	=	≡										20
MAYA *	•	••	•••	••••									ZERO
ETRUSCAN *	I	II	III	IIII	∧	I∧	II∧	III∧	XI	X		(X)	20 50
ANCIENT ROMAN *	I	II	III	IIII	V	VI	VII	VIII	IX	X	C	(X)	500
CHIOGGIA *	I	II	III	IIII	∧∨∪	VI	VII	VIII	IX	XOA	⊕		
CLASSICAL ROMAN *	I	II	III	IIII	V	VI	VII	VIII	IX	X	C	M	20
MEDIEVAL ROMAN *	7	77	777	7777	V	VI	VII	VIII	7X	X	L	C	500

* SELECTED

Conclusion 10. Numerical notation, preceding the arabic numerals.

437

Script / Source	1	2	3	4	5	6	7	8	9	0
Deva-nagari letters (2nd. cent A.D.)		?	?	?	?	?	?	?	?	
Arabic numerals (10th.cent.)	1	?	?	?	?	?	?	?	?	0
Arabic numerals (M S. A.D. 976) (Latin M S., Escorial Library)	1	?	?	?	?	?	?	8	9	
Arabic numerals (Western Type)	1	?	3	?	?	6	?	8	9	0
Arabic numerals (Eastern Type)	١	٢	٣	٤	٥١	٤	٧	٨	٩	.
	١	٢	٣	٤	٥	٤	٧	٨	٩	.
	١	٢	٣	٤	٥	٤	٧	٨	٩	0
To-day	١	٢	٣	٤	٥	٦	٧	٨	٩	.
"Apices" of Boëthius (11th & 12th centuries)	I	?	?	?	G	?	?	8	9	
	I	?	?	?	?	?	?	8	9	
	I	?	?	B	?	?	?	?	?	
	١	?	?	?	?	?	?	8	9	⊕
	١	?	?	?	?	?	?	8	9	
Numerals of John Basingestockes (d.1252)	?	?	?	?	?	?	?	?	?	
Arabic-Byzantine numerals (12th. to 15th. cent.)	١	?	?	?	?	?	٧	٨	9	
	١	?	?	?	0	?	٧	٨	9	.
	١	2	3	?	?	6	٧	?	3	0
M.S. from France 2nd. half of 12 cent.	١	?	?	?	B	?	٧	?	9	0
Italian M S., Florence, first half of 14th. cent.	١	2	3	4	?	6	7	8	9	0
Italian MSS. of 15th. cent.	1	2	3	4	٤	6	7	8	9	0

Conclusion II. Development of arabic numerals.

Conclusion 12. Medieval musical notation: *Mozarabic Antifonarium*, 11th century (Leon Cathedral, Spain).

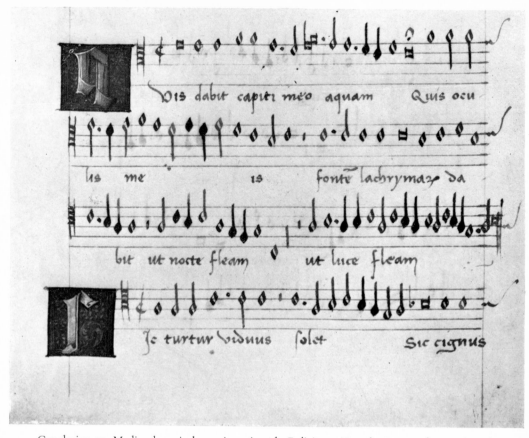

Conclusion 13. Medieval musical notation: Agnolo Poliziano, *Trenodio in morte* for Lorenzo the Magnificent, *c.* 1486 (Civic Library, Cortona, Italy).

Conclusion 14. Musical notation: Giuseppe Maria Angelieri, *Messa in Quattro*, Milan, 1691.

vector of magnitude A **A**

scalar product of **A** and **B**   **A.B**

vector product of **A** and **B**   **A** × **B**, **A** ∧ **B**

nabla or del, $\left(\mathrm{i}\dfrac{\partial}{\partial x} + \mathrm{j}\dfrac{\partial}{\partial y} + \mathrm{k}\dfrac{\partial}{\partial z} \right)$ ∇

Laplacian operator, $\left(\dfrac{\partial^2}{\partial x^2} + \dfrac{\partial^2}{\partial y^2} + \dfrac{\partial^2}{\partial z^2} \right)$ ∇^2

$$F_j \simeq F' + 2(f + \delta f_j)(\cos\theta - \delta\theta_j \sin\theta),$$

$$\Delta_j = 2f\{(\delta f_j/f)\cos\theta - \delta\theta_j \sin\theta\}.$$

$$\Delta_j = -2f\sin\theta\,\delta\theta_j.$$

$$\sigma_l^n = \sum_s m^s [\tfrac{1}{3}(\alpha_1^s + \alpha_2^s + \alpha_3^s) + \tfrac{2}{3}(\pm\beta_1^s \pm \beta_2^s \pm \beta_3^s)]$$

$$\sigma_t^n = \sum_s m^s [\tfrac{1}{3}(\alpha_1^s + \alpha_2^s + \alpha_3^s) - \tfrac{1}{3}(\pm\beta_1^s \pm \beta_2^s \pm \beta_3^s)]$$

Conclusion 15. Mathematical notation.

$$\xi = F(t) \cdot F(t+s)$$

$$\xi \neq 0 \text{ if } s < T \,; \ \xi = 0 \text{ if } s > T$$

$$Z = \frac{2\pi L^2}{h^3} (2mkT)^{3/2} \int_0^\infty z^{3/2} \, e^{-x} \, dx$$

$$Z = \left(\frac{2\pi mkT}{h^2}\right)^{3N/2} \frac{1}{N!} \int \exp\left(\frac{-\Phi}{kT}\right) . dV_N$$

$$\Phi = \sum_{pairs} \phi_{ij}(r_{ij}) = \sum_{i>j} \phi_{ij}(r_{ij}) = \tfrac{1}{2} \sum_{i=1}^{N} \sum_{j=1}^{N} \phi_{ij}(r_{ij})$$

$$\text{ZnSO}_4 . 7\text{H}_2\text{O} \rightarrow \text{ZnSO}_4 . 6\text{H}_2\text{O} \xrightarrow{100^\circ\text{C}} \text{ZnSO}_4 . \text{H}_2\text{O}$$

$$\xrightarrow{250^\circ\text{C}} \text{ZnSO}_4$$

$$\xrightarrow{750^\circ\text{C}} \text{ZnO} + \text{SO}_4$$

Conclusion 16. Scientific notation.

A Angström, answer. **A1**, first class (of ships). **A.A.**, Anti-Aircraft, Automobile Association. **A.A.A.**, Amateur Athletic Association, American Automobile Association. **A. and M.**, Ancient and Modern (hymnal). **A.A.U.**, Amateur Athletic Union (U.S.). **A.B.**, Able-bodied seaman. **A.B.A.**, Amateur Boxing Association. **Ab. init.**, *ab initio* (L., from the beginning). **Abl.**, ablative. **Abp.**, archbishop. **A.C.**, Aircraftman, alternating current, *ante Christum* (L., before Christ). **A/c**, account. **Acc.**, accusative. **A. Cdre**, Air Commodore. **A.C.F.**, Army Cadet Force. **ACTH**, Adrenocorticotrophic hormone. **A.D.**, *anno domini* (L., in the year of the Lord). **Ad.**, Admiral(ty). advertisement. **A.D.C.**, aide-de-camp. **Add.**, addenda. **Adj.**, adjective. **Ad. lib.**, *ad libitum* (L., as much as desired). **Adm.**, Admiral(ty). **Admin.**, administer(ed), administration, administrative(ly). **Adv.**, Advent, adverb. **A.E.A.**, Atomic Energy Authority. **A.E.C.**, Atomic Energy Commission (U.S.). **Aeg.**, *aegrotat* (L., he is ill). **A.E.I.**, Allied Electrical Industries. **Aet.**, *aetatis* (L., of the age). **A.E.U.**, Amalgamated Engineering Union. **A.F.**, audio-frequency. **A.F.L.–C.I.O.**, American Federation of Labor–Congress of Industrial Organizations (U.S.). **A.F.S.**, Auxiliary Fire Service. **A.G.**, air-gunner. **A.H.**, *anno hegirae* (L., in the year of the Hegira – Mohammedan calendar). **A.I.**, Appleton layer. **Ala.**, Alabama. **Alas.**, Alaska. **alt.**, altitude. **Alta.**, Alberta. **A.M.**, Air Ministry. **a.m.**, *ante meridiem* (L., before noon). **amp.**, ampere. **AMVETS**, American Veterans of World War II & Korea. **Anniv.**, anniversary. **anon.**, anonymous. **A.O.C.** (in-C.), Air Officer Commanding (in-Chief). **A.P.**, Associated Press. **approx.**, approximate(ly). **Aq.**, *aqua* (L., water). **arch.**, archaic, architecture. **archbp.**, archbishop. **Ariz.**, Arizona. **Ark.**, Arkansas. **A.R.P.**, Air Raid Precautions. **Arr.**, arranged, arrive(s). **A.S.**, Anglo-Saxon, anti-submarine. **a.s.l.**, above sea-level. **A.S.P.C.A.**, American Society for the Prevention of Cruelty to Animals. **assist.**, assistant. **assoc.**, associate(d). **assn.**, **assocn.**, association. **A.S.S.R.**, Autonomous Soviet Socialist Republic. **asst.**, assistant. **A.T.C.**, Air Transport Command (U.S.), Air Training Corps. **A/T**, anti-tank. **at. no.**, atomic number. **A.T.S.**, Auxiliary Territorial Service. **at. wt.**, atomic weight. **A.U.C.**, *anno urbis conditae* (L., 'in the year of the founding of the city' [Rome], 753 B.C.). **Aug.**, August. **aux.**, auxiliary. **A.V.**, Authorized Version (of the Bible). **avdp.**, avoirdupois. **A.W.O.L.**, absent without leave.

B Born, brother. **B.A.**, Bachelor of Arts, British Academy, British Association (for the Advancement of Science), Buenos Aires. **Bac.**, *baccalaureus* (L., bachelor). **Ball.**, Balliol College, Oxford. **b. and b.**, bed and breakfast. **B.A.O.R.**, British Army of the Rhine. **Bart.**, baronet. **Bart's**, St. Bartholomew's Hospital, London. **B.B.C.**, British Broadcasting Corporation (originally Company). **B.C.**, Before Christ, borough council, British Columbia, British Council. **B.Ch.**, Bachelor of Surgery (L., *chirurgiae*). **B.C.L.**, Bachelor of Civil Law. **B.Com.**, Bachelor of Commerce. **B.D.**, Bachelor of Divinity. **Bde.**, brigade. **b.e.**, bill of exchange. **B.E.A.**, British European Airways. **Beds**, Bedfordshire. **B.E.F.**, British Expeditionary Force. **B.E.M.**, British Empire Medal.

B.Eng., Bachelor of Engineering. **Berks**, Berkshire. **b.f.**, brought forward. **bk.**, book, bank. **b.l.**, bill of lading. **B.Litt.**, Bachelor of Letters (L., *Litterarum*). **B.LL.**, Bachelor of Laws (L., *Legum*). **B.M.**, Bachelor of Medicine, British Museum. **B.M.A.**, British Medical Association. **B.M.C.**, British Motor Corporation. **Bn.**, battalion. **B.O.A.C.**, British Overseas Airways Corporation. **B. of E.**, Bank of England. **bor.**, borough. **bos'n**, boatswain. **B.O.T.**, Board of Trade. **bot.**, botany(ical). **B.P.**, British Pharmacopoeia. **b.p.**, boiling point. **Bp.**, bishop. **B.R.**, British Railways. **Brec.**, Breconshire. **Brit.**, British. **Bros.**, brothers. **B.R.S.**, British Road Services. **B.S.A.**, Birmingham Small Arms (Company). **B.Sc.**, Bachelor of Science. **B.S.I.**, British Standards Institution. **B.S.T.**, British summer time. **Bt.**, baronet. **B.T.U.**, Board of Trade Unit. **Bucks**, Buckinghamshire. **B.U.P.**, British United Press. **bus**, omnibus (L., for all). **B.V.M.** Blessed Virgin Mary. **Byz.**, Byzantine.

C *Centum* (L., hundred). **C.** capacitance, Centigrade, Central, coulomb. **c.**, centimetre, chapter, cubic, *circa* (L., about). **C.A.**, Consumers' Association. **cal.**, calorie. **Calif.**, California. **Cambs**, Cambridgeshire. **Can.**, canon. **Cantab.**, *Cantabrigiensis* (L., member of Cambridge University). **cap.**, capital, chapter. **Capt.**, captain. **car.**, carat. **C.A.T.**, College of Advanced Technology. **cat.**, catalcgue. **C.B.**, confined to barracks. **C.C.**, Coastal Command, county council(lor), cricket club. **c.c.**, cubic centimetre, cubic contents. **C.C.C.**, Central Criminal Court, Commodity Credit Corporation (U.S.). **C.D.**, Civil Defence, Contagious Diseases (Acts), *Corps Diplomatique* (Fr., diplomatic body). **C.D.C.**, Commonwealth Development Corporation. **C.E.**, Chancellor of the Exchequer. **C.E.G.B.**, Central Electricity Generating Board. **C.E.M.A.**, Council for the Encouragement of Music and the Arts. **cent.**, century. **cet. par.**, *ceteris paribus* (L., other things being equal). **C.F.**, Chaplain to the Forces. **c.f.**, carried forward, cubic foot (feet). **cf.**, *confer* (L., compare). **C.G.**, centre of gravity. **cg.**, centigramme. **C.G.S.**, centimetre-gramme-second (system of units), Chief of the General Staff. **C.G.T.**, Confédération Générale du Travail (Fr., general confederation of work; equivalent of British T.U.C.). **C.H.**, Companion of Honour. **c.h.**, central heating. **Ch.**, chaplain, church. **Ches**, Cheshire. **C.I.**, Channel Islands. **C.I.A.**, Central Intelligence Agency (U.S.). **C.I.D.**, Criminal Investigation Department. **C.I.G.S.**, Chief of the Imperial General Staff. **C.-in-C.**, Commander-in-Chief. **C.I.O.**: see A.F.L.–C.I.O. **Cl.**, classical. **cm.**, centimetre. **C.M.G.**, Companion of the Order of St. Michael and St. George, Congressional Medal for Gallantry (U.S.). **C.M.S.**, Church Missionary Society. **C.N.D.**, Campaign for Nuclear Disarmament. **C.O.**, Colonial Office, commanding officer, conscientious objector, Crown Office. **Co.**, company, county. **c/o**, care of. **C.O.D.**, cash on delivery, Central Ordnance Depot. **C. of E.**, Church of England. **C.O.I.**, Central Office of Information. **Col.**, colonel, colonial, Colorado. **Col-Gen.**, colonel-general. **Coll.**, college. **Com.**, Communist, commissioner. **Comdt.**, commandant. **Comecon**, council for mutual economic aid (Communist).

Comm., commodore. **Comp.**, comparative, compositor, compound. **Compa.**, company (on £5 notes). **con.**, *contra* (L., against). **conf.**, conference. **conj.**, conjugation, conjunction. **Conn.**, Connacht, Connecticut. **Cons.**, Conservative. **contd.**, continued. **Co-op.**, Co-operative. **Cor.**, Corinthian(s), coroner. **C.O.R.E.**, Congress of Racial Equality (U.S.). **Corpn.**, corporation. **cos.**, cosine. **cox**, coxswain. **C.P.**, Common Prayer, Communist Party. **c.p.**, carriage paid, candle-power. **Cpl.**, Corporal. **cr.**, created, credit. **C.R.C.**, Civil Rights Commission (U.S.). **cresc.**, *crescendo* (Ital., becoming louder), crescent. **c/s**, cycles per second. **C.S.C.**, Civil Service Commission, Conspicuous Service Cross (U.S.). **C.S.E.**, Certificate of Secondary Education. **cts.**, cents, centimes. **cttee.**, committee. **cu.**, **cub.**, cubic. **C.U.P.**, Cambridge University Press. **C.V.O.**, Commander of the Royal Victorian Order. **C.W.S.**, Co-operative Wholesale Society. **cwt.**, hundredweight.

D Five hundred (Roman). **d.**, daughter, *denarius* (L., penny), died. **D.A.**, District Attorney (U.S.). **dat.**, dative. **dau.**, daughter. **dB**, decibel. **D.B.E.**, Dame Commander of the Order of the British Empire. **D.C.**, *da capo* (Ital., from the beginning), direct current, District of Columbia (U.S.). **D.C.L.**, Doctor of Civil Law. **D.C.V.O.**, Dame Commander of the Royal Victorian Order. **D.D.**, Doctor of Divinity. **deb.**, debenture. **dec.**, deceased. **Del.**, Delaware. **del.**, *delineavit* (L., he drew). **dele.**, delete. **Dept.**, department. **Deut.**, Deuteronomy. **D.F.**, Defender of the Faith. **D.F.C.**, Distinguished Flying Cross. **D.F.M.**, Distinguished Flying Medal. **D.G.**, *Dei Gratia* (L., by the grace of God), Director General, Dragoon Guards. **D.I.**, Defence Intelligence. **diam.**, diameter. **dim.**, *diminuendo* (Ital., becoming quieter). **dip.**, diploma. **dir.**, director. **dist.**, district. **div.**, division, divorced. **divi.**, dividend. **dl.**, decilitre. **D. Litt.**, Doctor of Letters (L., *Litterarum*). **D.M.**, Doctor of Medicine. **D. Mus.**, Doctor of Music. **D.N.A.**, deoxy-ribonucleic acid. **D.N.B.**, Dictionary of National Bicgraphy. **do.**, ditto. **D.O.M.**, *Deo Optimo Maximo* (L., to God the best and greatest). **Dom.**, Dominican, Dominion, *Dominus* (L., lord, master). **D.O.R.A.**, Defence of the Realm Act. **doz.**, dozen. **D.P.**, displaced person(s). **D.R.**, dead reckoning. **Dr.**, debtor, doctor. **dr.**, dram, drawer (of a cheque). **D.S.**, *dal segno* (Ital., [repeat] from the mark). **D.Sc.**, Doctor of Science. **D.S.O.**, Distinguished Service Order. **d.s.p.**, *decessit sine prole* (L., died without issue). **D.T.**, delirium tremens. **Dunelm**, *Dunelmensis* (L., of Durham). **Duo.**, duodecimo (12). **D.V.**, *deo volente* (L., God willing).

E Earl, east, eastern, English, second class (of ships). **e.**, eldest. **E. & O.E.**, errors and omissions excepted. **Ebor**, *Eboracensis* (L., of York). **E.C.A.**, Economic Co-operation Administration. **Eccl.**, (Book of) Ecclesiastes. **Econ.**, economics. **Ed.**, editor, edited, educated, Edward. **E.D.C.**, European Defence Community. **Edin.**, Edinburgh. **educ.**, educated, education. **E.F.C.**, European Economic Community. **E.F.T.A.**, European Free Trade Association. **e.g.**, *exempli gratia* (L., for the sake of example). **e.h.f.**, extra high frequency. **el.**, electric, element. **eld.**, eldest. **E.M.F.**, electro-motive force. **E.M.U.**, electro-magnetic unit. **E.N.E.A.**, European

Conclusion 17. Abbreviations. (Hutchinson's New 20th Century Encyclopedia)

444

Conclusion 18. Systems of shorthand from antiquity to the present day.

me
him
myself
himself
most
more
remark-ed
Mr.
mere
importance-ant
improved-d-ment
impossible
in
any
own
influence
influenced
next
nor
near
opinion
northern

information
hand
under
sent
language
owing
thing
young
Lord
your
year
yard
word
are
our, hour
ourselves
rather
writer
we
whether
wonderful-ly

a, an
ah!
the
aye, eh?
of
to
all
two, too
on
but
O! oh! owe
he
and
should
awe
ought, aught
who
how
with
when
what
would
beyond
you
why

significance
significant
signification
signify-ied
southern
speak
special-ly
spirit
subject-ed
subjection
subjective
sure
surprise
surprised
tell
thank-ed
that
the
their, there
them
themselves
therefore
thing

think
third
this
those
though
thus
thyself
till
to
to be
told
too, two
toward
towards
trade
tried
truth
under
usual-ly
valuation
very
was
we

what
when
whether
which
who
whose
why
wish
wished
with
within
without
wonderful-ly
word
would
writer
yard
year
you
young
your

Conclusion 19. Modern shorthand: Pitman system.

Conclusion 20. Stenography. Sample from a shorthand typewriter. The passage from *Hamlet*, act three, scene one, is read from top to bottom by columns, and from left to right (Courtesy Miss Vivien Rigden).

447

Conclusion 21. The semaphore alphabet.

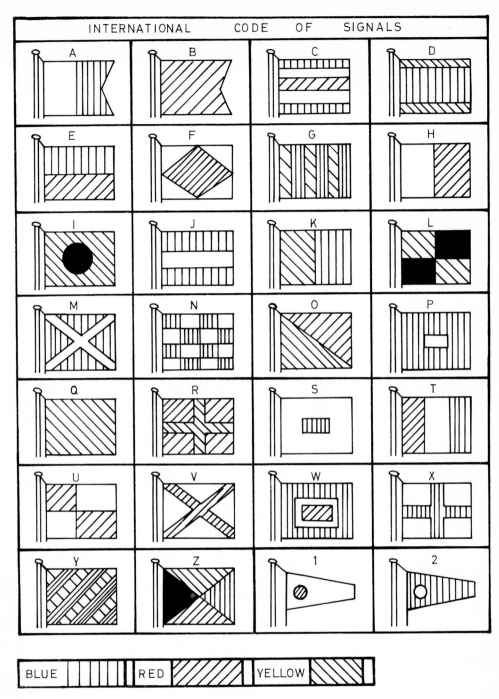

Conclusion 22. International flag code of signals.

449

MORSE CODE

A • ▬	H • • • •	O ▬ ▬ • ▬	V • • • ▬	3 • • • ▬ ▬
B ▬ • • •	I • •	P • ▬ ▬ •	W • ▬ ▬	4 • • • • ▬
C ▬ • ▬ •	J • ▬ ▬ ▬	Q ▬ ▬ • ▬	X ▬ • • ▬	5 • • • • •
D ▬ •	K ▬ ▬	R • ▬ •	Y ▬ • ▬ ▬	6 ▬ • • • •
E •	L • ▬ • •	S • • •	Z ▬ ▬ • •	7 ▬ ▬ • • •
F • • ▬ •	M ▬ ▬	T ▬	1 • ▬ ▬ ▬ ▬	8 ▬ ▬ ▬ • •
G ▬ ▬ •	N ▬ •	U • • ▬	2 • • ▬ ▬ ▬	9 ▬ ▬ ▬ ▬ •

Conclusion 23*a*. Morse Code.

BRAILLE

Conclusion 23*b*. Braille.

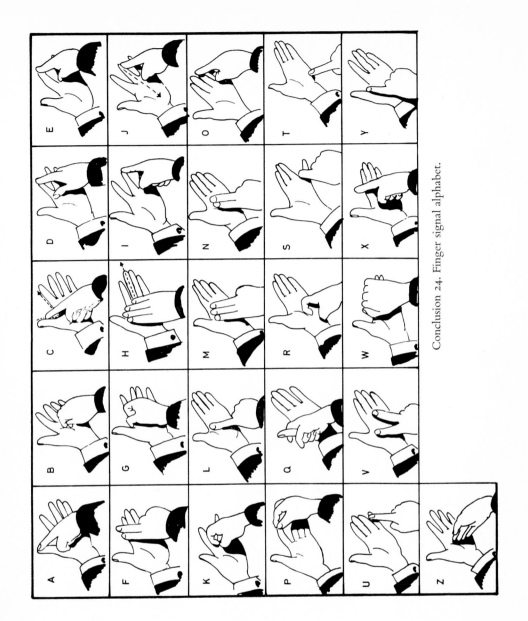

Conclusion 24. Finger signal alphabet.

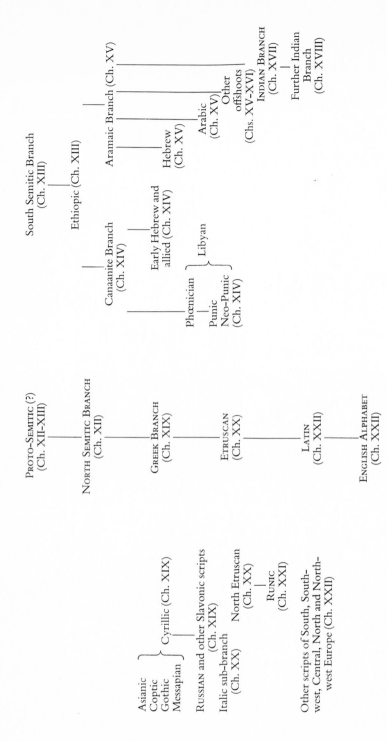

Conclusion 25. The origin of the English alphabet and its relationship to other main alphabetic scripts.